The Paradox Relational Database Advisor:
Elements of Database Design

First edition

The Paradox Relational Database Advisor:

Elements of Database Design

First edition

Kimberly M. Saunders

Windcrest®/McGraw-Hill

New York   San Francisco   Washington, D.C.   Auckland   Bogotá
Caracas   Lisbon   London   Madrid   Mexico City   Milan
Montreal   New Delhi   San Juan   Singapore
Sydney   Tokyo   Toronto

NOTICES

FIRST PRINTING

© 1993 by McGraw-Hill.
Published by Windcrest Books, an imprint of TAB Books.
TAB Books is a division of McGraw-Hill, Inc.
The name Windcrest is a registered trademark of TAB Books.

Library of Congress Cataloging-in-Publication Data

Saunders, Kimberly Maughan.
     The paradox relational database advisor / by Kimberly M. Saunders.
— 1st ed.
     p.cm.
Includes index.
ISBN 0-8306-3859-8 (pbk.)
1. Relational data bases.   2. Paradox (Computer file)   I Title.
QA76.9.D3S255 1992
005.75'65—dc20   92-41240
                                                                                        CIP

Acquisitions team: Ron Powers, Director of Acquisitions
                              Jennifer DiGiovanna, Acquisitions Editor
Editorial team: Mark Vanderslice, Editor
                         Susan Wahlman, Managing Editor
                         Joanne Slike, Executive Editor
Production team: Katherine G. Brown
Design team: Jaclyn J. Boone, Designer
                      Brian K. Allison, Associate Designer   WU1

Contents

To my husband, Raynard, and
children, Blake, Heath, Trent, Alanna, and Claire:
you are as always
my hope and inspiration.

Dedication

Acknowledgments

I would like to express my thanks:

to Genie Logan for persistent support on pushing the limits;
to Jenny Kluth for performance above and beyond the call of duty;
to Cheryl Paulin for willing-and-able drawing assistance;
to Martin Rudy for ongoing inspiration;
to Nan Borreson for timely help;
to Ann Lynnworth for the idea exchange;
and to all my students who continue to challenge and inspire me to a greater
appreciation of the ever-changing Paradox.

Foreword

If you use Paradox, you know just how intuitive a database product can be. For all the time we spend building tables and designing forms and generating reports and writing PAL code, we rely on the Paradox perspective. Paradox doesn't just allow work to go on—it facilitates and encourages the work, provoking new and creative solutions every step of the way.

Paradox's success is in part based on its fundamental nature: it is a relational database. Relational theory doesn't just support the product—in many ways the theory drives it. *The Paradox Relational Database Advisor* tears away the veil from that mysterious relational theory in order to give you, the Paradox user, a better understanding of the power behind the product.

Kimberly uses the process of database design as the starting point for a practical, nontechnical analysis of Paradox's relational underpinnings. She combines a rich appreciation for concept with a step-by-step exploration of how best to get the job done. It is a powerful perspective in an easy-to-digest package that will benefit both new Paradox users and experienced PAL programmers.

If you need to design a Paradox database from start to finish, this book should be your road map of choice.

Rob Dickerson
Senior Vice President, Client-Server
Borland International

Introduction

You bought Paradox. All the installation menu choices have been made, and you're ready to tap the power: your mouse is poised to attack! Suddenly the time you spent deciding to purchase this particular product doesn't seem adequate. You might have just realized that the hard questions lie still ahead.

The good news is that the answers are just ahead as well. This book is intended to provide practical guidance in the development and implementation of a database design in Paradox. This book will help a new developer identify and explore critical concepts necessary for successful design, and will assist the more experienced developer by regrounding him in the basics.

Part 1, "Preparing to design a Paradox database" (chapters 1 through 3), is intended to give you an overview of the process of designing a Paradox database. Chapter 1 addresses in detail the concept of an application and its various elements. Chapter 2 focuses on the steps of the database design process and reviews the basic terminology used by Paradox, identifying key concepts that will help ensure your success in developing your own design. Chapter 3 provides a series of snapshots of the process—essentially a quick walk-through of a real design project from beginning to end, including the tasks involved in implementing the design in Paradox.

Part 2, "Designing a normal database" (chapters 4 through 7), addresses the issues involved in designing a database to take full advantage of the power of relational theory (through normalization—the process of making your database conform to the theory). Chapters 4, 5, and 6 lay out a practical process for relational table development. Specifically, chapter 4 looks at big-picture considerations, while chapters 5 and 6 analyze the specifics of designing a field and modeling the relationships between tables. Chapter 7 briefly reviews the importance of data integrity and addresses the issue of how to ensure that the data stored in your tables is accurate and the relationships between the tables are valid.

Part 3, "Implementing a Paradox design" (chapters 8 through 11), addresses the issues involved in installing and fine-tuning a database design for optimal performance under Paradox. Chapter 8 is an overview of the issues specifically involved in realizing a design. (A realized design is one that acknowledges and incorporates Paradox (or other software) specific factors into the database design.) Chapter 8 also gives you an opportunity to look at the "relationality" of Paradox, i.e., how well it measures up against the relational model.

Chapter 9 examines the process of implementing a completed database design with Paradox. Detailed, step-by-step instructions lead you through table creation, application of `TableLookup` and other validity checks, and into development of PAL code to support additional business rules. Chapter 9 also touches on the concept of data dictionaries and other database design documentation, and provides practical suggestions for developing design documentation for applications that are already up-and-running. The concept of query templates is introduced, and ideas about using the templates are discussed in detail. Actual screen images of the entire implementation process in both Paradox 3.5 and Paradox 4.0 are provided.

Chapters 10 and 11 evaluate some of the issues involved in exploiting the database design through Paradox forms and reports. Fundamental concepts in form and report design are examined. Differences between single- and multitable forms and reports are highlighted, and options for handling complex relationships are detailed and examined. Chapter 10 also takes a look at some issues of form design under Paradox 4.0's windowing environment.

Part 4, "Optimizing a Paradox design" (chapters 12 through 14) focuses on issues which can help ensure the success of a Paradox database implementation. Specifically, chapter 12 addresses the overall concept of performance. How is the speed of a database application measured? When is the speed with which Paradox works an issue? Under what circumstances should you modify a design to take speed into consideration? What can you do to a database design in order to maximize speed?

Chapter 13 addresses the issue of costs in the database design process. What are the expenses that you reasonably can expect to be associated with the development of a database? Where are the hidden costs, and how can they be avoided? The cost of a Paradox database, and specifically of the design process, is evaluated both from a time and dollars-spent standpoint.

Finally, chapter 14 provides a toolkit of templates, forms, and other resources useful in supporting a Paradox database design specification project.

Conventions and case studies

This book addresses design issues for both Paradox 3.5 and Paradox 4.0. When a topic is handled the same in both products, the two are jointly referred to as "Paradox." If there are differences between the products which are either highlighted or simply addressed, each product is referred to with the inclusion of the version number (3.5 or 4.0).

 Important concepts and special terms used throughout the book are highlighted with a special key icon. The first time the concept or term is defined, the definition is highlighted in the text. Newly introduced key terms are repeated in the Key Terms section at the end of each chapter.

Four case studies will be developed as you move through this book. Each addresses a different type of database requirement. Case study 1 reflects the need of a sole proprietor to keep track of time and billing matters; case study 2 addresses the requirement of a purchasing group within a large corporation to deal with purchase order management; case study 3 takes a look at the need of a small zoo to track animals for breeding purposes; and case study 4 deals with a simple list intended to keep track of an individual's depreciable assets.

The intent of the case studies is to help you find and focus on your niche— which case study deals with a problem most like the one you're interested in? You'll find the examples most helpful if you identify the case study that fits your needs and follow it through from beginning to end. An issue highlighted especially well by one of the case studies normally is addressed in the body of the text as well, so don't be concerned that you'll miss something important if you don't keep track of them all. A complete database design for each case study can be found in the appendix.

Mistakes that are made within each case study are marked clearly and identified with a separate mistake icon and a description of the mistake that was made. Each case study is identified with an icon, so that you can quickly refer to the choice of greatest interest to you.

oops!

Case study 1: RTS
Type of business: financial planning sole proprietorship
Employees: 1 full-time, 1 part-time
Statement of purpose: This financial planner has a need to keep track of what he does and when. He needs to manage his spent time from a historical perspective for billing purposes, and he also needs a way to help him schedule his future time commitments. In addition, he needs to keep better tabs on his client contacts, including who he has talked to, when the contact took place, what recommendations he made, and what follow-up was required.

Case study 2: EB
Type of business: purchasing group within a large retail corporation
Employees: 11 full-time (within the group)
Statement of purpose: The purchasing group of a nationwide retail sales company needs to manage the process of buying nonmerchandise supplies for its stores and corporate entities. The group processes requests for supplies that are submitted by various users, and then forwards these requests to a vendor or a corporate warehouse location as indicated.

Case study 3: MH
Type of business: small zoo
Employees: 15 full-time, 9 part-time
Statement of purpose: The owner of this small zoo has a need to keep track of his animals. He needs to know the genealogy for each animal and where it is caged currently in order to plan mating schedules.

Case study 4: Household
Type of business: n/a
Employees: n/a
Statement of purpose: All you need to do is keep track of the total value for all your depreciable assets so you can give it to your accountant once a year.

Part One

Preparing to design a Paradox database

1 *Laying the foundation*

You're a Paradox user. Neophyte or guru, one-man band or large corporation, you've chosen a powerful and sophisticated software tool. Whatever the motivation, your choice of a relational database suggests that you need to manage data in some shape or form. You have a problem, and the challenge is to get Paradox to figure out the answer. You might need to decide whether or not to hire new staff. You might need to evaluate the growth your business has undergone in the past year in order to project next year's growth. You might need to give your accountant a payroll summary to ensure that your quarterly tax payments are accurate. Perhaps you need to track sales, to manage your contacts with your clients more efficiently, to make your patients' records more accessible, or to plan your schedule more than a day in advance.

Taking stock of your needs

What you really need is for Paradox to compile, analyze, and present the information you use in a way that makes the solution to your problem apparent. You probably need more than a simple view of a table: you need help in making a decision.

If your business is very small, the information you use might be limited in scope. You might only have a single employee, two sales per week, or ten patients total. The help you need might be as close as your RAM-resident SideKick calculator. You can rack up the numbers, jot down the results in your notepad, pull out last year's single-page history, and be done with it. Your decision might be obvious even without performing a single calculation.

After all, the human mind has powerful analytical abilities. It can assess intuitively the value of great amounts of information. Answers might be as close as a single one-table query.

In today's business world, the likelihood that any decision is obvious or easily made is slim. Even if all the details are available, are the implications of those details as clear? Can you bring added value to your information without help? Today information of value is more of a necessity than ever, because it is that added value that makes a decision simple—and accommodates the need to make that decision quickly.

Decision making has always been time-sensitive. Speed is crucial. Customers rely on an immediate response: will you extend me credit so I can buy this from you? When can I make my next appointment to see you? Where do I put my money when the term of this CD expires? How can I protect my customer base from my ever-expanding global competition? If you don't provide answers quickly, your customer will likely fly the coop. Even if you can do the analysis in your mind, with a calculator, or even with a complicated spreadsheet, can you do it fast enough to meet the competitive requirements for customer service in your industry? Are you equipped to take advantage of a narrowing window of opportunity (like that suggested by FIG. 1-1)?

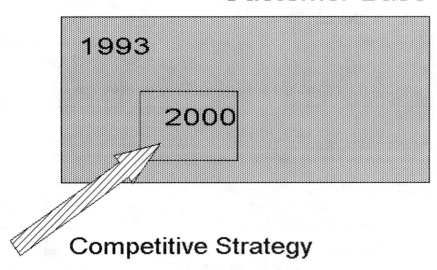

1-1
The narrowing window of opportunity

You've been surrounded by computers for years. Still, the vision of your computer as a decision-making tool is vague, and understandably so. Even Borland International's innovative technology doesn't provide you with hand-holding to ensure that you can make your computer do what you need it to do. There are so many elements that make up a PC that all vendors have almost unlimited opportunities to finger-point: you aren't getting what you want because of your hardware, because of limitations in Paradox, because of MS-DOS, because of your application, your hard disk, not enough memory, corrupted files, backup procedures, video limitations, cabling, or network protocols. The list goes on.

True, all of these elements must work together in order to solve your problem: to deliver information of value (see FIG. 1-2). However, what is often missing from the list is you. Your knowledge is essential; without it you can't tell the computer to do what you need. You must direct a PC just as you must punch the right keys on a calculator in order to arrive at the correct answer. Instructing a calculator can be simple; instructing a computer rarely is.

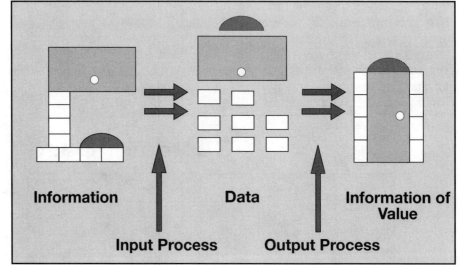

1-2
The goal of a database

Information **Data** **Information of Value**

Input Process **Output Process**

Help wanted in two languages

The problem is that a computer does not speak the same language that you do. Not even user-friendly, graphical-user-interface Paradox 4.0 speaks English. Making the leap from your own thought processes to the manipulation of databased information is no easy task. There is a process involved, a certain skill and definite art to making the translation from what you do to what a computer does.

You and Paradox work with the same information: names and addresses, customers and invoices, patients and records. However, where you have the ability to analyze and understand information from many sources presented in a variety of ways, Paradox is limited to manipulating the facts within a predefined set of storable types of data. You can understand information presented in a book, through a videotape, over the telephone, on a napkin, in a conversation. Paradox can deal only with information within the confines of very specific rules—some of which you establish but many of which are built into the product.

All computer software is intended to help translate your information into and back from the data that the PC actually stores and manipulates. As with any communication between two different languages, the translation must work two ways. Your information first requires translation into Paradox data (sometimes called *input*). Then the Paradox-stored data must be translated in order for you to understand it (sometimes called *output*—see FIG. 1-3). In general, different kinds of software help in the input, storage, manipulation, and output of different kinds of information. The information can range from the relatively simple to the very complex, and thus so can the software.

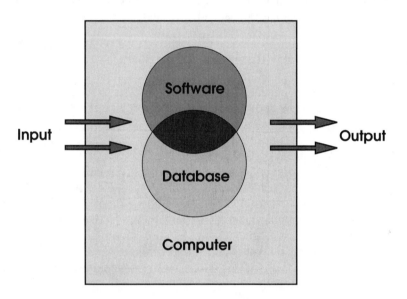

Input   Output

Word processing software helps translate a written document into computer-based information. A physical letter ready to fax and a simple word-processed document are fairly similar. You usually can begin to use a word processor without a lot of fuss; a few basic PC skills such as knowing how to save and to print allow you to be productive immediately. In this case, the translation from what you do to what the computer does is not a big leap.

More complex information requires more complex software. If instead of keeping track of documents, you must keep track of numbers, your word processor will be inadequate, because no word processor is designed to do that kind of job. You might have settled on a spreadsheet as the appropriate software for your needs. Spreadsheet software allows you to translate more complex information, such as that contained in a chart, into facts that the computer can store and manipulate. The translation required by a spreadsheet is more complicated than that of a word processor. In this instance, the information being translated goes beyond simple words into facts that are related to a structure (the cells in a spreadsheet).

Paradox is intended to translate even more complex real-world information into computer-based data. Not only can it support the same kind of data easily managed by a spreadsheet such as Quattro Pro or Lotus 1-2-3, it also can translate relationships between the different pieces of information into computer-based facts. Paradox can help you manage information, not just keep track of pieces of data. Customer management could involve a customer name and address, but also products that customer buys; medical office management might include knowing the age and sex of a patient, but also following the details of each and every contact that patient has had with you; library management must track the books in your library, but also must record who checks out the books, and who checked out which book when.

Paradox's ability to translate this more complex kind of information into usable computer-based data is what makes it powerful. But (not surprisingly) Paradox's power depends totally on your ability to wield it. Even Paradox, one of the easiest-to-use database software products available today, expects you to understand how to organize your information before you start. The organization you create before you even turn on the computer, before you input any of your information, will make or break the software's ability to do what it was designed to do. If you expect Paradox to help you make decisions, you must first understand how to direct it to do so. There are many books on the market which provide excellent tips and techniques for using both interactive Paradox and PAL. Even the documentation which comes with Paradox 4.0 contains valuable information on empowering both new and experienced users to take advantage of Paradox's many rich features. There is a robust third-party market which supports and expands upon the basic features of the product. But in the end, all of these resources rely on some level of previous knowledge.

Paradox's success in helping you to make a decision is dependent first and foremost on the design of your Paradox database. That design process is almost hidden within the wealth of resources on how to *use* Paradox. In making Paradox easy to use, Borland has effectively obscured the very real assumptions that Paradox (along with other relational database software) is based upon. All users should understand just how data structures are modeled and why; lack of this knowledge essentially excludes most nonprogrammers and even many PAL developers from ever getting full use from Paradox.

Using the drafting board

Paradox database design is a process that should result in a blueprint for building a Paradox database. A blueprint for a house specifies such information as the overall dimensions of the house, the sizes of the rooms, the positions of doorways and windows, and the intended use for each room. The blueprint includes essentially all the specifics that will allow a builder to go to work.

A Paradox database design should achieve the same level of detail. Without specifics, the database builder will be unable either to conceptualize the overall picture or to understand how each part will relate to any other part. The result could well be chaos.

Remember, your goal is to use the computer to help you make decisions. So the first step in defining a database is to outline the overall dimensions of your application: the big picture which announces and prioritizes the decisions that need supporting. An application design includes not only the database design but also the directions for how you intend to apply—to use—the database. This can be as simple as a description of the input forms and output reports you need for your database system, or as complex as details on multiple algorithms acting on data extracted for analysis from a SQL database server.

So, let's get to it. What are the tasks ahead? How do you create the set of directions necessary to make the computer do what you need?

First, you must identify what kind of information you expect. What kind of information will help you make that decision? What related decisions do you need to make? What is the scope of the help that you envision? In effect, what are the requirements for your application?

What an application is

An *application* is a customized use of database software intended to solve a business problem. An application can identify and formalize the elements involved in making decisions, and thus can provide a decision-maker with appropriate information of value relating to the available choices. Or an application might simply be the means for storing and retrieving data stored in a database.

application   A customized use of database software intended to solve a specific business problem.

All applications, whether simple or complex, involve a translation from information to computer-based data and back to information, which is now intended to be of more value (FIG. 1-3). Information is input into the application, is manipulated or managed as application data, and is then output as information of value, or decision information. A good application could be defined as one that manages this input-output process efficiently and without error, thus enabling you to make decisions efficiently and without mistakes.

Database software that is used to implement or to install an application on a PC is often called application-development software. Paradox is just one kind of application-development software. Paradox can be used both to create the tables for data storage and also to manage the actual input and output from those tables.

application-development software Database software used to implement or install an application on a PC.

You can look at the use of any application development software as having two phases. In the development phase, you build the tables and design input and output mechanisms (loosely called *objects*) that the application will need to use. In the implementation phase, you actually work with real data. The implementation phase allows you to put the development to the test—to use the objects your design process has yielded.

Developing an application is something like building a bridge: you design it, you build it, and only then can you actually use it to get to the other side. Only once an application has been created is it ready to be used; only then can you begin to input and output your information.

Application development focuses first on database design, because the database is truly the foundation of any application. Everything depends on the database: how you input and output, what you can input and output, and even how easy it is to input and output. Perhaps most importantly, the quality of your output—how useful it is—depends on the database. As FIG. 1-4 suggests, your ability to make a decision depends directly on the effectiveness of the database design. If you have built a solid foundation—a database designed for maximum usefulness, compactness, accuracy, speed, and cost effectiveness—how you get information in and out becomes a question of form rather than substance. The process of database design, and the content of this book, thus focuses on the five issues mentioned above:

Information of Value

1-4
*The database design
pyramid provides
information of value*

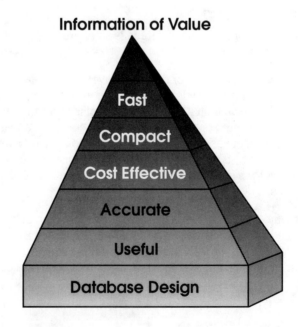

Fast

Compact

Cost Effective

Accurate

Useful

Database Design

- Usefulness
- Compactness
- Accuracy
- Speed
- Cost effectiveness

A database is most useful if it is clearly focused on achieving a goal (chapter 2). A database is most compact if it follows relational standards to reduce redundancy (chapters 4, 5, and 6). A database is most accurate if it adheres to rules of integrity (chapter 7). A database is fastest if it is optimized for a specific environment (chapters 8 through 11), and a database is most cost effective if it is evaluated in the context of both costs and benefits (chapters 12, 13 and 14).

Before getting into the details, it is important to understand the role Paradox plays in all this. What actually is database software, and what is it intended to do?

A database management system, or DBMS, is software which (like Paradox) is designed to allow you to manage data of a wide variety of types. In this text, DBMS is used in both the singular (to represent a single database-management system) and the plural (to represent multiple database-management systems).

What a database management system is

Remember, you and your computer speak different languages, and Paradox is intended to provide the translation. You can look at Paradox as a software universe in which you create an application customized to meet your specific needs (see FIG. 1-5). Paradox can give you access to a great wealth of information from a broad collection of data. However, to start, why are there

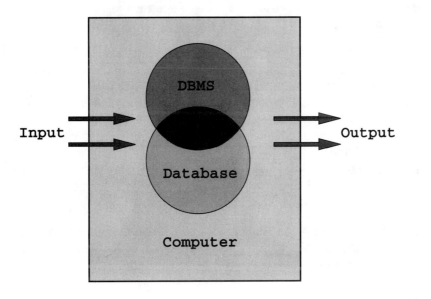

1-5
A database application under DBMS software

two terms: information and data? What is the difference between the two, and why is the distinction important?

🔑 **database management system (DBMS)**   Software designed to allow you to manage a wide variety of data types to meet a variety of needs.

**Storing data &
using information**

Data is facts. The word data is actually the plural of datum, but is used commonly as a singular description of something known or assumed. Data is meaningless because it provides no organization or context. Figure 1-6 displays data elements, which might or might not be related in some way. A jumble of alphabetic characters on a page explains nothing; those same characters grouped into words with a certain structure suddenly become a meaningful poem. Words and numbers randomly appearing on a page probably tell you nothing useful; organized words and numbers are immediately recognizable as the names and addresses of specific people. Data when organized is known as *information*. Information is what you use in your business. Information is what is created when data elements strewn across a page are grouped into employee names, identifiers, and telephone numbers (FIG. 1-7).

🔑 **data**   Facts (plural), or a fact (singular), meaningless because it lacks context.
information   Organized data.

**How Paradox
manages data**

Like other software, Paradox is intended to provide a translation between the information that you work with and the information that the computer can keep track of. Paradox is a database management system rather than an information base management system because all the information that you provide is translated into its component data elements by Paradox. These data elements then can be stored, modified, manipulated, or extracted back into information that you use. Paradox uses specific tools to perform each of these tasks.

Using Paradox 4.0 can be simple, much like making a sketch, filling in blanks on a form, or crossing an incorrect value off of a list. On the other hand, sometimes these simple tasks can be relatively hard to perform, and can require learning a whole language unique to Paradox (the Paradox Application Language, or PAL). Different DBMSs require you to have widely varying skills to get anything done. DBMSs like Paradox that are easy to use are intuitive and help you learn and get things done at the same time. Paradox gives you a lot of help through detailed menus with simple and well-defined choices, and screens that look something like (or sometimes a lot like) physical objects you are already familiar with.

🔑 **easy-to-use DBMS**   A DBMS that is intuitive and provides lots of help through detailed menus and well-defined choices, with screens that look a lot like the physical objects you are already familiar with.

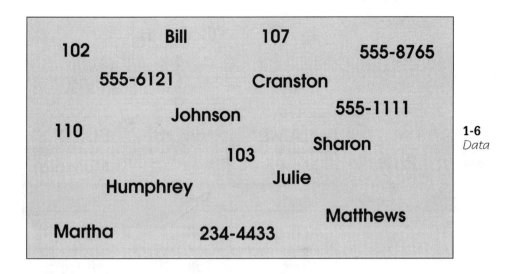

102
Bill Johnson
234-4433

103
Martha Humphrey
555-8765

107
Sharon Cranston
555-6121

110
Julie Matthews
555-1111

PAL   The Paradox Application Language, which is used to customize and extend the features available through the Paradox menu system.

The relational DBMS difference

The definition of a relational database is based on the concept that everything about an application (e.g., all the data that is to be managed by the application) can be stored in tables. For the purpose of this preliminary discussion, a table is nothing more than a single set of rows and columns (see FIG. 1-8).

C.J. Date, one of the earliest contributors to relational-database theory, defines a relational database as "a database that is perceived by its users as a

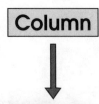

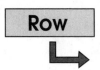

1-8
A table includes both rows and columns

NAME	HEIGHT	BUILD
Mark	Tall	Muscular
Mark	Short	Thin
Margaret	Tall	Thin
Karen	Tall	Athletic
Diane	Short	Thin

collection of tables (and nothing but tables)" (1990, 112). This concept is fundamental to a relational database because it allows for data independence, the isolation of data from the mechanisms Paradox or any other DBMS uses to access that data. When a system supports data independence, users of that system are not required to ever know how the data is stored or how to access it—only that it exists in some logical format (described more in detail below). We might know, for example, that the file formats supported by Paradox 4.0 are different than those supported by Paradox 3.5; but when we sit down to use the product that knowledge is irrelevant.

data independence   A quality of data that describes the fact that it is accessible through a logical format, and whose users need never know how it is physically stored.

Other types of databases, including structured or hierarchical databases, also manage data in tables. However, nonrelational databases usually relate or link the data in different tables through a program. A program is nothing more than a set of directions you create and save that a DBMS then can follow once or many times (in Paradox, a program is called a *script*). A relational database is by definition more flexible than other types of databases, because changes to a relational application often can be made by changing the data, not the program. Changes to data are easily made; changes to programs usually are not.

program   A set of directions you create and save that tell a DBMS what things to do and in what order. In Paradox, a program is called a script.

Relational theory, initially developed by E.F. Codd in the late 1960s, is unique in that it applies mathematical logic to the realm of database management (Codd 1970). In fact, the term relational is used in this context because of the theory's basis in relational algebra. The theory itself is a set of rules that define different aspects of the ideal relational DBMS. This idealized DBMS is known as the *relational model*. Originally, the model was defined by 12 basic rules, but over time it has been expanded and now encompasses over 300 rules (Codd 1990).

relational model   A set of rules based on relational algebra that describe data structures using mathematical principles. The model describes three aspects of database management: data structures, data integrity, and data manipulation. The data structures are intended to reduce redundancy in data storage, and also to provide efficiency, security, and integrity across databases that are both shared and integrated.

DBMS software that is advertised as relational is usually only relational to one degree or another—only to the extent that it follows the rules established by relational theory. There currently is no commercially available software (not even Paradox!) that follows all the rules, either for a PC or for any larger minicomputer or mainframe system. However, for the purposes of this book, a relational DBMS (sometimes called an RDBMS) is simply software that is intended to manage data stored in relational tables (see chapter 4 for more detail on relational tables). To this degree, Paradox is also a RDBMS.

relational DBMS (RDBMS)   DBMS software that (to one degree or another) follows the rules laid out by the relational model.

Most applications built with a relational database management system (including Paradox applications) rely on data encompassed within multiple tables. As suggested by FIG. 1-9, the data in these tables define actual objects and processes, while at the same time also defining the relationships between the tables.

DBMS functions can be divided into five basic categories (see FIG. 1-10). Every DBMS should allow you to:

What a DBMS does

- Create and modify data structures
- Add, modify, manipulate, or delete data
- Manage data security and integrity
- Customize data input and output
- Automate or enhance the use of the other features

Paradox, like most DBMSs, allows you to work with data elements that can be extracted and manipulated independently of any other data elements. Unlike elements (words) in a word-processed document, Paradox data elements usually are not linked sequentially. Instead, they are stored within a

Creating & modifying data structures

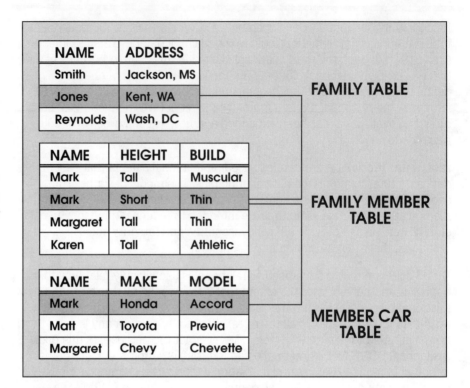

1-9
A relational database

FAMILY TABLE

NAME	ADDRESS
Smith	Jackson, MS
Jones	Kent, WA
Reynolds	Wash, DC

FAMILY MEMBER TABLE

NAME	HEIGHT	BUILD
Mark	Tall	Muscular
Mark	Short	Thin
Margaret	Tall	Thin
Karen	Tall	Athletic

MEMBER CAR TABLE

NAME	MAKE	MODEL
Mark	Honda	Accord
Matt	Toyota	Previa
Margaret	Chevy	Chevette

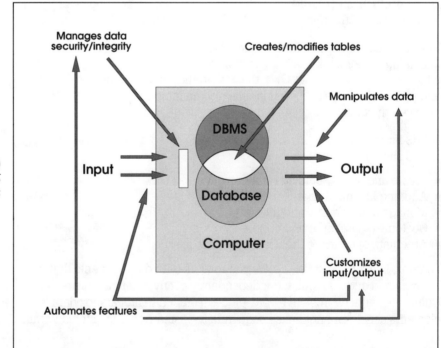

1-10
The functions of a DBMS fall into five categories

Manages data security/integrity

Creates/modifies tables

Manipulates data

Input

DBMS

Database

Computer

Output

Customizes input/output

Automates features

separately defined database structure known as a *table*. This database structure is discussed in greater detail later in this chapter.

Paradox allows you to build a new structure through the `Create` menu option or the PAL `Create` command. Once built, that structure can be modified through `Modify|Restructure` or through the PAL equivalent commands.

Once a table has been created, you can use Paradox to enter data, make changes to data, or delete data. Paradox also has powerful tools for manipulating, summarizing, and analyzing data. These capabilities allow you to perform calculations, combine data, and translate data (import and export) directly to and from other DBMSs or related software.

Adding, modifying, manipulating, or deleting data

Data manipulation also includes data extraction, or the capability to ask questions about the data. Paradox supports very sophisticated tools in this area through query-by-example (QBE). Querying is a crucial feature in any DBMS, because most applications rely heavily on queries as the basis for outputting information of value. Paradox's QBE is particularly easy to use and in fact was one of the pioneers of the QBE concept, which utilizes a special blank version of the table which the user then fills out in order to demonstrate what the result of the query should look like.

query   A technique for asking questions or doing analysis on data managed by a DBMS.

query-by-example (QBE)   An implementation of querying which utilizes a query form which the user then fills out to demonstrate what the result of the query should look like.

Paradox's data-manipulation features also include the capability to handle multiple sets of data at the same time. Paradox can combine or separate data from more than one structure through a single QBE operation, through menu choices, or via PAL.

Paradox includes the capability to control who can use the data structure and data-manipulation features described above. Password protection is easily available at the table level. In addition, Paradox (through PAL) also supports specifying under what circumstances the use of such features is allowable. This kind of control is usually a critical aspect of your application. Without accurate and valid data, any information compiled by the application and provided as output to you will be unreliable, and thus useless as a tool for making a decision.

Managing data security & integrity

Data security describes the control the DBMS exerts over who can do what in an application. Security can be seen as a matrix that compares each user to each item of data. In its simplest form, data security defines data table by table, and each user's ability to access the data is specified through a yes or no (see Table 1-1). In reality, data security usually is enforced through a more complicated set of PAL definitions that can identify specific data elements (not just tables) and which of several types of access are allowable.

Table 1-1
The simplest kind of data security:
is access allowed to the rows?

User	Mark	Steve	Judy
Family	Yes	Yes	Yes
Member	No	No	Yes
Member car	No	Yes	Yes

One of the reasons that data security is a primary concern in an application is that without it, the validity of the data can be compromised quickly. Even with appropriate security in effect, data entry and modification will always include inadvertent errors. Whenever possible, Paradox should and will help you to reduce the frequency of these kind of errors.

Data integrity describes the accuracy and validity of data in an application relative to the requirements of the business. As discussed in more detail later in this chapter (and in chapter 2), the database design specifies what data you will keep track of and how that data is related. The design also specifies details about what makes the data being tracked correct—in other words, what you expect for each data element (see chapter 5). A DBMS should help make sure that these details are applied consistently, and thus that the data will be accurate. In other words, a value you think is a social security number is in the appropriate format, a date for a newly purchased item is within the current month and year, and an invoice number falls within an allowable range of values. The combination of Paradox's data types and validity checks can be used to increase data accuracy. Paradox's validity checks can also help ensure that the data reflects what is true, i.e., that a two-digit state abbreviation describes a real state, or that a department number represents a real department in the business system.

 data integrity   The accuracy and validity of data in an application relative to the requirements of the business.

Customizing data input & output   In addition to the basic features necessary to maintain the data, most DBMSs provide a wide variety of features that enable you to control how you actually work with the data. These features allow you to control the organization and format of what you work with in order to help you use information, rather than merely data.

In effect, these features enable the translation of your information to and from data. Even if a query is used to compile the information, a printed report or plotted graph or displayed window on the screen actually will deliver it. The closer the appearance of that image is to the information you need, the more readily you will be able to derive information of value from it (and, not coincidentally, the easier the application will be to use).

Paradox's ongoing development in this area is helping to keep the product at the forefront of its RDBMS competitors. One of the most obvious enhancements available through Paradox 4.0 is in the on-screen appearance of the software. Applications running under 4.0 now can have a look-and-feel that is similar to other software you might be using today. This kind of organization and formatting is fundamentally different from the type of organization developed through a database design. As described in detail in chapter 2, the database design deals with relational logic applied to your data. Customized data input and output, on the other hand, address your need to deal with this data as information. Each user of the data might (and probably will) have a different need for information. Even as a single user of your application, you will probably want to enter (input) or gather (output) different information from the system at different times. You might need to enter a new patient and his appointment time today, but tomorrow you might need to print a list of all the patients and their addresses. The next day you might want to print your appointments for next week. Each different need is associated with different information.

At one level, customization of data input and output involves identifying the information you need for a specific purpose. In conceptual terms, this kind of specification is called a *view* (see FIG. 1-11). In some DBMSs, views are

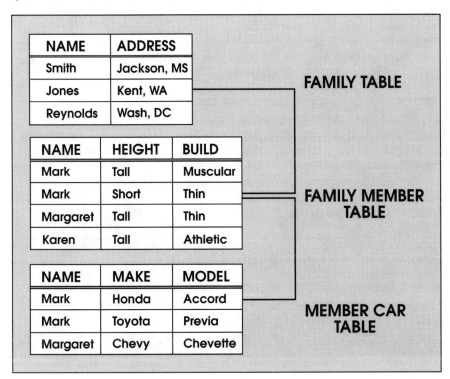

NAME	ADDRESS
Smith	Jackson, MS
Jones	Kent, WA
Reynolds	Wash, DC

FAMILY TABLE

NAME	HEIGHT	BUILD
Mark	Tall	Muscular
Mark	Short	Thin
Margaret	Tall	Thin
Karen	Tall	Athletic

FAMILY MEMBER TABLE

NAME	MAKE	MODEL
Mark	Honda	Accord
Mark	Toyota	Previa
Margaret	Chevy	Chevette

MEMBER CAR TABLE

1-11
A relational database combines data in multiple tables through combining specific rows of data

created and modified in a way similar to tables. The only difference is that the elements of a view are not data elements themselves; views just identify where among the tables the actual data elements can be found. In Paradox, a conceptual view can be created through a query, a multitable form or a multitable report. In all of these cases, what can be stored is the definition of the view, not the combined data. The Paradox View menu option is only one way to access data in tables. Paradox's support for conceptual views extends well beyond that single menu choice.

conceptual view A combination of fields from tables that acts like a table itself. A view normally is used for a specific input or output process.

You should be aware, however, that Paradox support for conceptual views is somewhat tainted. The same combination of data elements must be redefined (sometimes three or more different times) in order to utilize the view's data. From a purist perspective, a single view definition (like a multitable query) should be able to build a conceptual view which is then reusable in all appropriate contexts. This would allow data to be entered, or modified, or graphed, or reported on, or analyzed, from within the view in the same way that it can be accessed through the source table. In today's Paradox, once a query has been performed to create the view, the data elements in the view (the Answer table) are now separate and independent from their source tables. It can require substantial programming in order to reconnect Answer data back to its source, and even then there are no guarantees. Similarly, once a multitable form has been defined to create the same kind of view as the query, yet another definition must be created to support a multitable report; yet all of these views are conceptually identical. Even if another report or another form or another query acts on the same view, it must again redefine the view, over and over again.

Paradox's form and report generators might eventually be able to work on a predefined view. A form is an image on the computer screen that is used to access data, to input new data, or to look at or modify data that already has been input. A report, on the other hand, is used to create output which is separate from the source. The form generator is used to build a form, and it works much like a report generator for output on the screen. A form usually specifies details such as the placement of the data on the screen, the order in which you enter or move through the data elements, and cosmetic details, such as the colors of different areas of the screen or what kind of borders will surround them. A report simply defines the data, how it is organized, and also cosmetics including fonts, spacing, etc.

form An image on the computer screen that is used to access data; to input new data, or to look at or modify data that has already been input.

report A type of output used to create a stored, printed or displayed image of the data.

The last category of DBMS features allows you to customize the way that your application works. Remember, the intent is to deliver information of value. You can see from the discussion of the other DBMS features that the delivery of this information might well be dependent upon not one, but several features of the DBMS.

Without help, you would be forced to go through several steps in order to get what you need. For example, to determine your schedule for today, you might need to build a query to select only those appointments for today, design a report to lay out each appointment against a grid of the available appointment times, and finally output that report to your printer or onto your screen.

However, Paradox supports features that enable you to automate this kind of task. Automation involves creating a script, simple as it might be, that tells Paradox what to do so you don't have to. Instead of going through each step every time you need a printed copy of your schedule, you perform one step, `Scripts|Play|Schedule`, relying on Paradox to follow through with the rest of the steps. Automating thus can be seen as creating a layer of control that customizes how the DBMS interacts with you (see FIG. 1-12). Automating allows you to use Paradox to perform a task without your having to remember all the steps every time. Once you've created a menu structure (written the script), you can ignore the details of the steps, and making a simple choice can allow input, output, or some combination of both to occur.

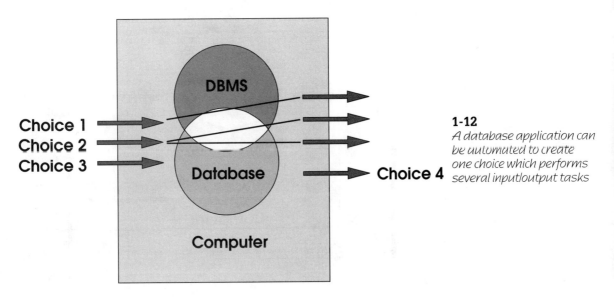

1-12
A database application can be automated to create one choice which performs several input/output tasks

This category of DBMS features is often called a *programming language* because it allows you to create and save the necessary instructions as a program. The DBMS will then follow these instructions each time you direct it to. DBMS programming tools, even Paradox's PAL, are often the most difficult features to understand and work with, because they are essentially similar to any other programming language, such as BASIC or PASCAL or C.

programming language   Those features of the DBMS that allow you to automate or customize the use of the other features.

All the features of the DBMS should be used to accomplish the overall goal of the application: to deliver information of value to you. A DBMS programming language gives you the power to define what you need just once, and then rely on the DBMS to get it done.

However, how do you go about defining what you need? Specifically, what kinds of things does Paradox have to do for you in order to deliver information of value? Although you now should have a sense of what a DBMS is or should be able to do, it might not be so clear which of these features you need for your application. The features that will be important to you depend on what you need to accomplish, or more to the point, what you need the application to do.

What an application does

The things you need Paradox to do usually are nothing more than inputs and outputs, and sometimes internal manipulations. These operations taken together can be called *application tasks* (see FIG. 1-13).

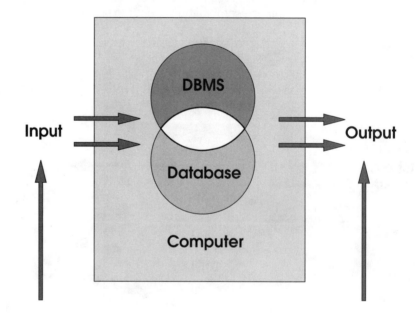

1-13
Application tasks include both inputs and outputs

application tasks   Things you need the DBMS to do, usually involving input or output from the database.

C.J. Date, along with other database theorists, draws a distinction between operational and decision support databases. Operational databases, according to Date, focus on "routine, highly repetitive applications . . . executed over and over again to support the day-to-day operation of the enterprise." Decision-support databases "frequently [consist] of summary information (e.g., totals, averages), where that summary information in turn is extracted from the operational database on a periodic basis—say once a day or once a week" (1990, 10–11). In this sense, the tasks an operational database might be expected to perform would differ dramatically from those expected of a decision-support database. However, for the purposes of this discussion, both types of databases are assumed to be encompassed within a single, decision-oriented database. Practically speaking, most small to mid-size applications do combine both types of requirements into one. For example, you'll probably use just one application—one database—to both help you track current activity and predict upcoming activity. An application normally includes the following decision-oriented tasks:

- Generating reports
- Displaying graphs
- Answering questions
- Performing analyses

These tasks are clearly focused on getting you information of value, and they basically define the output of the application (see FIG. 1-14).

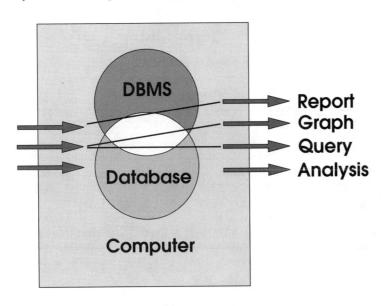

1-14
Automating application output tasks

In addition to the decision-oriented tasks, an application must support the maintenance of the data itself. Without the mechanisms in place to keep the data up-to-date, any business system will quickly fail. The information will not be of value because it will be obsolete.

The data must be entered, edited where appropriate, and deleted when necessary. From your point of view, these tasks often are the most time-consuming in an application, and thus weigh heavily in any cost analysis (see chapter 13). Data input and maintenance can, however, be streamlined by taking advantage of different options supported by Paradox. In addition to entering data from the keyboard, Paradox supports the entry of data through file import from other software, by moving data from one table to another within the database or from other physical sources, such as a scanner or a bar-code reader. These jointly define the input for the application (see FIG. 1-15).

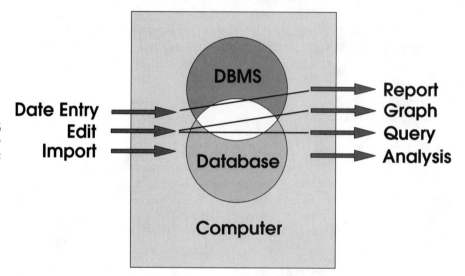

1-15
Automating application input and output tasks

In addition to those tasks specifically related to data maintenance, other tasks are necessary to support the application itself. These tasks usually include the development of backup and recovery procedures to protect against the time when the computer will fail. Backup refers to the process of making a copy (often in some kind of compressed mode) of the application programs and data (the output side). Recovery refers to the process of returning the application to its original state (the input side).

backup   The process of making a copy of the application programs and data (often in some kind of compressed mode).
recovery   The process of returning an application to a prefailure state after a problem has occurred.

Backup and recovery tasks all relate to the process of entering and maintaining data within the structures of the database.

What data structures are   All DBMSs manage data (see FIG. 1-16). Data managed by an RDBMS like Paradox is always managed in tables. A table, in its simplest form nothing

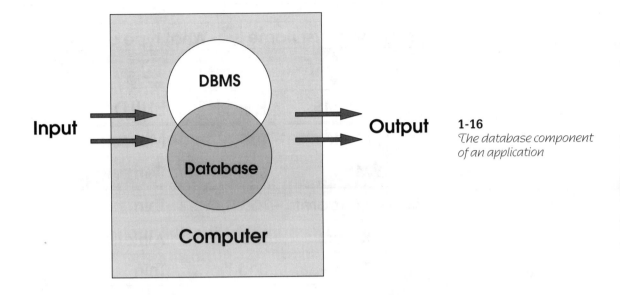

1-16
*The database component
of an application*

more than a set of rows and columns, is commonly used to keep information
in an organized format. You have already encountered and intuitively
understood tables in many contexts completely unrelated to databases, such
as sports box scores, tide tables, and questionnaires.

A Paradox table is a lot like these other kinds of tables. However, a relational
table (the data structure used by any RDBMS) is unique in several important
ways. In fact, a relational table differs enough from what people commonly
regard as a table that the relational model uses different terms entirely to
describe it, such as relation, or R-table (see chapter 4 for a more detailed
discussion of relations). However, in this book I use the more familiar term
table when referring to a relational table.

A table consists of a grid of rows and columns and looks a lot like a simple
spreadsheet. Each row contains data, all of which relate to a single object or
process. Each column contains data that describe one attribute of that object
or process (see FIG. 1-17).

For example, data about members of your family could be stored in a
table that listed each member's name, height, and build. Each family
member's data would be represented by a single row, and each type of
stored data would be represented within a single column, i.e., *Name*,
Height, or *Build*.

For the purpose of simplicity, thus far the term table has been used to
describe the way a DBMS, and specifically Paradox, manages and stores
data. In fact, there is a big difference between the concept of a table and
the way data actually is stored by Paradox on a hard or floppy disk.

**Working with
logical tables**

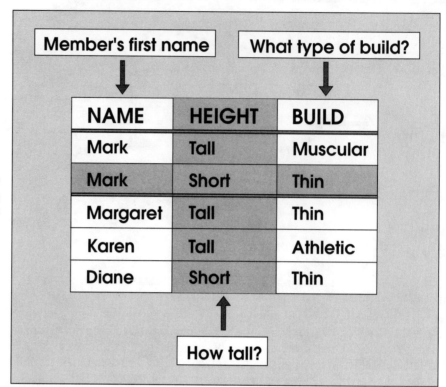

1-17
*The columns in a table
contain attributes*

The terms *logical table* and *physical table* describe these two different ways of understanding the way a DBMS manages data. A table (as this book uses the term) is more specifically a logical table, because it is really just a disciplined way of thinking about how the data is stored. Each DBMS manages the physical storage of the data in its own way. Thus, a single logical table could be stored in many different physical table formats. To you, or any other user of Paradox, the data will look the same, regardless of the particular physical table format being used. For example, a Paradox 3.5 table will look exactly the same to you as a Paradox 4.0 table. This follows directly from the data independence achieved by the relational model; you can ignore the physical format as long as the integrity of the logical tables is preserved (see FIG. 1-18).

logical table   A table that is conceived by application users to think about and manipulate data.

Understanding physical tables

Some DBMSs translate each table into an individual file. Some DBMSs combine all tables in a given database into a single file. Paradox combines table data and all associated activities regarding that data into a related group of files (the table's *family*).

physical table   The organization for data as it is stored.

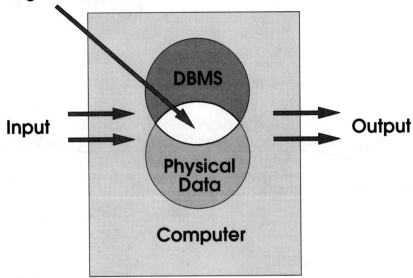

Logical Tables

DBMS

Physical Data

Input

Output

Computer

1-18
Logical tables are used by Paradox and users to conceptualize the physical storage of the data

family   The group of DOS files which all relate to a single set of data stored in a single Paradox table.

This separation between logical and physical tables sometimes is described in slightly different terms. A physical table can be considered part of an internal level or storage view that is concerned primarily with the way the data is stored on the disk; a logical table is sometimes regarded as existing on a conceptual level. In other words, a logical table consists of all the tables and their relationships; a third level, known as the external level, is used sometimes to describe the way individual users access the data, roughly equivalent in scope to the definition of a view given earlier in this chapter (Tsichritzia and Klug 1978).

Regardless of terminology, the physical structure of the data is one feature that differentiates one DBMS from another. Many RDBMSs use proprietary structures that cannot be accessed by any other software. Data from this kind of RDBMS must be translated in order to be usable by any other kind of DBMS, or by any other kind of software. A translation of this kind often is called *exporting* (my software to yours) or *importing* (your software to mine).

export   A translation of data from your DBMS to the format of another software program.
import   A translation of data from another software program into your DBMS.

Some RDBMSs use a more standard structure, with data stored in physical files with the DBF (database file) extension. This specific kind of file name describes an arguably nonproprietary type of physical data structure. The class of DBMS known as XBase products utilizes this rather generic form of physical storage. DBF data structures are accessible directly by a variety of DBMS products. Borland International is currently pursuing a vision of database software which would make several different file formats available to Paradox users (not just the standard Paradox .DB format). Borland's SQL Link product takes one step in that direction by allowing Paradox users to get access to data stored in different file formats supported by Structured Query Language (SQL).

Again, any RDBMS that supports data independence should allow the physical structure of the data to be of little importance to you. After all, it is Paradox's job to act as the interpreter between the computer and you; translating data between the physical and logical realms is a perfect example of this interpretive kind of task.

To review briefly, Paradox manages data in tables. A table is thus the only kind of Paradox data structure. If no other qualifier is used, in this book the term table refers to a logical, relational table.

Remember, the DBMS controls the application. It both manages the data in the tables and allows the input and output to occur. However, even the most highly automated application will still rely on you to make it work. After the design process is over, you must still play a role, but what role is that? What kinds of things should you expect to contribute to ensure your application's success?

Using an application

Any functioning application involves a combination of human and automated resources. Even those tasks that are managed clearly by the computer depend, to a greater or lesser degree, on the people who interact with it. The automated part of the business system depends on the people to gather the necessary information, to convey this information to the computer in some way, and to demand information in return.

The people who work with an application fall into two categories: those who support the maintenance of the data (the gathering and conveying, or input), and those who rely on the data to make decisions (the demanding, or output). Both categories of people can be considered system users. In a smaller system, most users assume both roles. In a larger system, management-level people usually have little responsibility for day-to-day data maintenance, while staff workers have little need for decision-oriented information.

user A person who works with an application, either to maintain the data or to rely on it, to aid in the decision-making process.

In a small business system, the application developer also might be the focus for the delivery of the information of value. Obviously, you are your own designer here. Depending on the degree of automation (sometimes called *sophistication*) of your application, obtaining input and output might be very simple or very complicated, either fast or very slow. Don't confuse sophistication with complexity; the most sophisticated applications are often deceptively simple to use.

sophistication The degree of automation of an application that makes use of the system as easy as possible.

An application that meets its goal will allow a user to demand, and to obtain, information of value. However, in order for that to happen, the application must be maintained. Any system, computer-based or not, requires monitoring on an ongoing basis. Data that is input must be kept up to date, work in process must be copied (backed-up) in case of system failure, and useless or out-of-date data must be archived or removed. These tasks and others like them are called *system maintenance*, and they can occupy a substantial portion of the time required to make the system work. If your application is used by more than one individual, these tasks likely will occupy an even greater amount of time.

maintenance The ongoing work done to an application that is required in order to ensure that it continues to work.

Summary

In this chapter, you encountered some basic concepts that should help you understand the foundation of any database management system and of Paradox in particular. Specifically, you learned that:

- Data and information are not the same. You work with information while a computer deals with data.
- A Database Management System, or DBMS, stores and manipulates data of many kinds to provide you with a wide range of information.
- An application usually involves tasks directed toward decision-assistance (delivering information of value), but also must involve data input and maintenance tasks.
- Data storage describes the way a computer keeps track of the data, while input and output involve how you move data in and out.
- Paradox stores data in tables consisting of rows and columns.
- You and all other users are integral to the success of your business system.

Key Terms

application A customized use of database software intended to solve a specific business problem.

application-development software Database software used to implement or install an application on a PC.

application tasks Things you need the DBMS to do, usually involving input or output from the database.

backup The process of making a copy of the application programs and data (often in some kind of compressed mode).

conceptual view A combination of fields from tables that acts like a table itself. A view normally is used for a specific input or output process.

DBMS (database management system)   Software designed to allow you to manage a wide variety of data types to meet a variety of needs.

data   Facts (plural), or a fact (singular), meaningless because it lacks context.

data independence   A quality of data that describes the fact that it is accessible through a logical format, and whose users need never know how it is physically stored.

data integrity   The accuracy and validity of data in an application relative to the requirements of the business.

data security   The control the DBMS exerts over who can do what in an application.

easy-to-use   A DBMS that is intuitive and provides a lot of help through detailed menus and well-defined choices, with screens that look a lot like the physical objects you are already familiar with.

export   A translation of data from your DBMS to the format of another software program.

family   The group of DOS files which all relate to a single set of data stored in a single Paradox table.

form   An image on the computer screen that is used to access data, to input new data, or to look at or modify data that has already been input.

import   A translation of data from another software program into your DBMS.

information   Organized data.

logical table   A table that is conceived by application users to think about and manipulate data.

maintenance   The ongoing work done to an application that is required in order to ensure that it continues to work.

PAL   The Paradox Application Language, which is used to customize and extend the features available through the Paradox menu system.

physical table   The organization for data as it is stored.

program   A set of directions you create and save that tell a DBMS what things to do and in what order. In Paradox, a program is called a script.

programming language   Those features of the DBMS that allow you to automate or customize the use of the other features.

query   A technique for asking questions or doing analysis on data managed by a DBMS.

query-by-example (QBE)   Paradox's implementation of querying which utilizes a query form which the user then fills out to demonstrate what the result of the query should look like.

relational DBMS (RDBMS)   DBMS software that (to one degree or another) follows the rules laid out by the relational model.

recovery   The process of returning an application to a prefailure state after a problem has occurred.

relation   A special kind of table that has been modified to follow the rules of the relational model.

report   A type of output used to create a stored, printed or displayed image of the data.

relational model   A set of rules based on relational algebra that describe data structures using mathematical principles. The model describes three aspects of database management: data structures, data integrity, and data manipulation. The data structures are intended to reduce redundancy in data storage, and also to provide efficiency, security, and integrity across databases that are both shared and integrated.

sophistication   The degree of automation of an application that makes use of the system as easy as possible.

user   A person who works with an application, either to maintain the data or to rely on it, to aid in the decision-making process.

2 The database design process

You've taken a look at the boundaries of what an application can do. This perspective is certainly interesting and very helpful in concept, but what about your needs? How does all this relate to what you want to get done?

Now you need to start getting specific. You need to be able to imagine what your own application will look like. You need to begin creating an application design (to draft the blueprint for your application), but understanding the components of a generic application isn't enough. It doesn't really equip you to begin the process of creating your own.

What you need is a methodology for application design. A methodology in this sense is nothing more than a series of steps that you can follow. At this point you need to understand the process as well as the result.

Developing an application

You might imagine that application development is a straight-line process. Follow step one, step two, and step three, and you'll arrive at a point where your application is complete. This assumes that the application is a product, a result of the development process.

Let's take a closer look at the definition of an application. As defined in chapter 1, an application is a customized use of database software intended to solve a business problem. Because an application is a product, application development follows the classic cycle. The life cycle is so called because it spans the life of the business system, from beginning to end (see FIG. 2-1).

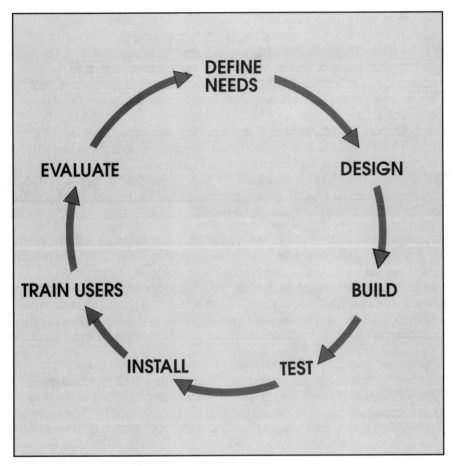

2-1
The application development life cycle

life cycle   A development process that spans the life of the system being developed and usually encompasses steps from the identification of the requirements through the installation, training, and evaluation of the system.

In many ways, application development is not a true cycle. It begins with the conceptualization of the target: the end result, or what the system will do. From that point on, the development proceeds through the design, building, and testing of the application, installation and training, and evaluation of the implemented system. Evaluation usually happens naturally, as people complain about problems: invalid results, slow processes, awkward tasks. The evaluation thus leads to a redefinition of the requirements, which starts the cycle again. However, now the requirements are closer to the end result, and thus the cycle should take less time. Note that this quickening development cycle only really applies in a relational database system. It is, in fact, part of the power of a relational system that it is flexible enough to allow for redesign—in fact, to encourage it. Nonrelational systems are so rigid that redesign often involves as much time as designing the first time around.

In practice, a life cycle can continue indefinitely. A final end result, so carefully evaluated and planned for, is often unreachable. This might be true for several reasons. First, once an application is implemented, the end result (the target) is bound to change. It is always much easier to conceptualize an end result when you have pieces of it already available than when everything is still on paper. Second, the requirements for a system could become obsolete before the system is even implemented. The computer industry is changing so quickly that the cost/benefit to making a different hardware selection or integrating several applications can justify a substantial change in the requirements. Third, the development could end prematurely because the benefit to be realized in continuing to make modifications just doesn't justify the cost. In effect, the application might not be ideal, but it works.

You might find this kind of process unsatisfying, or even unacceptable. It certainly isn't mathematically pure, in the sense that A (identified end result) plus B (application development process) always equals C (ideal application). The process of building an application is not now, nor will it ever be, an exact science, because what you are trying to do is translate human thought into computer processing. The languages are different, and thus the translation will never be exact.

This isn't an insurmountable problem; it shouldn't scare you to think that you are shooting at a target you'll never hit. The process has its own benefits. First, you'll probably discover things about your business that you never had time to contemplate before. Second, you might be surprised to uncover better ways of doing business, even for those tasks that aren't computer-based. Finally, even a rough-and-ready application is likely to prove invaluable.

The database design step in system design

As mentioned earlier, database design is only one component of the application development phase. This is because the database is only one component of the application itself, albeit the most important one. This book is not intended to cover the entire scope of application design, but just as a matter of perspective, application design should include the following:

- Specifics of hardware (what kind of computer will be used)
- Operating system(s)
- Software (Paradox and other)
- Communications (within the same business system or between business systems, locally or over a distance)
- Integration (controlling relationships between different hardware, software, operating system, and communications elements)

The human components of the application design include the specifics of who will use the system and for what purpose, how those users will relate to one another, who will be responsible for what area of the application, and what kind of training will be required initially and in the long-term for those users.

The development of the database design will need to take some of these elements into consideration. The hardware and software components that are proposed will have a large impact on the type of database design used. For the purposes of this book, the business system design is assumed to include implementation on a PC-based system (either with one or multiple users), using Paradox 3.5 or Paradox 4.0.

Input and output will need to be identified in order for you to decide appropriately what type of data will need to be managed by Paradox. However, you can't make those assessments until you've taken a closer look at database design.

A database design is an object: an actual, physical document that describes in textual and graphic detail the data structures required for a given business system. Note that the term *object* is used by this industry in a very specific way, to describe the software analog of a real-world thing (Mullin 1989). The usage here does not relate to that definition; *object* here is used simply to describe a material thing that occupies space. These structures include both a definition of the logical tables and a description of the boundaries of the data to be found within those tables. In many ways, a database design is a model of the data itself. The model must be very detailed, detailed enough that the entire application can be built confidently on this foundation. However, the model also should be real enough so that you can describe it without special terminology, and straightforward enough so that you can summarize it on a single piece of paper.

What a database design is

Don't be misled—database design is still a part of application design cycle. The design will be modified and enhanced and tweaked. Simply regard the first cycle as being highly dependent on the quality of the database design. If you do a good job with the design the first time, you're starting out on a firm foundation.

The process of database design begins with a concept of the overall application. The application should be able to take what you know and translate it into what the computer can handle. What you know in this situation relates not only to the information you work with, but also to the work flow that you live every day, the process of doing business.

An overview of the database design process

The database design process starts with a firm grounding in relational theory, and then when necessary, moves to optimize the design (see FIG. 2-2). You start by defining the input/output, designing the tables, and identifying the integrity constraints on the data, but you could discover that this initial design doesn't meet your requirements from a performance or cost standpoint. Thus, after you apply a dose of reality, you'll likely revisit those initial definitions. The theoretical side of the process is completely independent of any hardware or database product specifications, while reality remains oblivious to any restrictions of relational database modeling.

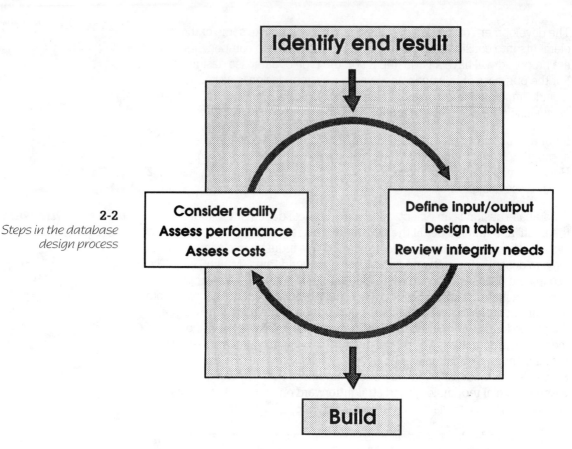

Identify end result

Consider reality
Assess performance
Assess costs

Define input/output
Design tables
Review integrity needs

Build

2-2
*Steps in the database
design process*

The first time around, the theoretical design is addressed first. Even though you have selected Paradox as your RDBMS product of choice, the theoretical design should remain independent of Paradox, insofar as that is practical. This is true for several reasons. First, it helps to keep an open mind about the implementation so that brainstorming is not adversely impacted. Second, it is always possible that a particular relational design is just not suited to Paradox implementation. Luckily, this is rarely the case, but it is possible, and certainly should always be considered an option. Third, if a theoretical design has been accomplished and is untainted by practical considerations such as those imposed by Paradox, this theoretical design will be readily portable to any other database platform that you might move to at some later date. Once the theoretical design is complete, the process continues with the consideration of the practical aspects of the design's implementation. Paradox does has different requirements that will immediately have an impact on the design. Performance issues, which address how fast different aspects of the implemented system must happen, also should be considered (see chapter 12). In addition, the costs of the system must be evaluated continually, because design decisions will have a major impact on the long-term cost of any business system (see chapter 13).

Any business solution must be preceded by a specific, identifiable need. If you can't express the requirement, you surely won't be able to conceptualize a solution. The first step in the process of designing an application thus involves identifying and capturing the need. The output of an up-and-running application intended to meet this need could be called the *end result*: the target in the life cycle.

Your end result might be nothing more than a summary of what you want your application to do. You should be able to summarize your end result in a single, simple sentence. In a decision-oriented application, the end result normally will involve the delivery of information of value: an output.

end result   The output of an up-and-running application, and the goal of the application development process.

To figure out your end result, ask two very specific questions: What do I need to know that this system will tell me? What will this information allow me to do? Table 2-1 asks and answers these questions for each of the case studies. Note that three out of the four cases specify the management of a given business function as a goal for the application.

Table 2-1
Information needed.

Need to know	Need to do
Who is scheduled when	Manage time
Who ordered what	Manage purchase orders
Which animals should be mated	Find mates
How much assets are worth	Keep list of assets

The application should be there to help the job get done. In a very real way, the end result of your application might well be parallel to the end result of your job. Asking the question "What do I do?" could lead directly to the answer, "What must my system help me do?" Even if you don't need a system to support you in every area of your job, understanding the scope of what your job entails often will help put the requirements for your application in perspective. This perspective is essential in looking at the cost versus benefit equation examined in some detail in chapter 13.

Table 2-2 lists some additional examples of end results. You'll note that many of these examples, like the case studies, include the term *management*. This term is used frequently in regard to applications, for the same reason that it is used frequently to describe job responsibilities. In an application, information management usually spans the spectrum of Paradox tasks, including the input, processing and maintenance of the data, as well as the development of the required output, just as your job might span a similar spectrum of responsibilities.

Table 2-2
Database design end results.

Management of inventory
Archiving sales orders
Management of patient information
Management of employee information
Tracking attorney work flow
Management of vendor relationships
Management of daily tasks
Considering growth

Considering growth

You need to evaluate potential changes in your business when developing an application design. If growth is planned, or especially if rapid growth is likely, you should design to include future requirements as well as those for today. If your business has gone through the process of building a two-year or five-year business plan, growth projections could be as available as that document. However, if you haven't developed a written plan, this is a good time to take a look at this issue. A business plan is critical to the success of a business, and is at least as important to the success of a business system. If you're just starting out, there are many valuable references to assist you in the process of building a business plan, including pamphlets published by the Small Business Administration and many state business-assistance agencies.

Growth can impact several areas of an application, including:

- Number of users
- Speed of access to data
- Data storage requirements
- Data summaries

The users

As your business grows, so can the number of employees. More employees usually means more and different users for an application. If your system is designed for a single user, changing it to allow for multiple users can be a very painful process. This pain will arrive in the financial area; the costs associated with a multiuser system are substantially greater than those for a single-user system (see chapter 13). However, it will arrive also in the area of management and coordination. For example, you might have designed a database with unique names that only you understand. Training another user to your naming conventions could be nearly impossible.

More generally, you might not have considered security issues in the design, and adding another user could involve creating password or other protection features to isolate sensitive information to or from the appropriate user(s). The issue of security often is addressed naturally at the point you have to install a multiuser system (a local-area network or larger). A *local-area network* (LAN), is simply a group of computers physically linked together with cables. Most LANs have PCs linked together, while some also link Macintosh, minicomputers, or other kinds of terminals together with PCs as well.

local-area network (LAN)   A group of computers physically linked together with cables, usually utilizing a special operating system to manage the interactions of the multiple users.

When evaluating your initial investment, you might have considered yourself the only potential user. This could have led you to decide to keep your investment in consultants or other programmers to a minimum. You might have planned to rely on your own skill to perform any computer-related tasks. Once other users are added, however, you might find that they don't have your competence nor your inclination toward supporting a computer-based system. This could wreak havoc in a loosely structured application that depends heavily on a well-trained user, in which the program doesn't provide a lot of help at getting things done. Table 2-3 describes the potential user-oriented difficulties encountered by the growth anticipated by RTS.

Table 2-3
RTS problems in personnel growth.

Current user plan:
RTS intends to do all the system maintenance himself. He will be inputting the required data and preparing all the reports. He intends to use the system at least two hours per day. RTS wants this system to be the foundation for all his work products, as well as provide him with a simple way to prepare bills using his verified schedule.

Growth expected:
Plans to double his client base within two years.

Problems anticipated:
Unable to manage the business on a one-man basis. Business system must be expanded to include at least one additional user (employee or partner).

Solutions explored:
Focus on application development that will make the business system as easy to use as possible, so when new users must be added, training time is minimized.

Consider making application easily modified from single to multiuser.

Even an application initially designed for multiple users can be impacted dramatically by growth. Most multiuser systems have a limit to the number of users that they can support. This limit can be enforced through the hardware or software, i.e., no more than 50 users for a particular type of file server or no more than five users per purchase of a Paradox netware pack. Frequently a practical limit is reached through the degradation of performance (speed) when the number of users approaches some critical point. Degradation of performance is nothing more than the application slowing down. At some point, slowness will cause a system to fail, because users will elect not to use the system.

performance   The speed of an application measured against the application's requirements.

Speed   The speed of the different components of your application must be a factor in designing it. Even though speed is often difficult to assess, and particularly so when you are implementing an application for the first time, this evaluation is extremely important to the success of the system. An application that takes five seconds to react when you enter a keystroke, a report that takes overnight to print, or a query that takes three hours to process can cause a user to elect not to use the system.

Many issues impact the speed of a system, including the number of system users and the amount of data stored by a system. Chapter 12 takes a more detailed look at speed and directly addresses the issue of when you should modify a database design to maximize performance. Table 2-4 identifies the issues to be considered by EB, whose growth as planned will dramatically impact the speed requirements.

Data storage requirements   The data stored by an application should reflect the business being done. The more business transactions that occur, the more data usually will be generated, and thus the more data will need to be stored. Business growth can involve increased numbers of clients, increased numbers of jobs for clients, increased numbers of patients, or increased numbers of sales, all of which will result in the need for greater data storage.

Business growth also could be reflected in the need for storing additional types of data. If all your clients are in a single industry, categorizing them is unimportant. If your business grows to encompass several industries, keeping track of which client is in which industry likely will become important.

Estimating the size of the data storage required can be a challenge, but it is important to the database design process. Generally speaking, when the volume of data to be stored is high, the importance of the relational model is proportionally high. A system task performed on one big table might work okay when there isn't very much data to be evaluated; the same task attempted when that table is very large could take a very long time, or could even cause the computer to *lock up* (an expression describing what often happens when the computer doesn't have enough resources, such as memory or disk storage, to complete a task). The amount of data stored has a strong impact on both the speed and efficiency of an application (see chapter 12 for more details).

Table 2-4
EB growth problems.

Current user plan:
EB will name a single system administrator who will have primary responsibility for the maintenance of the multiuser network, as well as for the routine system maintenance chores. Each of the ten other group members will be required to utilize the system on a daily basis in order to input newly received requests, process purchase orders, and answer questions from vendors and users.

Growth expected:
Overall company has doubled its number of retail stores in the past 18 months and plans to continue this growth rate for the next two years (again doubling the number of stores).

Problems anticipated:
Purchasing activity must be able to keep pace with the additional demands of the new stores. Hiring freeze in nonmerchandise related activities means that the current users must be equipped to handle the growth. The purchasing system must be efficient (and fast) enough to allow each group member (buyer) to increase productivity to keep pace with the growth for a minimum of two years.

Solutions explored:
Focus on design issues that will maximize performance. Consider batching (processing only once per day or less frequently) certain noncritical activities to allow essential transactions to occur without interruption.

Investigate hardware upgrades to assist in speeding up processing tasks.

Put in place procedural mechanisms to ensure any available software upgrades are implemented immediately.

Consider phasing in additional system development that will reduce each user's impact on the other users.

Data is stored on a part of the computer called a storage disk, and both the size of the storage disk and the amount of data stored is measured in bytes. One byte is roughly equivalent to a single character of data. For example, the word *margarine* would take approximately nine bytes to be stored.

Originally, PCs had only floppy disk drives, and all data had to be stored on floppy diskettes. Older floppy diskette can hold 360,000 bytes (360 kilobytes) of data. Today, high-density diskettes can hold up to a standard 1,200,000 bytes (1.2 megabytes) of data. Smaller, better-protected diskettes are also standard today, such as the newer, 3.5-inch diskette, which comes built into its own case and can hold up to a standard 1.44 megabytes of data.

Data on almost all PCs today is stored on a hard disk drive that is often internal (inside the computer itself). This disk often is mounted permanently and can hold 40, 80, 100, 200, or more megabytes (up to 9.6 gigabytes) of data. Newer technologies for disk storage involve laser disks (like the CD you use to listen to music) and optical disks. These types of disks usually can store much larger volumes of data than the standard magnetic disks described previously.

One of the advantages of a LAN is that it allows multiple users to have access to data stored in a central location on the LAN (often called a *file server*). Thus, the data storage used by an application can be a combination of data stored at individual local PCs and data stored at a remote central location (or locations). In this scenario, an increase in the amount of data stored can be handled at one rather than many locations if this is desired.

It is difficult, if not impossible, to make even a rough assessment of the volume of data the system will need to store at the time you begin your database design. However, as the database design process continues, you should be aware that data storage is an issue. Be prepared to take a closer look at your data storage requirements when the table designs are complete (see chapter 8).

Depth of detail

As the volume of data increases, so does the need to summarize that data. Reports that display the data in all its detail become more and more difficult to evaluate. The organization, combination, and analysis of data become a higher priority. In fact, the computer's facility at summarizing data is often a driving factor in developing an application in the first place.

In many cases, more data also leads to a need for graphic representation of data. Graphs display summarized data in a format that is more easily interpreted than a detailed report. Task specifications that include detail-level reports might need to be modified to include summarized reports and graphs.

To summarize, potential changes in the volume or types of data to be stored should be evaluated when beginning the design. If rapid growth is likely, you should design for future requirements wherever possible.

How to begin the design process

Once you have identified the end result and addressed some of the growth issues, now is the time to start breaking down what you know into manageable chunks. You must begin to organize your information in a way that can be used logically to describe that information. Remember that your design eventually will be implemented using the features of Paradox.

Now that you've done all this preparatory thinking, you're ready to sit down and begin the design. Your ideas might not flow easily, or they might not have any logic to them at first. However, there are a couple of tips that you can use to get started, and to help you maintain continuity once you've begun.

Sketching concepts on paper

A sketch is by far the easiest way to describe information about a database design. Remember, the design itself will end up in both written and graphic form; both formats can and should originate from rough sketches. You might feel that designing a simple database is a straightforward exercise. You could whiz through the table and field designs, briefly pause at the development of table relationships, and be ready to create the structures within Paradox within moments of opening your newly purchased 4.0 box.

However, you should be aware that even the simplest of designs will benefit from a sketch. Remember, the database design process isn't even computer-based until after the design is complete. You might want to turn your system on and get going, but your solution no doubt will be a short-lived one.

If you are concerned that your database design will be complex, a sketch is a first step toward providing simplicity. Even the most complex data and relationships can be described with a simple sketch. Even if you oversimplify, you can use a sketch to establish the boundaries for the different components of your application. Figures 2-3 through 2-6 illustrate preliminary sketches for each of the case study applications. Chapter 14 includes several templates for forms to utilize in conjunction with a database design project.

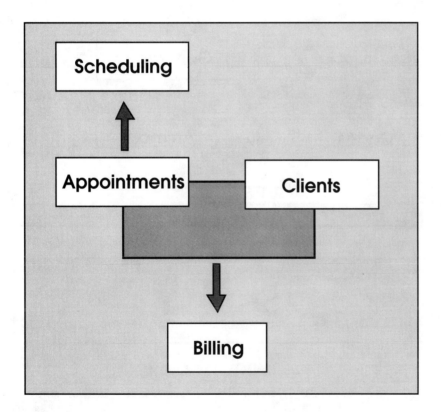

2-3
Sketch of the RTS database application

Throughout the process of creating your database design, assessment of the widest variety of possibilities is crucial. At this early point, the possibilities might only include problems to be solved, but within each problem identified

Brainstorming

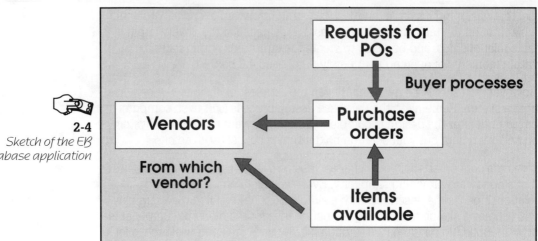

2-4
Sketch of the EB database application

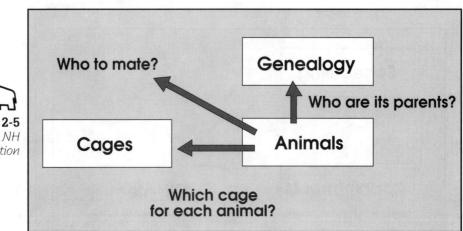

2-5
Sketch of the NH database application

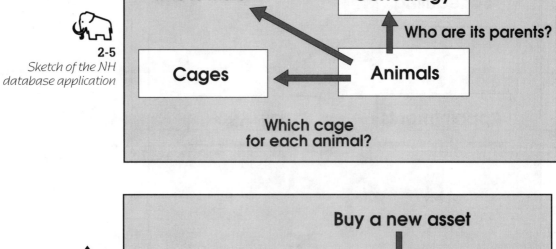

2-6
Sketch of the Asset Manager application

early on lies the seed of its later solution. Brainstorming is a proven method for provoking new and creative ideas. Taking the time to brainstorm might be difficult, but whatever time you can lend to the process up front will only be of benefit. Even with limited time, devoting a few minutes to brainstorming with a pencil in hand should be a high priority.

Consider for a moment what other long-term goals this application could meet. Does my business plan depend on application development for its success, and if so, what can I do to ensure that it happens? Is there any way to integrate more of my job into the application design? Are there tasks unrelated to my end result that might benefit from being computerized? Do I want to spend more time at the computer, or is my intention to use the application to free me from that kind of drudgery? Is there anyone in my group or professional contacts who might be willing to act as a sounding board for my database design?

Questions like these should help you keep an open mind as you progress through the database design process. You might discover that although there can be more than one right answer, or even several potential database designs that meet your basic requirements, the best solution might not be the most obvious one. Unless you allow yourself to explore alternative ways of thinking, you might never discover that less obvious, but better, solution. In this case, *better* refers to the degree to which the application meets the goal established by the end result.

Documenting the design process

Throughout the process of developing the details of your database design, be prepared to record them on paper. Simple sketches and notes from your brainstorming are really all that is necessary. Recording your design as it evolves helps the process in two ways. First, taking the notes can help you think. The activities of drawing and writing often will provoke unique thoughts or unexpected solutions. Second, having a written record of your thoughts and plans, even in the earliest stages, will prove invaluable. These notes and diagrams, rough as they might be, will become the basis for system documentation. System documentation is the written-in-English, published version of what the system does. System documentation can include two parts: user documentation, which details what the system does from a user's perspective, and internal program documentation, which explains how the code (any programmed part of the system) works.

system documentation   The written-in-English, published version of what the system does, usually including details from the user's perspective as well as from the programmer's perspective.

One of the most difficult parts of any system to document is its goals. Having the details of its development in writing will aid you or anyone to whom you delegate the task. Documenting the process as it occurs is valuable from a historical standpoint as well. Your design might be very broad to begin with, but could narrow as you continue the design process. If the system ever needs redesigning because of growth or migration to another type of system, the design documents will help provide a blueprint for evaluating the necessary enhancements or translations.

Creating a one-page database design diagram

You should keep in mind that one of the goals of the database design process is to develop a straightforward way to communicate the design. This is accomplished normally through the development of a single-page diagram that lays out the various tables in the design, the relationships between the tables, and any pertinent restrictions on the data. The critical areas of the completed system should be obvious on the sketch.

One sign that there is a problem with a database design is that the design cannot fit onto a single page. You should be sure to keep your design sketches close at hand. If at any point the overall sketch becomes too complex, reduce its complexity: summarize it. Figure 2-7 provides an example of a single-page preliminary database design (early in the design process). If you get stumped along the way, take a look at the appendix to see where each of the case study designs will be ending up.

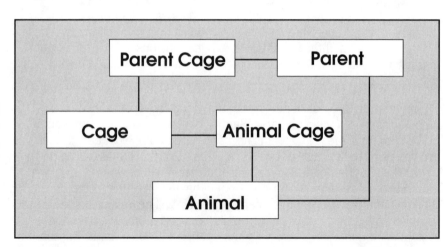

2-7
Intermediate database design sketch

Defining the requirements

The database design will need to address two specific components of the application design: inputs and outputs. The inputs and outputs for an application are crucial to the design of the database because they form the foundation for identifying the data that needs to be maintained. If an output is required, it needs data in order to occur, and the database design must take this fact into consideration. In fact, the process of designing the database begins here because it is much easier to remember inputs and outputs than it is to conceive of data elements in a vacuum. Remember, you deal with information while you work, and that information that you depend on must be available in the computer, in the database that you are designing. A complete business-system design would require an evaluation of the specific mechanisms for accomplishing these tasks, including the user skills and Paradox programming required, if any.

Table 2-5 describes a variety of input and output tasks that an application might be expected to accomplish. In developing your database design, it can be useful to lay out the tasks in a matrix like that in Table 2-5. The questions at hand are: who will do what, and how often will they need to do it? To make this kind of assessment for your application, you must first identify the tasks involved.

Table 2-5
Task/user matrix with expected
frequency of performance.

Task	Manager	User 1	User 2
Print report		Daily	
Display graph	Weekly		
Print graph		Weekly	
Ask questions	Daily		Monthly
Do analysis	Daily	Weekly	Monthly
Input data		Daily	Daily
Modify data		Daily	

oops!

The system tasks are the input and output required to support the application. As suggested by the Table 2-5 matrix, a list of tasks normally includes the following:

Identifying the input & output

- Reports to be generated
- Graphs to be developed and displayed
- Questions to be answered
- Analyses to be performed
- Data to be input and maintained

Table 2-6 identifies the tasks for each of the case studies.

Before you can identify which tasks will or should be performed by the users, it is important to take a look at who the users are. Remember, users can fall into two categories: those who maintain the data, and those who rely on the data for decision support. Some users could, of course, do both. Table 2-7 identifies the users of each of the case study systems, while Table 2-8 identifies the task/user matrix for each of the case studies.

Identifying users & their tasks

Pay special attention to the mistake icon in Table 2-6. The most common problem encountered when evaluating the users and tasks associated with an application lies in underestimating the time it will take to manage the system. Even if MH believes that he will be able to make the time to support a new system, this is extremely unlikely, especially considering that he is not replacing a manual system with his new application. In his case, all these

Table 2-6
Case-study tasks.

 RTS needs to:

- Print a daily/weekly/monthly schedule
- Print invoices for clients
- Display a daily schedule on screen
- Display client information on screen
- Enter new appointments
- Modify the appointment schedule
- Enter client contacts
- Update client information

 EB needs to:

- Print a list of purchase orders by user or item category
- Print a list of vendors
- Print an analysis of processing time by buyer
- Enter new purchase requests
- Modify current purchase requests
- Create purchase orders
- Close purchase orders
- Display purchase orders by user, vendor, or order date
- Maintain vendor, item and buyer data

 MH needs to:

- Print a list of animals
- Print a genealogy for each animal
- Print a list of available cage space
- Enter new births
- Modify animal records
- Display all available data about an animal
- Maintain cage data

oops! Mistake: Not using the system to accomplish the end result: identify appropriate mates. A well-designed system is not only able to store data but to analyze it as well. Not to utilize that capability dramatically reduces the effectiveness of the system.

 You need to:

- Print a list of assets and depreciated values
- Enter newly purchased assets
- Delete assets that have been sold

tasks are new and will take time away from his current job responsibilities. Unless he had time to spare before system implementation, he will be putting himself immediately in a situation that will lead quickly to application failure: lack of maintenance time.

Table 2-7
Users of the case-study systems.

RTS is currently the sole user of the system.

EB will name a single system administrator who will have primary responsibility for maintenance of the multiuser network as well as other system-wide maintenance chores. There are 12 other users, of whom six are buyers who maintain their own relationships with vendors, with four being data entry personnel. The last two, the department head and the vice president in charge of the department, will do no data maintenance but will be using the output generated by the business system to aid in decision-making.

MH will be the manager of the system. He intends to use two of his part-time staff to input the data when the system is set up and one of this staff to print reports once the system is up and running. He expects to use this part-time help only once a month, when he needs to generate the reports. His staff will notify him about births as they occur, and he will update the data himself.

You will be the sole user of the system.

Summary

In this chapter, you encountered some basic concepts that should help you understand the overall process of database design. Specifically, you learned that:

- The business-system design process is a cycle that begins with the identification of the end result and continues with the design and implementation of the design. Database design is the foundation for the overall process, and its success helps speed up the movement toward the end result.
- A database design is a document that provides a detailed description in both text and graphics of what the data structures for a business system will look like.
- The database design process starts with the identification of the end result, continues through the development of tables, including the design of fields and table relationships, and ends with an evaluation of the impact of reality on the theoretical design.
- Application requirements include a description of the users, the tasks to be accomplished, and who will be responsible for what task.
- The growth of your business should always be considered during a database design process. Specifically, growth can affect the number of users of a system, the speed with which a system does what it needs to, the volume of data storage required, and how much detail is needed to make the system usable.

- The database design process can be initiated by sitting down and making a sketch, and it can be facilitated through ongoing sketches and brainstorming. The process should always be documented, if through no other means than with simple notes and sketches.
- An important goal of the database design process is the creation of a one-page database design diagram.

Table 2-8
Case-study task/user matrix.

 RTS is the sole user of the system, so each task will be performed by him.

Task	Frequency
Print a daily/weekly/monthly schedule	Daily
Print invoices for clients	Monthly
Display a daily schedule on screen	Daily
Display client information on screen	Daily
Enter new appointments	Daily
Modify the appointment schedule	Daily
Enter client contacts	Daily
Update client information	Weekly

EB Task	System Admin	Buyers	DE Staff	Dept. Head	VP
Print PO list by user/item	Weekly				
Print vendors list	Weekly			Weekly	
Print process time analysis by buyer				Weekly	Weekly
Enter new requests		Daily			
Modify current purchase requests		Daily			
Create PO	Daily				
Close PO	Daily	Daily			
Display POs by user/vendor/date		Daily			
Maintain vendor/item/buyer data			Daily		

MH Task	MH	DE Help	Report Help
Print a list of animals			Weekly
Print a genealogy for each animal			Monthly
Print a list of available cage space			Daily

Enter new births	Daily (start-up)
Modify animal records	Weekly (start-up)
Display all available data about an animal	Weekly
Maintain cage data As needed	

You will be the sole user of the system. You need to:

Task	Frequency
Print a list of assets and depreciated values	Yearly
Enter newly purchased assets	As needed
Delete assets that have been sold	As needed

Key Terms

end result   The output of an up-and-running application, and the goal of the application development process.

local-area network (LAN)   A group of computers physically linked together with cables, usually utilizing a special operating system to manage the interactions of the multiple users.

life cycle   A development process that spans the life of the system being developed and usually encompasses steps from the identification of the requirements through the installation, training, and evaluation of the system.

performance   The speed of an application measured against the application's requirements.

system documentation   The written-in-English, published version of what the system does, usually including details from the user's perspective as well as from the programmer's perspective.

3

Snapshots of the database design & implementation process

The database design process encompasses many steps and even more concepts. As a design unfolds—and a good design will tend to make itself known (to unfold) in a very real way—you might find it difficult to stay focused on the end result. There are so many different issues to consider that in some ways database design becomes a challenge characterized by the difficulty of keeping the different steps in mind and in sequence.

To help prevent this type of brain fatigue, this chapter will give you a brief overview of the whole process. The Family database used throughout the book to demonstrate problems, techniques and solutions is used in this chapter to give you a quick set of snapshots of the design process. This procedure will give you the opportunity to focus on the "why" rather than the "what" issues. In addition, this should help focus your attention with a glimpse of what is to come, giving you some perspective on what you're working toward in the end.

These snapshots of the process are provided in a fairly graphic format. Each step is described briefly, the section of the book that addresses the topic is identified, and the implementation of that step is laid out in a diagram. Most of these figures will reappear later in the book at the appropriate time.

Steps in data-base design

Step 1: Identify the requirements. See chapter 2, "Defining the requirements." Make a list of the inputs and outputs that you expect the database to support. If you have reports or graphs, get copies. Be as specific as possible (see Table 3-1).

Table 3-1
Family-database requirements.

End Result: Manage contacts with family members

Identify a previously met family member, using hair and eye color, height, glasses (or not), and clothing pattern preference.

List all family members' cars by make and model.

List family members without a car.

List families who live in California.

Analyze family members by clothing pattern preferences.

Add a new family.

Add a newly met family member.

Update family member information.

Update member car information.

Step 2: Create a master list of info elements. See chapter 4, "Creating a master list of info elements." Make a list of all the elements of information suggested by the input and output tasks (see Table 3-2).

Table 3-2
Family database information elements.

Task	Info elements
Identify a previously met family member, using hair and eye color, height, glasses (or not), and clothing pattern preference	Name Hair color Eye color Height Build Glasses Pattern preference
List all family members' cars by make and model	Member name Family Make Model
List family members without a car	Member name Family (no car)
List families who live in California	Member name Family Address
Analyze family members by clothing pattern preferences	Member name Family Pattern preference

Table 3-2   Continued.

Task	Info elements
Add a new family	Family name
	Address
Add a newly met family member	Family name
	Member
Update family member information	Family name
	Member
	Age
	Build
	Glasses
Update member car information	Family name
	Member
	Make and model

Step 3: Identify the entities. See chapter 4, "Dividing the elements into entities." Assess what entity (what object or process) is being described by each info element, group the like elements together, and give each group the name for a table (see Table 3-3).

Table 3-3
Family-database entities.

Info elements	Entity
Name	Family member
Address	
Hair color	
Eye color	
Height	
Build	
Glasses	
Pattern preference	
Age	
Family name	Family
Address	
Car make	Member car
Car model	

Step 4: Identify the primary key. See chapter 4, "Assigning a key to the unique element." Figure out which info element makes each thing unique, and define it as the primary key for the table (see Table 3-4).

Table 3-4
Family-database primary keys.

Table	Primary key
Family member	Member ID (surrogate)
Family	Family ID
Family car	Car ID (surrogate)

Step 5: Isolate the fields. See chapter 5, "Isolating the fields" and "Naming a field." Take each info element one by one and break it down into nondecomposable components—as individual as they can get. Name each isolated component as a field (see Table 3-5).

Table 3-5
Family-database fields.

Info elements	Field(s)
Name	Member ID
Address	City, State
Hair color	Hair color
Eye color	Eye color
Height	Estimated height
Build	Build
Glasses	Glasses
Pattern preference	Pattern preference
Age	Age estimate
	Family ID
Family name	Family name
Address	City, State
	Car ID
Car make	Car make
Car model	Car model

Step 6: Describe each field. See chapter 5, "Defining a field's data type," "Defining a field's domain," and "Reevaluating the fields." Take each field and individually determine the appropriate data type, domain, and rules for the field (see Table 3-6).

Step 7: Relate the tables. See chapter 6. Identify the type of relationship by analyzing the connection from both sides (see FIG. 3-1), model the connection with the appropriate fields (see FIG. 3-2), and refine the database design diagram to reflect these relationships (see FIG. 3-3).

Step 8: Modify the design to reflect the requirements of the environment. See chapters 8, 12 and 13. In this example, modification is unnecessary, because the database is so small.

Table 3-6
Family-database fields described.

Field	Data type	Domain	Rules
Member ID	Integer	Values 1-500	Unique
First name	A20	First names uppercase, all others lowercase	First letter
City	A20	US cities	Required
State	A2	US states	Required
Hair color	A8	Brown, blonde, auburn, grey, black, red	
Eye color	A8	Brown, blue, black, albino	
Rough height	N	0-100 inches	Rounded to nearest inch
Build	A5	Thin, heavy, muscular	Default to thin
Glasses	A3	Yes, no	Default no
Pattern preference	A10	Patterns	Required
Age estimate	A10		Required
Family ID	S	1-50	Required
Family Name	A15	Names	Required
City	A20	US cities	
State	A20	US states	
Car ID	S	1-400	Unique, required
Car make	A15	Japanese or Chevrolet (models)	Toyota, Honda, Chevy
Car model	A25		

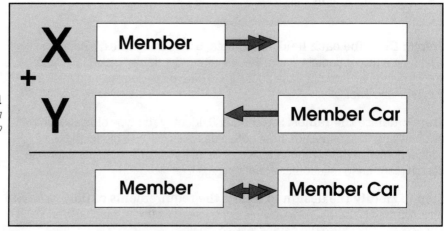

3-1
Looking at both sides of a relationship

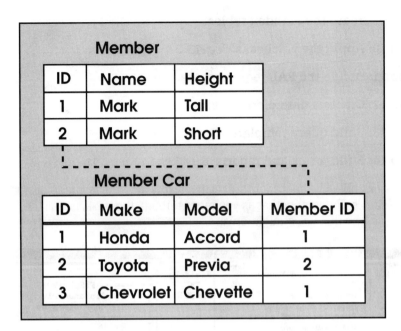

3-2
A modeled One-to-Many relationship

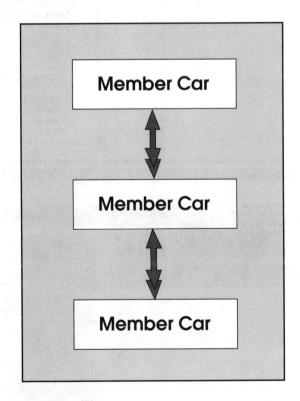

3-3
The Family database design

Step 9: Create the Paradox tables. See FIGS. 3-4 and 3-5.

Step 10: Apply the valchecks. See FIG. 3-6.

Step 11: Define the PAL requirements. See FIG. 3-7.

Step 12: Create a data dictionary. See FIG. 3-8.

Step 13: Build query templates. See FIG. 3-9.

Step 14: Build forms and reports. See FIGS. 3-10 and 3-11.

In this example, the snapshots are relatively few, and the resulting design quite simple. Remember that as you move through the book, not all the issues will be quite so straightforward.

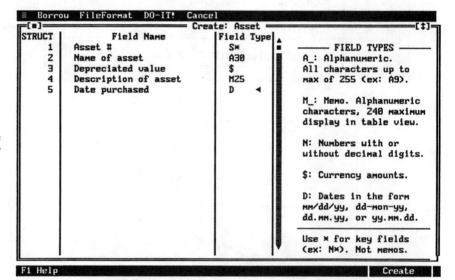

3-4
Creating a Paradox table

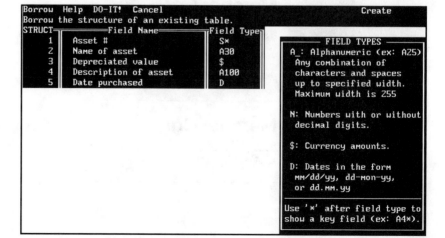

3-5
*Creating a table in
Paradox 3.5*

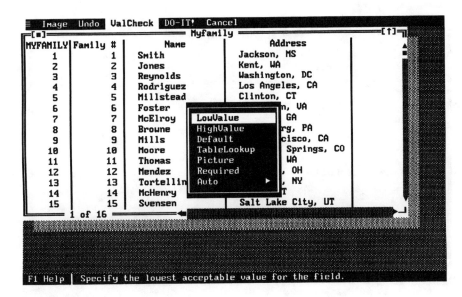

3-6
Validity check menu choices

```
;Val.sc
;Required values only

PROC check_validity()
 PRIVATE v

vmess = "OK"
IF TABLE () = "Myfamily" THEN                    ;Required fields in
                                                      family table

 IF ISBLANK([Name]) THEN
  vmess = FIELD()
 ENDIF
 IF ISBLANK([Address]) THEN
  vmess = FIELD()
 ENDIF
ELSE                             ;Required fields in member table
  IF ISBLANK([Member #]) THEN
   vmess = FIELD ()
  ENDIF
  IF ISBLANK([Pattern]) THEN
   vmess = FIELD ()
  ENDIF
ENDIF
IFF NOT vmess = "OK" THEN
 vmess = "You must enter a value in"+vmess
  RETURN false
ELSE
 RETURN true
ENDIF

ENDPROC
WRITELIB "Main" check_validity
RELEASE PROCS check_validity
```

3-7
Integrity checking through PAL

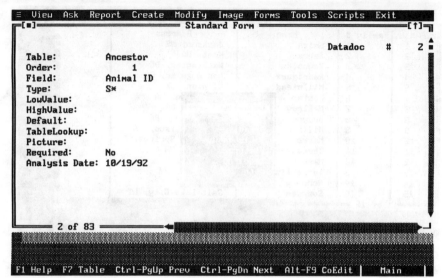

3-8
*Using a data
dictionary table*

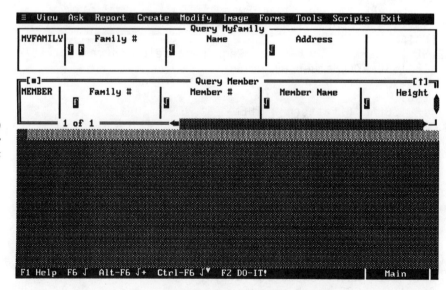

3-9
*Building a query template
using Family tables*

Preparing to design a Paradox database

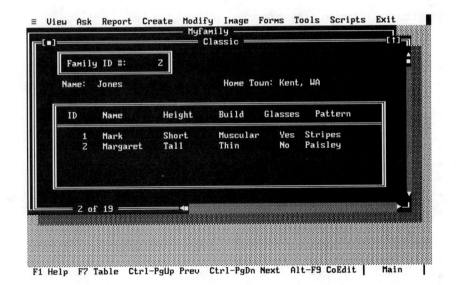

3-10
A multi-table form for the Family database

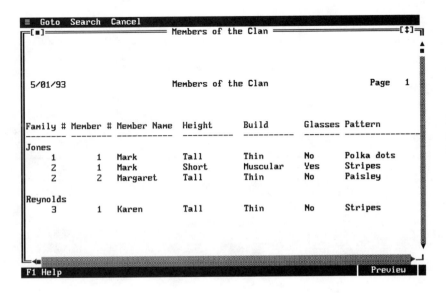

3-11
A multi-table report for the Family database

Summary   This chapter provided a quick overview of the entire database design process. To summarize, the steps involved in the process include the following:

- Identify the requirements.
- Create a master list of information elements.
- Identify the entities.
- Identify the primary key.
- Isolate the fields.
- Describe each field.
- Relate the tables.
- Modify the design to reflect requirements of the environment.
- Create the Paradox tables.
- Apply the valchecks.
- Define the PAL requirements.
- Create a data dictionary.
- Build query templates.
- Build forms and reports.

Part Two

Designing a
normal database

4 *Developing a table design*

The specific process that ensures your database tables conform to the rules of the relational model is called *normalization*. Part 2 of this book is intended to help you create a normalized database design, but without once using the term normalization. Thus, the database you design through Part 2 will meet the standards of relational theory: each table will be normal, if not specifically normalized. This normal database could be the end result of your database design; although you might want to optimize it (the subject of Part 4), in many cases you won't have to.

By now you probably have a good idea of what is involved in the database design process. You've got the tools in hand for building the design: your pencil and paper are ready to catch the flow of creative ideas. You stand poised to create an application and the documentation that goes along with it. To provide some perspective, thus far the discussion of database design has focused on the database design environment. You might feel virtually inundated by all the factors that can affect the design. Now you need to shake off some of that necessary background noise and focus your attention on the heart of any database system: the table designs.

Understanding the elements of a table

You've already encountered the rough-and-ready definition of a table in previous chapters. Now you need to look more closely at this definition. Specifically, what makes up a table?

As discussed in chapter 1, a table is a two-dimensional grid of rows and columns. A table contains data about individual occurrences of a specific object or a process. Some DBMSs refer to a table as an *entity*. A table containing data about objects can list data about a person, a place, or a thing. A table describing a process could contain data about purchases, sales, transactions or other activities.

table   A set of columns and rows that describes a single object or process and that is the fundamental data structure of any relational database.

A table's name usually describes the object or process in a single word. The table in FIG. 4-1 is named Member; other tables could be called Invoice, Client, Contact, Equipment, or Transaction, to list a few examples.

Column names

NAME	HEIGHT	BUILD
Mark	Tall	Muscular
Mark	Short	Thin
Margaret	Tall	Thin
Karen	Tall	Athletic
Diane	Short	Thin

4-1
The Family Member table

What a row is

A row represents a single occurrence of the object or process defined by the table. All of the data in a row are related to that single occurrence. As suggested by FIG. 4-2, each row represents a single member of the family. A row is often called a *record* (in this context, the terms are completely interchangeable). A row is less frequently known as a *tuple*, a term used in relational theory.

Each row in an Invoice table represents an individual invoice; a row in a Client table describes a single client; Contact, one contact with a customer; Visit, one visit by a patient; Equipment, one piece of equipment; and Transaction, one general ledger transaction.

row   Used interchangeably with record to refer to one occurrence of an object or process within a table (the horizontal of the table).
record   Used interchangeably with row to refer to one occurrence of an object or process within a table (the horizontal of the table).

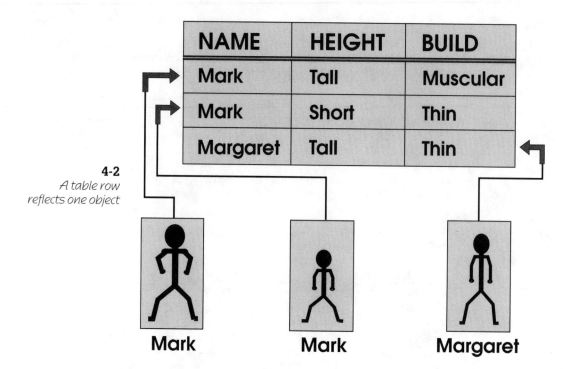

NAME	HEIGHT	BUILD
Mark	Tall	Muscular
Mark	Short	Thin
Margaret	Tall	Thin

4-2
A table row reflects one object

Look at this another way. Imagine that you are meeting some members of your extended family for the first time. You want to make note of each new member you meet, so you jot down his or her name. To represent these people in your Member table, you would need to add a new row for each new person that you met. You could create a sketch of this, which might look something like FIG. 4-3.

The table has three rows, one for each person that you've been introduced to. Note that your list shows you've met two people named Mark. In reality, remembering that there really are two Marks is not difficult. All you need to do is look at the two men in order to recognize this fact; what's more, in one glance you can easily differentiate between them. Drawing this kind of distinction is impossible for a computer, at least without your providing the mechanism to do so.

What a column is
A column represents one descriptive element of each row. In the context of this example, columns are a lot like a list of different adjectives that describe a noun. Take another look at your list of family members. You want to remember who is who, beyond the fact of each person's name. When you met the first Mark, you assessed what you saw—you described him to yourself. If you had to write this description, you might use adjectives such as tall, muscular, and youthful. Each adjective describes one feature, or attribute, of the person. In the Member table that you are constructing, each

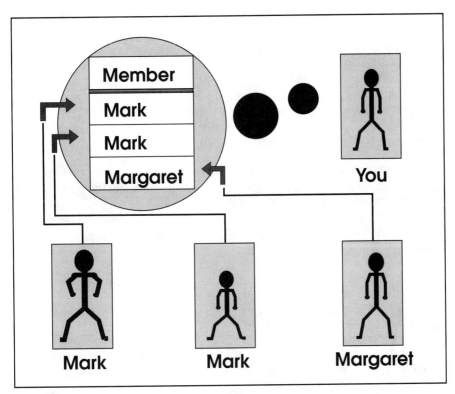

4-3
Thinking about creating the Family Member table

of these adjectives would be found in its own column, which identifies the feature that is being described. This Member table might have columns like those described by FIG. 4-4.

NAME	HEIGHT	BUILD	AGE
Mark	Tall	Muscular	Youthful
Mark	Short	Thin	Teenager

Mark   Mark

4-4
Adjectives to describe each Family Member

The column name identifies the feature, while the data in the column describes that feature for a specific individual. All the features in a given row describe one person—in this case, each of the Marks.

You can describe features in terms that go beyond simple adjectives. One of "tall" Mark's distinctive features might be the fact that he wears glasses. Another feature might be the fact that he always wears stripes. Columns are not limited to adjective descriptions; anything that explains or describes the entity (member) can be contained in a column.

Within a single column, the value in every row will be the same kind of data and will describe the same attribute of the row (in this case, the same feature of the family member). Each column should contain data that describes only one attribute. A column is often referred to as a *field*; like row and record, column and field also are interchangeably used. Less frequently, a column is called an *attribute*.

column   Used interchangeably with field to refer to one descriptive element or attribute of a table (the vertical of the table).
field   Used interchangeably with column to refer to one descriptive element or attribute of a table (the vertical of the table).

In FIG. 4-5, the Member table has been expanded to include Glasses and Favorite Pattern columns. The columns for an Invoice table might include items such as Invoice #, Customer Name, Address, Equipment Type, G/L Account #, Purchase Date, and Contact Phone Number. The column name usually indicates the type of data that the column contains—the name of the feature that is being described or identified.

Rows and columns in combination create the grid that is a table structure. Different DBMSs represent this grid to a user in different ways. In some

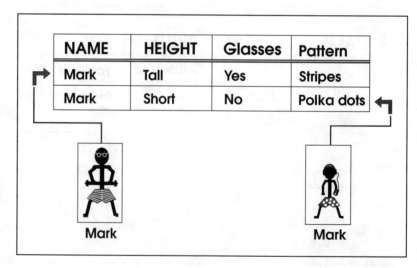

4-5
More about each Family Member

NAME	HEIGHT	Glasses	Pattern
Mark	Tall	Yes	Stripes
Mark	Short	No	Polka dots

Mark   Mark

Designing a normal database

products, a table is bounded by a visible horizontal and vertical grid. In others, the columns of a table are separated by vertical lines, but the rows have no separators. Paradox supports both horizontal and vertical gridding. In any case, a grid is not an integral part of a table; it simply helps you to visualize the relationships between the different data elements. Vertical lines, or rules, help reinforce the commonality of each value in a column, while horizontal rules help focus your attention on the fact that all the data in a given record relate to the same entity or occurrence.

RDBMS theory defines a table much more specifically. In fact, since table is such a well-used term (see chapter 1), relational theorists have coined another term entirely to describe a table that conforms to the relational model: a relation.

A *relation* is a special kind of table. All relations are tables, but all tables are not relations. More specifically, a relation is always a theoretical table that conforms to all of the rules established by the relational model. The relational model currently specifies 14 general rules, and many other specific rules, that a relation must conform to. One of the first general rules specifies "freedom from positional concepts" (Codd 1990, 32). By this rule, a relation identifies each record independently of the next; there is no relative ordering of the rows. There is no such thing as a record being located next to another. In other words, each row can be accessed for a specific output without regard to its relative position in the table. Also by this rule, a relation contains fields that have no relative positioning. The fields are independently named, and they are theoretically unordered. As with a relation's records, a relation's columns have no "nextness."

What a relation is

It would seem that a relation can exist only in theory, because in practice a table that exists will contain rows and columns in a specific order. However, remember that a table doesn't exist in a physical form either—it is only a logical concept. The data being stored physically is always managed by Paradox in some unimportant way. Thus, it is possible to conceive of Paradox tables that are relations, and in practice to treat these tables under the rules of the relational model.

The goal in defining relational database structures is to develop tables, that is, relations, that conform to the relational model. Consideration of the requirements of Paradox that will be used to implement the database design is reserved to the end of the database design process (see chapter 8), and should not have an impact on development of the table designs.

The group of relational tables that jointly form a database design also can be termed a relational database. In other words, a relational database is a collection of relations that all work together to define the data involved in a particular business system or a single application (see FIG. 4-6).

4-6
The big picture of a relational database

Paradox can be used to create and manage any number of databases, or more to the point, any number of different applications. Because each table in a database remains a separate and unique entity, the question of whether it is a part of a given database is not always easily answered. For this reason, many DBMSs require that each database be given a name, that can be associated then in some way with the appropriate database tables. This association is usually by context only; the data in the table won't refer to it at all. Paradox simply recommends that all the tables in a single database be stored within one DOS subdirectory, a specific area of disk storage. Thus the subdirectory location of a table can provide a clue as to the database it is associated with. Part of the power of a relational database lies in the fact that a single table—or even a set of related tables—can be copied or moved from one database to another without any loss of meaning. However, this requires that critical relationships are preserved, and that the database designs are essentially compatible.

Designing the data structures (tables) to support an application is known as *database design* because all of the tables designed will be conceived of as one unit, working together toward the specified goal of the business system: the end result. Thus, the table-design process is more correctly the tables design process; each table in a database should be developed with the scope of the entire database in mind.

An overview of the table-design process

The process of developing table structures takes you in a direction opposite to the processes you've seen before. Although table development begins with the big picture, it immediately leaps into great detail. The big picture is then gradually reconstructed, this time in an organized, relational fashion. Basically, all this overwhelming detail is organized into groups that are formalized, enhanced, and grown to create individual tables (see FIG. 4-7). Overall, you should cover the following steps:

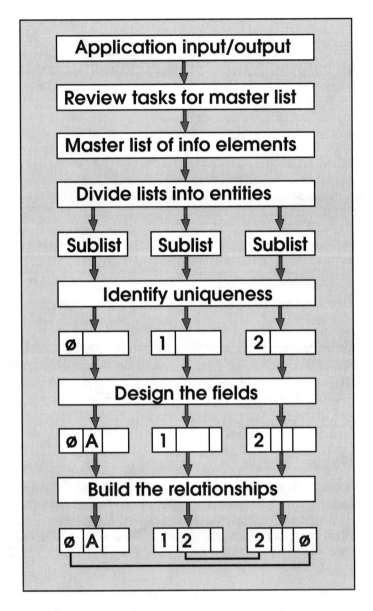

4-7
The table design process

1. Review the application tasks.
2. Create a master list of information elements.
3. Divide the elements into entities.
4. Determine what makes each entity unique.
5. Assign a key to the unique information element.
6. Design the fields.
7. Identify the table relationships.

The first five steps are addressed in this chapter, while steps 6 and 7, which are often the most time-consuming, are covered in detail in chapters 5 and 6.

Reviewing the application input/output requirements

The place to begin is with your layout of the tasks you intend the application to perform. Each input or output task is in itself a goal. Ask yourself what information you need to achieve this goal. You should find clues to the answer within the statement of the task itself. The more descriptive the phrase that describes that task, the more obvious the answer will be. Again, refer to templates in chapter 14 for a look at that form.

Each item of information that you uncover will be called an *information element*, or in abbreviated form, *info element*. Each info element you identify will have some meaning associated with it. For example, the output task "Print client labels" assumes that you know the right address, but the right address is not just any address; it is the specific address of one (or each) of your clients. The info element is thus not a simple address, but instead a client address. Be descriptive; the more detail that you retain at this point in the process, the more likely it is that the application you create will be able to retain it as well. Focus on the information content, not just an item of data stripped of meaning.

information element (info element)   An item of information that has not yet been defined or broken down into a specific field or fields.

A task that requires printing a report should give you some indication of what that report should look like. What are the info elements you'll need in order for the report to tell you what you want to know? If you are already producing the report manually or with some other system, get a copy of it. If that's impossible, make a sketch. Chapter 11 discusses some tips you can use in the design of new reports.

Give each info element a descriptive name, one that uses your own words and the specific terminology of your business. If your source report already contains some kind of header or name for the element, use it. For example, if you need an employee's name, a simple "Employee Name" description will be enough detail for now. However, if you need the name for each job the employee has worked on during the period 1/1/88 through 1/1/92, specifying a simple "Job #" won't be enough. You'll need to make sure you include "Dates Worked" and "Jobs by the Employee" as info elements.

Don't overlook information that you need to get the task done, but that might not appear on a resulting report or graph. Ask yourself: in what order will this report print? Does it need to be sorted? A sort is simply a rearrangement of values into a specified order, usually following numeric, then alphanumeric order. Is the sort on a value that you've already defined, or on some other value? If you want to see a list of employees in the order in which they were hired, you'll need to know the Hire Date information for each employee. If you want to print your client labels in zip code order, you'll need to have the zip code available for each client. Table 4-1 describes the tasks for each case study along with the info elements required to get each task done.

Table 4-1
Case-study tasks and associated info elements.

Task	Info elements
Print a daily/weekly/monthly schedule	Dates covered
	Date printed
	Appointment times
	Appointment clients
Print invoices for clients	Client name & address
	Invoice number
	Hours worked
	Services performed
	Total due
Display a daily schedule	Current date
	Appointment times
	Appointment clients
Display client information	Client name
	Address
	Telephone number
	Primary contact
	Secondary contact
Enter new appointments	Appointment date
	Appointment time
	Client
	Service to perform
Modify the appointment schedule	Appointment date
	Appointment time
	Client
	Service to perform
Enter client contacts	Client name
	Client contact
	Primary or secondary?
Update client information	Client name
	Address
	Telephone number
Print a list of purchase orders by user or item category	Purchase order number
	PO date
	Vendor
	User
	Prices
	Total PO amount
Print a list of vendors	Vendor name
	Address
	Telephone number
Print an analysis of processing time by buyer	PO date issued
	PO date closed

Table 4-1   Continued.

Task	Info elements
Enter new purchase requests	Buyer
	User
	Items
	Date requested
Modify current purchase requests	User
	Items
	Date requested
	Date updated
Create purchase orders	Purchase order number
	PO date
	Vendor
	User
	Items
	Quantities
	Prices
	Total PO amount
	Buyer
Close a purchase order	Purchase order number
	PO date closed
Display purchase orders by user, vendor, or order date	Purchase order number
	PO date
	Vendor
	User
	Items
	Quantities
	Prices
	Total PO amount
	Buyer
Maintain vendor, item, and buyer data	Vendor name
	Vendor address & phone
	Item name
	Item description
	Buyer name
Print a list of animals	Animal name
	Age
	Cage
Print a genealogy for each animal	Animal name
	Father's name
	Mother's name
	Grandfathers' names
	Grandmothers' names
Print a list of available cage space	Cage
	Number of spaces available

Table 4-1 Continued.

Task	Info elements
Enter new births	Date of birth
	Animal name
	Mother's name
	Father's name
Modify animal records	Animal name
	Cage
Display all available data about an animal	Animal name
	Cage
	Mother
	Father
	Grandparents
Maintain cage data	Cage name
	Location
	Number of spaces
Print a list of assets and depreciated values	Name of asset
	Depreciated value
Enter newly purchased assets	Name of asset
	Description of asset
	Date purchased
	Purchase price
	Depreciation period
Delete assets that have been sold	Name of asset
	Date sold

sort The arrangement of values into a specified order, usually following the ASCII key-code order.

Once you have gone through all the tasks one by one and have identified the info elements for each, you should combine all the info elements into a single list. This list could be quite lengthy, or it could be relatively short. Don't be concerned about the number of info elements, or any relationships between them that might leap out at you. When you first create the master list, you should take care to copy the info elements straight from your list of tasks, and ignore any other concerns. In addition, you should retain your documentation regarding the association of info elements with each task. This documentation will be invaluable when you are ready to write scripts for the tasks.

After you have made the master list, go through the list and mark out those elements that are duplicated elsewhere on the list. Be careful to eliminate only those elements that exactly match. If "Client Name" appears once and "Name" appears elsewhere, look closely to see if both descriptions relate to the name for each of your clients. Table 4-2 describes a master list for each of the case studies.

Creating a master list of info elements

Table 4-2
Master list of info elements.

Dates covered
Date printed
Appointment times
Appointment clients
Client name and address
Invoice date
Hours worked
Services performed
Total due
Current date
*Appointment times
*Appointment clients
*Client name
*Address
Telephone number
Primary contact
Secondary contact
*Appointment date
*Appointment time
*Client
Service to perform
*Appointment date
*Appointment time
*Client
*Service to perform
*Client name
*Client contact
*Primary or secondary?
*Client name
*Address
*Telephone number

Purchase order number
PO date
Vendor
User
Items
Quantities
Prices
*Total PO amount
Vendor name
Address
Telephone number

Table 4-2   Continued.

*PO date issued
 PO date closed
 Buyer
*User
*Items
 Date requested
*Users Items
*Date requested
 Date updated
*Purchase order number
*PO date
*Vendor
*User
*Items
*Quantities
*Prices
*Total PO amount
*Buyer
*Purchase order number
*PO date closed
*Purchase order number
*PO date closed
*PO date
*Vendor
*User
*Items
*Quantities
*Prices
*Total PO amount
*Buyer
*Vendor name
*Vendor address and phone
*Item name
 Item description
*Buyer name

 Animal name
 Age
 Cage
*Animal name
 Father's name
 Mother's name
 Grandfathers' names
 Grandmothers' names

Table 4-2   Continued.

*Cage
  Number of spaces available
  Date of birth
*Animal name
*Mother's name
*Father's name
*Cage
*Animal name
*Cage
*Mother
*Father
*Grandparents
*Cage name
  Location
  Number of spaces

  Name of asset
  Depreciated value
*Name of asset
  Description of asset
  Date purchased
  Purchase price
  Depreciation period
*Name of asset
  Date sold

At this point in the development of a nonrelational system, you might feel prepared to take each identified info element, turn it into a column or set of columns, and be done. You already have come up with a description of everything you need to know, or more exactly, everything you think Paradox needs to know. What more is there to do except start implementing?

At this point you should take a step back and review what your goal in this database design process is. You want to create a business system that delivers information of value, information that will help you make a decision. To do this, it is obvious that your application must know what is information of value, and what isn't. You need to be able to rely on your application to tell the difference. For example, suppose you are at the family reunion the year following your first gathering. A man walks up to you: who is he? Because your family member system keeps track of all these people for you, you quickly pose a question to the system: who is this? Your system must be able to sift through all the data floating around and match up all the right pieces. You need to be sure that the name and the descriptive features really pertain to the same person. Obviously, if they don't, you'll be unable to make a good decision and you won't know who this is. If your family member system is still residing in your brain only, you run a risk: you could have forgotten those connections you built a year ago. However, if you've transferred the information to a computer, the connections will still be intact, and finding the right row (you do know this man is tall and is wearing stripes) will guarantee you coming up with the right name.

Your application will be acting on (that is, finding, manipulating, and retrieving) individual items of data—remember, that is all a computer can deal with—but what you want is information. The only way to make this work is to have you associate the information you need with the data Paradox will store. That is exactly the point you are at right now in designing your database. You need to determine how to retain the information content of each info element, while still handing it to Paradox to manage as data. You know that "2047 Marina Lane" is the address for "MRT Manufacturing," one of your clients (this is information). However, you must apply this knowledge to a table structure that will contain only data.

Remember, in a relational database, everything that is known about the application is contained in tables (and only tables). You must thus define the right column in the right table, a definition that will allow Paradox (and your application) to always associate that address with that client.

The table structure consisting of rows and columns is all you have to contain the information you want. So you must plan carefully to take full advantage of the intuitive relationships a table provides. Remember that a row contains several pieces of data, all of which describe the same object or process. So if you need to describe an object, use columns in the same table to contain the information. If your application can find the name "MRT Manufacturing" in a table, you can bet that the address the application finds in that same row will be for that same client.

However, there is a hook: an info element that describes one object could be an object in its own right. What if one of the info elements that describes Mark is the type of car he drives, but he owns two cars? How in the confines of a single table can you describe this information? Obviously you've got three choices: two entries into a single column, separated in some way; two separate columns (first car, second car); or a new row containing a different car than the first row. Relational theory calls this kind of information a *repeating group*. Each method of expressing a repeating group in a single table (multiple-valued single column, multiple columns, or rows) causes problems. With multiple values in a single column, the basic table structure of one value per row and column combination is violated. With a new column, the assumption is made that every family member will have the same number of cars, and thus every row for every member will have to reserve space for that potential information. With a new row, all the data for that member (name, height, build, etc.), except the name of the car must be repeated in every row, because there is no way in the table itself to associate one record with any other record. In a relational database, the solution to this problem is straightforward. Each repeating group is broken out into its own table, and a relationship is defined between the new and old tables. In this example, the Member table would be related to a new MemberCar table (see chapter 5 for a thorough discussion of table relationships).

This is by far the most difficult concept in relational database design, and modeling it is the toughest task in the database design process. It can be expressed simply: break the info elements into logical tables. Unfortunately, it isn't simple: how do you know what tables to create, and where to put which info elements?

Dividing the elements into entities

You can break down the process into three distinct steps:

1. Assessing what entity is being described by each info element
2. Grouping each entity's info elements together
3. Naming each entity as a single table

Assessing entities described by info elements

Once you've created a master list of info elements, you should begin to assess which entities are being described by each of the elements. An entity is any "thing which has definite, individual existence in reality or in the mind; anything real in itself" (Guralnik, ed. 1976). An entity can be a Member, or a MemberCar. Each entity that you uncover will be represented in the database design as a separate table.

 entity   A thing that has a definite, individual existence in reality or in the mind; anything real in itself.

Remember that in a database design two types of things are usually entities:

- An object (a person, place, or thing)
- A process (a transaction, occurrence, or activity)

Look for similar phrases that are being used to describe different aspects of the same object or process. For example, "Employee Name" and "Employee Address" would likely describe two different features of the same entity: an employee. "Sales Order Date" and "Order Amount" might well be two different info elements relating to a specific sales order.

If an info element occurs more than once for a given entity, pull it out and create a separate table to hold that information. For example, if a single employee had two dependents, your info elements list would likely contain an element called "Dependents" along with the rest of the information about the employee. You should extract this repeating group and create a new, separate table to hold the information associated with any dependent.

Grouping each entity's info elements together

Once each info element has an identifiable entity associated with it, you should reorganize your master list to bring each entity's elements together. As you continue the database design process, each entity will be identified as a single table, and the info elements you've collected will be the basis for the fields of that table.

Note the continued use of the term *info element* here. Remember, you have not yet broken out the data from the info element. Each info element still contains vital information that you need to preserve in the application. There is no need to bring any arbitrary descriptive data into the system; if there is no need for a data item, in that there is no information of use associated with it, then the application should not recognize it or include it.

Once you've established the groups of info elements, you need to identify each entity with a unique name. Naming conventions, rules for naming that you follow as standard practice rather than by necessity, differ between DBMS products. Naming rules also vary. In particular, Paradox stores each table in a set of files (the family), and because of that a Paradox table name must be consistent with the rules imposed on a DOS file name, including the maximum length of eight characters (not including the extension, which Paradox reserves for the identification of each family member). See Table 4-3 for a listing of Paradox's table naming requirements.

Naming each entity as a single table

Table 4-3
Paradox table-naming requirements.

A table name:
  can be a maximum of 8 characters in length
  can contain letters, numbers and special characters like $ and __
  can't contain spaces
  can't duplicate the name of another table in the same subdirectory
  shouldn't include characters in the IBM extended character set
  should not be the name of any directory
  should be descriptive

naming conventions Rules for naming that you follow as standard practice rather than by necessity.

In any case, a theoretical table name should always be singular: "Member" and not "Members," "Employee" and not "Employees," "Client" and not "Clients," and so on. This is because the table name is intended to describe each one of the rows in the table; one row in the Employee table describes one employee, while a single row in the Client table describes a single client.

Paradox also reserves several table names for its use either as ordinary temporary tables or internal temporary tables. You can create a table with the same name as a Paradox temporary table, but it will be deleted at the same point that any other temporary table is:

- When you exit Paradox
- When you change to another subdirectory (Tools|More|Directory)
- When you perform the task that creates the table

Table 4-4 provides a listing of all table names to be avoided under Paradox. Table 4-5 describes the info element groups for each of the case studies. Take particular note of the mistake icon in case study 1 (naming a table with a nondescriptive name). Each table should have a name that is meaningful. The name should provide you and any other user with a sense of what information likely can be found within that table structure. Most of the time the name of a table is fairly obvious. If it isn't, there is a good chance that the information you are trying to lump together really doesn't belong together in a single table; that is, it doesn't describe a single object or process.

Table 4-4
Paradox temporary
table names.

Answer
Changed
Chantemp
Crosstab
Deleted
Entry, Entry01, Entry02, etc.
Family
Inserted
Instemp
Keyvio, Keyviol1, Keyviol2, etc.
Kvtemp
List
Password
Passtemp
Problems
Probtemp
Resttemp
Sortques
Struct

Also review the mistake icon for case study 3 (naming a table with a plural name). A table name always should refer to one record in the table, or one occurrence of the entity.

Determining what makes each table unique

Once you've identified the basic tables needed, the next step in the design process is to figure out which info element will be used to individually describe each row in the table. What makes each entity unique? Specifically, what feature of this entity is different for each and every row? What makes each row unique? In my Family Member table, what makes each relative unique? In my MemberCar table, what makes each car unique? In my Invoice table, what makes each invoice unique?

Table 4-5
Info element groups.

Table1:
Dates covered
Date printed

Table2:
Date
Time
Client
Services performed

Table3:
Client name
Client address
Telephone number
Primary contact
Secondary contact

Table4:
Invoice date
Hours worked
Total due
Services performed

Mistake: Naming each table with a nondescriptive name. Rename each table **oops!** to indicate the entity being described by the table

Table1: REPORT
Table2: APPT
Table3: CLIENT
Table 4: INVOICE

Purchase order (PO):
Purchase order number
PO date
Vendor
User
Total PO amount
PO date closed
Buyer

Items (ITEMS):
Item
Quantity
Price
Item description

Vendor (VENDOR):

Table 4-5   Continued.

Vendor name
Address
Telephone number
Purchase request (PURCHREQ):
Date requested
Date updated
User

oops! Mistake: Naming a table in the plural. A table name should always be singular, describing the contents of a single row. Rename the table.

Rename ITEMS to ITEM

Animal (ANIMAL):
Animal name
Age
Date of birth
Cage
Father's name
Mother's name
Grandfathers' name
Grandmothers' name

Cage (CAGE):
Cage name
Location
Number of spaces
Number of spaces available

Asset (ASSET):
Name of asset
Depreciated value
Description of asset
Date purchased
Purchase price
Depreciation period
Date sold

Make a note of the selected info element for each table. Each record in the table must be uniquely identifiable with the use of this element. The element you choose to identify each row of a table sometimes is called the *identifier* (or ID) for that table. For example, each employee in an Employee table should be identifiable in some unique way. An employee's social security number might be selected intuitively as a field that could uniquely identify that individual.

identifier (ID)   The field or fields (or during the design process, the info element) that can be used to identify uniquely each row of a table.

The info element that you choose to be the identifier must have (or be assigned) a different value for each record in the table. Thus, an element like "Name" would not be appropriate, because a name could be shared potentially by several different people. A unique identifier is crucial to the design of any table because the identifier becomes the "name tag" for that individual (or specific process or object) throughout the rest of the database design. Because a family member is associated with a specific family, the family's unique identifier is used to describe that association; the member is tagged with the family's ID (see FIG. 4-8). Also, if an invoice is created for a specific client, that client is referred to by its unique identifier: the invoice is tagged with the client ID. These cross-references, or *tags*, are the links that define relationships between tables in a relational application (see chapter 6).

ID	Name	Height	Glasses	Pattern
1	Mark	Tall	Yes	Stripes
2	Mark	Short	No	Polka dots

Name Tags

Mark

Mark

4-8
Tagging each row

Because identifying values are used for linking, or tagging, in the examples above, identifiers are crucial to the relational model. In the model, the identifying element for a table (the field in which you find the name tag) is known as that table's primary key. For the purposes of this discussion, a primary key is assumed to be contained within a single field of the table. A discussion of multifield keys is reserved for later, after the concept of atomic field values has been introduced.

Once assigned, a key can be used throughout the database to refer not only to a particular entity but to a specific record in that table; because the key value is always unique, each row in the table is also unique. Remember, an entity is a real thing. In the model, each of these things is tagged with the key value, which is used to refer to that thing everywhere else it is found in the database.

Assigning a key to the unique element

Paradox (along with most RDBMSs) supports the designation of a primary key for each table. The designation of a primary key occurs as part of the table creation (`Create`) or modification (`Modify|Restructure`) process. Once a primary key has been designated for a table, it can impact the application as follows:

- Each record in the table is forced to be unique because the primary key value is forced to be unique.
- The table will be kept in sorted order by primary key value.
- Database operations involving the table work faster.

Once the user has identified the primary key, Paradox will respond by creating an index on the selected field(s). More specifically, a primary index (a separate and relatively small file with the .PX extension) is created and used to keep track of the primary key values and where in the table they are located (see FIG. 4-9). Once created, the primary index allows Paradox to get at specific records in a table without having to search the whole table itself. (Refer to chapter 7 for a further discussion of Paradox implementation of primary keys.)

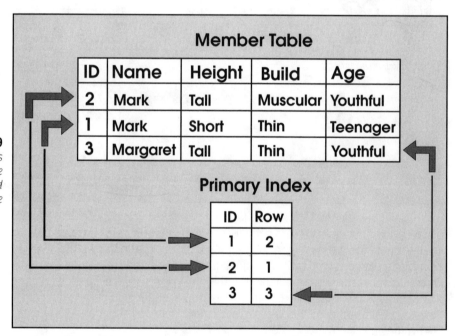

4-9
A primary index relates the primary key value to its associated place in the table

index A separate and relatively small file used to keep track of values (in the case of a primary index, it tracks primary key values), and which allows a DBMS access to a particular value without searching the table itself.

There could be more than one info element that uniquely identifies an entity. Each potential primary key value is known as a candidate key. Even if there are several candidate keys for a table, only one should be selected. However, how do you choose the best element for the job?

Review for a moment the way a primary key value will be used. Like a name tag, it will appear anywhere (and everywhere) that entity is referred to. In practice, this means that primary key values are often found in more than one table—sometimes in many tables—within a single database. Because the primary key is used everywhere, a bad key choice can haunt you.

So what is a good key? First, a good primary key is as small as possible (e.g., #1 rather than #100000000). A smaller primary key value will occupy less storage space and will be accessed more easily by Paradox. The ideal primary key will thus be both short, and if possible numeric, because in general numeric values (numbers) occupy less space than alphanumeric values (letters or other characters).

Second, a good primary key is unchanging. Remember, the primary key value will be used as a reference to the entity everywhere else in the application. When a primary key value must change, you are forced to make the change not only in one table, but in all the other tables in which the reference to that entity might have occurred (called a *cascading effect*). It is easy to avoid the problem of changing the primary key value by simply making the primary key meaningless. There is usually no incentive to change a value that has no relationship to the real world and that is meaningless. Thus, the ideal primary key should be both meaningless and unchanging.

It might be possible for you to make your life easier by using certain Paradox features in conjunction with primary keys. An application can force you to depend on Paradox to keep track of primary keys, even to the point of automatically numbering each new row as you add it. Autonumbering is often of great benefit, because it usually provides a primary key close to the ideal: short, numeric, meaningless, and thus unchanging. Autonumbering is not a feature available through Paradox's menu system, but is easily implemented using PAL. See chapter 9 for details on a simple autonumbering routine for a numeric field.

autonumbering   A DBMS function that builds a primary key value without the need for user input.

Some tables might not have an obvious primary key value. In those cases in which an info element does not exist that would make an appropriate primary key, you might choose to create a special element specifically to act as the primary key for the table. This created element is known as a *surrogate key*, because the primary key value is not really an attribute (a feature or description) of the given entity. Take the Member table as an example. Is there anything in the Member table that you can use to identify uniquely each family member? Is it "Favorite Color," or "Age," or "Name?" Obviously the data doesn't support any of these choices. The solution is to create a surrogate key for the table. You can add a new column to the table to act as this key; "Member #" would be an obvious column name (or ID, as described in FIG. 4-8). "Member #" is a surrogate key because it has no existence in reality; it is created and used strictly by the application.

Note that defining a surrogate key should not make your life harder. Many users complain when they have to keep track of this kind of meaningless number. It seems to add a layer of complexity to the use of an application. However, a truly relational DBMS will shield the user from ever having to know anything about a surrogate key. If your application requires you to know an employee's number, and cannot accept your information in the way you use it (by employee name, for example), it is more likely a problem with how you have designed your application than with Paradox. Table 4-6 provides a listing of all the database tables and their primary keys for each case study.

Table 4-6
Tables and their primary keys.

REPORT:	Report ID
CLIENT:	Client ID
APPT:	Date
	Time
	Client
PO:	Purchase Order number
ITEM:	Item
VENDOR:	Vendor ID
PURCHREQ:	Request number
ANIMAL:	Animal ID
CAGE:	Cage Number
ASSET:	Asset ID

The next step in the database design process lies in reevaluating the specific info elements in each table. This involves turning the info elements into fields and is the subject of the next chapter. A detailed discussion of table relationships is deferred until chapter 6.

Summary   To review, designing a table begins with an understanding of the table structure itself. You should now be comfortable with the row/record and column/field terminology, and also with the following concepts:

- A relation is a special kind of table that conforms to the rules established by the relational model.

- The table design process begins with an evaluation of the tasks the business system will perform, then continues with a breakdown and regrouping of the information elements suggested by those tasks.
- A master list of info elements must be created that lists out (in no particular order) the items of information that the application will be required to manage.
- The info elements should subsequently be divided into entities that form the foundation of relational tables.
- Each entity identified should then be isolated and named as a single table.
- Each table must then be evaluated to determine what makes it (and each record in it) unique. The unique element is then identified as the primary key for the table.
- A primary key acts as the enforcer of the uniqueness requirement of a relational table.
- The ideal primary key is short, numeric, meaningless, and unchanging.
- A surrogate key can be built to help identify each row in a table (to tag each occurrence of an entity).

Overall, a table should describe occurrences of only one object or process; have a descriptive, singular table name; and include only unique records by applying a key.

Key Terms

autonumbering   A DBMS function that builds a primary key value without the need for user input.

column   Used interchangeably with field to refer to one descriptive element or attribute of a table (the vertical of the table).

entity   A thing that has a definite, individual existence in reality or in the mind; anything real in itself.

field   Used interchangeably with column to refer to one descriptive element or attribute of a table (the vertical of the table).

index   A separate and relatively small file used to keep track of values (in the case of a primary index, it tracks primary key values), and which allows a DBMS access to a particular value without searching the table itself.

information element (info element)   An item of information that has not yet been defined or broken down into a specific field or fields.

identifier (ID)   The field or fields (or during the design process, the info element) that can be used to identify uniquely each row of a table.

naming conventions   Rules for naming that you follow as standard practice rather than by necessity.

record   Used interchangeably with row to refer to one occurrence of an object or process within a table (the horizontal of the table).

row   Used interchangeably with record to refer to one occurrence of an object or process within a table (the horizontal of the table).

sort   The arrangement of values into a specified order, usually following the ASCII keycode order.

table   A set of columns and rows that describes a single object or process and that is the fundamental data structure of any relational database.

5 Designing the fields

You have several groups of info elements in front of you. Each group, which you have roughly defined as a Paradox table, has a name and some element that you have selected (or created) to represent its primary key. These rough groups contain what information you need your application to manage for you.

You probably have guessed that each info element corresponds roughly to a column definition (remember, the terms column and field are completely interchangeable). However, translation of that info element into the precise parameters of one (or more) Paradox column definition can be more delicate an operation than you expect. Why is this the case, when a table structure is such an intuitive one, and the contents of a column seemingly so obvious?

This question returns you to the truth underlying the entire database design process: it is very difficult to isolate what you know about an item of data from the data itself. A simple description of an info element can come with an entire host of associations that are known to you or other users but are not obvious to your application. The task in defining the field that will contain this data is to build those expectations—those things that you know about the data, or in other words, the information that you know—into the field definition itself.

This process has already begun: you have applied your knowledge of the different info elements to organize them into groups that you believe represent different entities: real life objects or processes. Now you must apply more rigorous analysis to uncover additional assumptions that you work with and which add value to the information you know.

Field design, in contrast to the more common term, field definition, is a term used very appropriately to describe this process. In a very rough sense, you already have completed the field definition; you've identified what you need Paradox to manage. Remember, however, a field definition only represents one piece of a structure for what will be managed. A column that is to hold accurate and useful data must have identified those questions (what is accurate and what is useful?) in the design process. Thus, field design is an art; it involves both skill (how do I communicate my expectations to my application?) and intuition (what do I know that I need to communicate?).

The field-design process begins with the isolation of individual data components from an info element. Figure 5-1 identifies each step of the field design process. Each isolated component, now more appropriately called a field, is then described in detail. The description identifies the name of the field, as well as details about the field data type and domain. Both of these

An overview of the field-design process

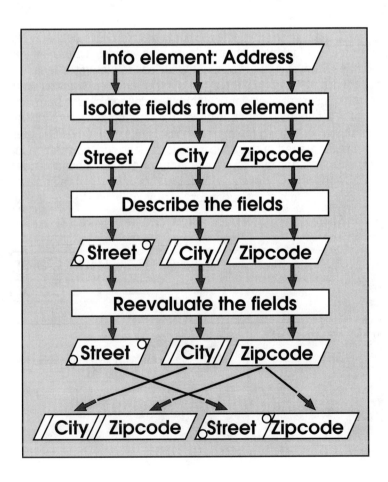

5-1
The steps in the field design process

terms are defined and thoroughly discussed later in this chapter. Once the field has been described, it must be reevaluated to determine if it is appropriate to the current table. Does this field truly describe the entity? Or does it describe something else—is it dependent on some other value in the table? Refer to FIG. 5-1 as it explores the process of designing fields to contain address information. Once three fields are isolated from the info element Address, each is described by name and type of data expected, and the range of possibilities for the field is exposed. Once each is reevaluated, however, it is clear that two of the fields, City and Zip Code, have a relationship that wasn't obvious on first glance. In reality—in real life—the Zip Code field defines the value in the City field. Your zip code and city name are both descriptive of where you live; each zip code area is in effect a subset of each city area. Relational theory thus would indicate that the City field is inappropriately placed in the current table. A solution that conforms better to the relational model would be to create a second, separate table that accurately reflects the dependency. The second table would contain each zip code along with the city that is always associated with it (remember, this is still theory, not practice!). The City field would be removed from the current table entirely.

Isolating the fields

Starting with the first group of info elements that you have defined, take a look at each individual info element in turn. Ask yourself: can I isolate any components within this single element while still retaining the meaning associated with it? Relational theory calls a "no" answer *atomicity*, and it is integral to the concept of a relational table. As defined by C.J. Date, an *atomic value* is one that cannot be decomposed or broken down into any smaller unit without losing the meaning associated with it (1990). I prefer to use the term isolate rather than decompose, because decomposition implies a loss of value; isolation of different elements, on the other hand, tends to reinforce the concept that each element is independent and valuable on its own (see FIG. 5-2). Note that the concept of atomicity is very questionable

5-2
Data elements are independent pieces of an info element

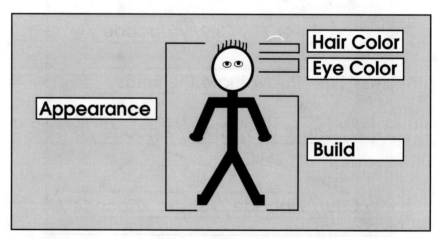

when applied to more sophisticated types of information such as Memo or Binary Large Object (BLOb) values.

atomicity   A quality of a value that indicates that it cannot be broken down into components without the loss of its meaning.

BLOb   Binary Large Object, any type of data which is storable in binary format.

For example, the Address info element described earlier does contain three specific components: Street Address, City, and Zip Code. The Street Address component could be broken down into subcomponents (e.g., Street Number and Street Name). If you isolated these subcomponents, however, meaning would be lost, because that meaning is dependent on the order in which the two components appear. The Street Address value only retains meaning (is only accurate and reflective of reality) if the number and street name appear in their proper order, with the proper spacing. Thus, this first step, which might seem the simplest, is not always straightforward. Refer to Table 5-1 for some examples of field isolation through an analysis of case study 2 (EB).

Also note that an atomic value also can be regarded as one that does not exist elsewhere in the database, regardless of the form it might take. In other words, if you can calculate a value based on another value, don't store both. Only the source value is necessary, because you always can construct the other value when you need it. You might note in case study 3 that the Age field is really another version of the Date of Birth field: they represent the same information. The Date of Birth field would be the one to keep, however, because you always can calculate the Age from the Date of Birth; you can't calculate the other way. All the fields for case study 3 are found in Table 5-2.

Once an atomic component has been isolated from within an info element, it more accurately can be called a field. The task of describing that field then falls into the two major categories:

- Naming the field
- Identifying the values that you expect the field to contain

Naming a field

First, the field name should be descriptive. Paradox supports field names up to 25 characters in length, including spaces, and thus is only mildly restrictive in the creation of a completely descriptive name. See Table 5-3 for a complete rundown on field naming requirements for both Paradox 3.5 and 4.0. Referring back to the Member table described earlier, Age is probably an inappropriate name for the values in that column. Because the descriptive values that are known for the column include Youthful and Teenager, the name of the field more appropriately would be Age Estimate or even Age Attitude. The column describing the Height of each Member more appropriately would be labeled Relative Height or Rough Height, because the

Creating a descriptive name

Table 5-1
Isolating the fields for case study 2.

Info element	Field(s)
PO:	
Purchase order number	Purchase order number
PO date	Purchase order date
Vendor	Vendor ID
	Vendor name
User	User name
Total PO amount	Total purchase order amount
PO date closed	Purchase order date closed
Buyer	Buyer name
ITEM:	
Item*	Item number
Quantity	Quantity ordered
Price	Price
Item description	Item description
VENDOR:	
Vendor ID*	Vendor ID
Vendor name	Vendor name
Address	Street address
	City
	State
	Zip code
Telephone number	Area code
	Phone number
PURCHREQ:	
Request number	Request number
Date requested	Date requested
Date updated	Date updated
User	User name

values known to be included in the field are Tall and Short (see FIG. 5-3). If the field name accurately and completely describes what is expected in a column, following the basic relational column-naming rule (RN-3) is easy enough. Specifically, Codd mandates that "all columns . . . within any single relation must be assigned names that are distinct from one another, and distinct from the names of relations and functions" (1990). Thus, if the Member table were to contain another column describing the person's favorite color of shoes, the design would have to take into consideration the fact that Favorite Color already existed as a column, and thus a new column would have to be named more specifically (e.g., Favorite Shoe Color). Table 5-4 identifies field names for fields in case study 1. Note that the field-isolation process can yield additional

Table 5-2
Isolating the fields for case study 3.

Info element	Field(s)
ANIMAL:	
Animal ID*	Animal ID
Animal name	Animal name
	Age
Date of birth	Date of birth
Cage	Cage number
Father's name	Father/animal name
Mother's name	Mother/animal name
Grandfathers' names	Paternal grandfather/animal name
	Maternal grandfather/animal name
Grandmothers' names	Paternal grandmother/animal name
	Maternal grandmother/animal name
CAGE:	
Cage number	Cage number
Cage name	Cage name
Location	Cage building
	Cage row
	Cage level
Number of spaces	Number of spaces total
Number of spaces available	Number of spaces available

Table 5-3
Paradox field naming requirements.

A field name:
  can be up to 25 characters in length
  cannot start with a space but can contain spaces
  can contain any printable character except the following:
    "(double quotes)
    [] (square brackets)
    # (number sign as the complete Field Name by itself)
    () (left or right parentheses)
    -> (the combination hyphen and greater than sign)
  can't duplicate the name of another field in the same table
  should be descriptive of the field's contents
  should not be the same as the name of a Paradox temporary table

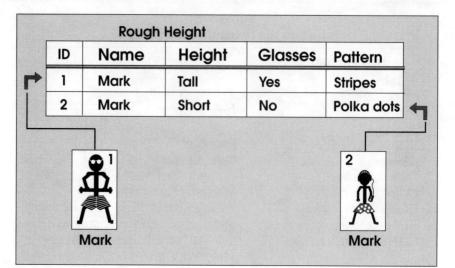

5-3
Field names should be as specific as possible

fields, or even additional tables, that you didn't consider the first time around. For example, a given appointment conceivably could cover more than one service, and thus a separate table (Appointment Service) would need to be created to handle each specific service that was performed. In another change, the service changed from a descriptive field to a coded field (Service Code) in order to accommodate the numerous times that description would have been required in other tables. Also, Total Due was a value required for the Invoice table, but its source (a billing rate) was nowhere to be found. Thus, Service Rate was added as a new field to contain the rate at which each kind of service would normally be billed (the assumption in this business is that all clients share the same rate for the same service).

Because each column name within a given table must be unique, it follows that each combination of table and column name will be unique. As a matter of convention, some DBMSs other than Paradox always identify a particular column (or depending on circumstance, a particular value in a column) relative to its table. Thus, the Favorite Color column from the Member table could be described as Member.Favorite Color, with the period indicating (by convention only) the relationship between the table and field names. In referring to a value in a field within a specific table, Paradox requires that the table and field name be separated by an arrow (a hyphen and greater-than sign in combination). Thus, the above field from the Member table in Paradox could be described as [Member->Favorite Color]. This is only one of several alternative ways to describe values found in a particular column. See Table 5-5 for field referencing alternatives.[1]

• • • • • • • • •

[1] Notice that there is a "current" field position in a table other than that where the cursor is now located. This is a *shadow cursor* holding a position in each table in the workspace or desktop, and to which your active cursor moves when you execute an Image/Move command.

Table 5-4
Isolating the fields for case study 1.

Info element	Field(s)
SCHEDULE:	
Schedule date*	Schedule date*
Dates covered	Schedule start date
	Schedule end date
Date printed	Schedule date printed
APPT:	
	Appointment number*
Date	Appointment date
Time	Appointment start time
	Appointment end time
Client	Client ID
APPTSERV (new):	
	Appointment number*
Services performed	Service code performed*
	Hours worked
SERVICE (new):	
	Service code*
	Service description
	Service rate
CLIENT:	
Client ID*	Client ID*
Client name	Client name
Client address	Client street address
	Client zip code
Telephone number	Client telephone number
Primary contact	Primary contact name
Secondary contact	Secondary contact name
CITY (new)	
	Zip code*
	City name
	State abbreviation
INVOICE:	
Invoice number	Invoice number*
Invoide date	Invoice date
Total due	Total amount due
Invoice Detail	INVDET (New):
	Invoice number*
Services performed	Service code performed*
Hours worked	Hours worked

Table 5-5
Field Referencing Options in Paradox.

Identify a value from a Paradox table on the workspace or desktop as follows:

[ ]	Value that cursor is currently on (current field and current record)
[#]	Value in current field of # record number in the same table
[Field]	Value in same record of same table, but in a different field
[Table->Field]	Value that is currently in record and field, but in a different table
[Table->]	Value in current field in named table
[Table(n)->Field]	Value in named field in nth image of named table
[Table(n)->]	Value in current field in nth image in named table
[Table(Q)->Field]	Value in named field in query image of named table
[Table(Q)->]	Value in current field in query image of named table

Beyond the specified rule, Codd suggests that a column name should contain a reference to the domain from which the column values are drawn (1990). See the discussion on domains later in this section for details. This concept is not currently supported by Paradox.

Using the singular rather than the plural

Like a table name, a column name is intended to describe one occurrence of the feature being described. More specifically, a column name should describe one atomic value. Thus, the Zip Code field name describes one value in that column: a single zip code. The City field describes one value in that column: a single city name. If more than one value is needed to describe that element for a single row (e.g., a person in the Member table has not only one but two favorite colors), this qualifies the value as a repeating group. As with all repeating groups, a new and separate table should be created to handle that information. Refer to Table 5-4 for examples where fields must be broken out into other tables. Note that the breakdown of the Services Performed field requires not only field isolation into individual services performed per appointment, but actually the creation of two new tables: an Appointment Service table and a Services Code table. Also note that the Schedule Date info element required two components, Start Date and End Date, to be isolated. Similarly, the Appointment Time info element required two components, Start Time and End Time, to be isolated.

🗝 **repeating group** The relational model's term for a feature of an entity that can include more than one value.

Defining a field's data type

Once a field has been named, you already should have evaluated the data that you intend to keep in that field, and you are probably familiar with what that data will look like. In effect, both the validity and the appearance of the data will contribute to its value to you as information in your application. To refer back to the earlier discussion, you have developed knowledge that your field definition must convey to Paradox. In this case, that knowledge relates to the values that you expect to find in a given column.

One way to describe each value you expect to find in a column is through a convention known as a *data type*. A data type is a description of a value that Paradox (along with other DBMSs) uses as a way to understand some fundamental qualities of that value. A data type is just that: a type, or category, of data. The specific category that you select for each field depends on two factors:

- What a value is
- What Paradox can understand

data type   A description of a value that the DBMS uses as a way to understand some fundamental qualities of that value.

Describing what a value is

There is a difference between what a value is and how it appears. What a value is falls into a few, relatively limited categories, and in the purest sense reflects nothing more than how we perceive it (bear with me; this is not an attempt to delve into existential philosophy). We can use any of our five senses to perceive information:

- Sight
- Sound
- Smell
- Taste
- Feel

These categories probably don't look much like any data type that you've encountered in the past. This is simply because the translation of information (in this case, a specific value) into computer-based data is still in a rudimentary phase. Humans are able to perceive information through all five senses, but today's RDBMS products (partially because of the computers they are designed to operate on) are able to understand only a very limited subset of that. Today's computer can know basically only what you can describe in words (and sometimes images), but this cannot reproduce the experience being described. Once again, the basic problem is that you can make intuitive connections between information received in a variety of forms. A smell can invoke a vivid visual memory. The feeling of a plastic apple easily can change your opinion about whether it would be a good apple to eat. The sound of glass shattering immediately can bring the image of a broken window to mind. Even the most formidable writer would be hard pressed to find language to describe all that you can perceive.

A computer cannot make these intuitive connections. In fact, a computer's language is so simple it has only two words: yes and no. The binary nature of computer processing (literally using only 0 and 1 to describe everything) makes the expression of complex information a matter of thousands of connections—thousands of yes's and no's in combination. Given this context, it is fairly easy to see how this fact impacts the types of data that the computer can manage. The more powerful the hardware is, that is, the more thousands, or millions, of connections it can manage at once, the more complex the data is that it can handle.

Paradox supports a limited variety of categories of data, basically extending only through the visual (sight) realm. Paradox 4.0 introduced two major new data types which are intended to expand those categories dramatically. The new BLOb data type can handle any type of binary data, from graphics to sound to actual interpreted program code. Paradox supports the following specific types of values:

- Numbers (Numeric)
- Text (Alphanumeric or Memo)
- BLOb
- Short integers
- Dates
- Dollar values
- Logical values (true/false, yes/no, or 0/1, but only in PAL)

Table 5-6 identifies these different possible data types along with examples of values that might be labeled appropriately with the type. Alphanumeric and Memo data types require that you specify a maximum length, A.. for the total number of storable characters, and M.. for the total number of characters to be viewed in the source table (not the external Memo file). Review pages 268–270 in the Paradox 4.0 User's Guide or pages 19–20 in the Paradox 3.5 User's Guide for more details on data types.

The specific types of data that Paradox supports has something to do with how it manages the translation from logical table to physical data. Values of different data types occupy different amounts of disk space and make Paradox do more or less work to manipulate them. In general, numbers are easier to deal with than text values and also occupy less space. Enhancements in data types directly impact Paradox's file format, and specifically contributed to the change in format between Paradox 3.5 and Paradox 4.0.

***Differentiating
between data
types & formats***

Paradox separates how the data in a particular table and field is stored and managed from how the data is displayed on screen or in a report. The difference is subtle. Each Paradox data type actually controls what data is allowable in a field defined with that type. For example, Paradox maintains an internal calendar against which any date entered into a Date data type field is evaluated—if it isn't a real day, the value is excluded from the field. A date that is legal, however, can appear in many formats (again, reality versus the computer). A day exists on a calendar (and in real life), but it can be described in several ways—"1/1/91," "January 1, 1991," or "1 Jan 1991," etc.[2]

•••••••••

[2] In this context, the use of quotation marks does not follow the assumption that a value surrounded by quotes is a string (text) value. In this usage, the quotation marks simply indicate that within is found a value, regardless of data type.

**Table 5-6
Paradox data types.**

Data type	Description	Restrictions	Sample value
D	Date	valid date between 1/1/100 and 12/31/9999	1/1/93
S	Short Number	integer only between -32,767 and 32,767	101
$	Currency	same as N but formatted differently, with display to include whole number separators, negative numbers in parentheses, and rounded to 2 decimal places	$1,004,333.99
N	Numeric	floating point number; up to 15 significant digits; larger numbers are rounded and stored in scientific notation	10059.352
A	Alphanumeric	1-255 characters	"Any string value"
M	Memo	1-240 characters to include in initial display; actual field size variable length up to 64MB in size; Paradox 4.0 only	
B	Binary	Variable length; can hold any binary value; Paradox 4.0 only	
U	Unknown	Field type created automatically when value of imported field is unrecognizable to Paradox; Paradox 4.0 only	

These different descriptions all represent the same value (the same real thing), but use different conventions to display that value. Each different convention is called a format; like a book's format, it reflects the shape, size, type of binding, paper stock, and type face (cosmetics), and has little, if anything, to do with the contents (see FIG. 5-4). Don't be deceived by the example drawn by FIG. 5-4. Paradox does differentiate between uppercase and lowercase letters; they are considered different values. The idea here is just that the different descriptions don't change the fact; what is being described remains the same.

Some RDBMS products draw a fine line between different formats and different data types. For example, Paradox manages all numbers the same way; but it also recognizes that you use numbers to mean different things, such as quantities, prices, salaries, ages, etc. Because you are accustomed to

5-4
The substance of an entity is the "real thing," while the format is only one particular appearance or version of it

seeing currency values with a certain format ($###,###.##), Paradox assumes that all currency values you use should appear in that format. This is true regardless of the fact that a currency value is essentially no different than any other number. The Currency data type is more a formatting option than the reflection of data with a different set of qualities.

Fundamentally, the intent of a data type is simply to help you describe the values that will be managed within a given field. The more specific that description is, the more likely it is that the data that is entered into the field will retain its information content, and that it will be usable as information of value.

Deciding on a data type

Again, the data type for a given field is less a definition than a description of a value. As in most areas of database design, the more specific you can be, the better. Theoretically, all DBMSs, or at least all RDBMSs, should support all potential types of data. Practically speaking, none do.

At this point you should utilize the data types supported by Paradox. You should take a look at Table 5-7 in order to assess what types of data might be handled in theory; Paradox does not support some of these. In particular, Paradox does not support a Time data type (you should utilize an A5 data type (e.g., 07:00, 11:53 or 12:00) to handle time within Paradox today). Paradox also does not support Logical data within a field definition. Logical values are supported through PAL.

Table 5-8 provides a summary of the fields and selected data types for the case studies. Note that zip code values are identified as Alphanumeric values, even though they can contain only numbers. This is because Paradox specifies that numbers cannot contain any leading zeros; zip codes, of course, must have that option.

Table 5-7
Theoretical data types.

Data type	Abbreviation	Example value
Number	N(2,1)	5.6
number of digits	N(9,3)	888901.983
number of decimal places	N(2,0)	33
Dollar	M(5)	$333.55
number of digits	M(1)	$.07
Character	C(2,F)	Up
number of characters	C(14,V)	My mother . . .
(F)ixed or	C(10,F)	(555)-XRXT
(V)ariable	C(1,F)	z
Graphic	G(1)	[1 picture]
number of characters	G(3)	[3 pictures]
Date	D	3-14-93
(month-day-year)		2-20-1887
Time	T	11:30:10
(hour:minute:second)		

Table 5-8
Case-study field and data types.

Field name	Data type
SCHEDULE:	
Schedule date*	D
Schedule start date	D
Schedule end date	D
Schedule date printed	D
APPT:	
Appointment number*	S
Appointment date	D
Appointment start time	A5
Appointment end time	A5
Client ID	S
APPTSERV:	
Appointment number*	S
Service code performed*	S
Hours worked	$
SERVICE:	
Service code*	S
Service description	A25
Service rate	$

Table 5-8   Continued.

Field name	Data type
CLIENT:	
Client ID*	S
Client name	A25
Client street address	A25
Client zip code	A10
Client telephone number	A12
Primary contact name	A40
Secondary contact name	A40
CITY:	
Zip code*	A10
City name	A25
State abbreviation	A2
INVOICE:	
Invoice number	S
Invoice date	D
Total amount due	$
INVDET:	
Invoice number	S
Service code performed*	S
Hours worked	N(
PO:	
Purchase order number	S
Purchase order date	D
Vendor ID	S
Vendor name	A25
User name	A40
Total purchase order amount	$
Purchase order date closed	D
Buyer name	A40
ITEM:	
Item number	S
Quantity ordered	N
Price	$
Item description	A15
VENDOR:	
Vendor ID	S
Vendor name	A25
Street address	A25
City	A25

State	A2
Zip code	A10
Area code	A3
Phone number	A8

PURCHREQ:
Request number	S
Date requested	D
Date updated	D
User name	A40

ANIMAL:
Animal ID★	S
Animal name	A20
Date of birth	D
Cage number	S
Father/animal name	A20
Mother/animal name	A20
Maternal grandfather/animal name	A20
Paternal grandfather/animal name	A20
Maternal grandmother/animal name	A20
Paternal grandmother/animal name	A20

CAGE:
Cage number★	S
Cage name	A20
Cage building	S
Cage row	S
Cage level	S
Number of spaces total	S
Number of spaces available	S

ASSET:
Name of asset	A30
Depreciated value	$
Description of asset	M25
Date purchased	D
Purchase price	$
Depreciation period	N
Date sold	D

Beyond the description of the values in a column that you have identified as a data type, the theoretical model supports an additional description of the values. This extended description is actually much more precise than a data type, which is normally just a rough description of what is expected.

Defining a field's domain

What a domain is

A domain is a concept so precise that it assumes each and every possible value for a field can be known—and specified—at the time a field is created. In fact, a *domain* is nothing more than a pool of values from which actual values in the field can be drawn (Date 1990) (see FIG. 5-5). This assumes that there is a distinct difference between a domain (in effect, a separate set or table) and a field (one use of the domain).

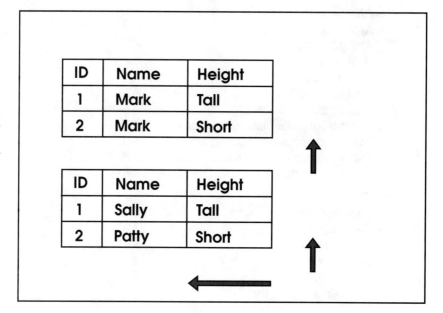

5-5
Each domain describes the pool of values from which any field value must be drawn

domain   The pool of values from which actual values in a field might be drawn.

Working from the general toward the specific

In some products domains have been labeled "extended data types" because they extend the description that a data type provides into a greater level of detail. Conceptually, a domain provides the most powerful tool in an RDBMS for retaining information content within a data element. The theoretical importance of this cannot be overstated. When domains are enforced, the RDBMS maintains control over what values are allowable or not. When control is maintained at that level, comparisons between values in different fields become possible. If you know that the Family Name in the Member table comes from the same domain as the Family Name in the Family table, you can make a meaningful comparison between the values. Support for domains give the data manipulation features of a RDBMS a firm theoretical foundation.

Although domains are not directly supported by Paradox, you can still consider applying the concept to your database design. After you've described a field with a specific name and data type, expand on the description by analyzing what specific values (not just categories of values) you expect to find in the field. An important support for domains that might not be obvious is through the relational nature of your database design itself. Assume, for example, that you have broken your Member and MemberCar information into two separate tables, as suggested. The MemberCar table will have to include the Member's ID (the name tag for the family member who owns the car). In order for the name tag to be valid, it must exist already in the Member table. In other words, the Member table defines the domain for the allowable Members. This kind of relationship is explored more fully in chapter 6. Paradox supports this kind of domain restriction through the use of the TableLookup validity check (also discussed in more detail in chapter 6). For now, suffice it to say that relationships depend on domains.

Reusing a predefined domain

Outside of the concept of support for a list of allowable values (domains), Paradox does support more specific descriptions of field values than those provided by the data types. In particular, analyze your field for the following qualities:

Specifying additional restrictions

- Range of values (minimum and maximum)
- Unique values
- Required values
- Defaults
- Expected formats

These additional features of a field are definable through Paradox's validity checking process. A valcheck can be attached to a single field in a table and acts much like a screen on the field's window: the screen prevents nonconforming data from being entered. However, the screen on the window does not provide complete protection from nonconforming data (you can always get in through the door). In this case, the "door" might be any type of nonkeyboard data entry or modification. Paradox valchecks only apply when data is being added or modified through DataEntry, Edit, or CoEdit; not through Tools|More|Add, not through an insert query, and not through an import process. Paradox validity checks also do not apply to data entered into a table before the validity check was defined. Validity checks are addressed in more detail in chapter 9.

Note that this kind of attribute of a field can be inherent in the value itself or can be enforced as a matter of business policy. For example, in the example of the MemberCar, one field you want to track is the cost of each car owned by the Member. Thus you design a Car Cost field. You might recognize the fact that no value in the Car Cost field will ever be lower than $5,000, but the reason for that truth is debatable. On the one hand, it could just be a matter of fact (i.e., no car on the market today costs less than $5,000). Or it could just as easily be a business rule that is being enforced (i.e., no one in this family is allowed to buy a car that costs less than $5,000). Regardless of source or intent, the range of values is still valid.

Range of values Do the values in the field always fall into a specified range? Specified ranges usually are based on one of the five mathematical comparison operators—equals, greater than, less than, greater than or equal to, or less than or equal to. These operations are indicated by the standard mathematical signs: =, >, <, >=, or <=. Paradox utilizes two different valcheck options to control the range of values: High and Low. The High option allows you to specify the largest allowable value for a field; the Low supports the smallest allowable value. Each option is established independent of the other. Thus, a range could be open-ended on either end. If the valcheck specifies a High value of 5, an attempt to enter a 6 into the field will be unsuccessful; if the Low value of 0 is specified, an attempt to enter a negative number into the field will be rejected. A range can be applied against any one of many different data types, including dates, numbers, currency values, or even alphanumeric (character) strings. Paradox does support a specific order for characters, usually based on the ASCII key-code order, a standard sort order for the United States that sorts numbers before uppercase characters, which are before lowercase characters. You could conceivably specify a range such as <F that would imply a range of uppercase characters which came before the letter F. Similarly, ranges can be applied against dates, with the understanding that if date 1 is "less than" date 2, date 1 occurs first on the calendar.

Uniqueness Refer to the discussion in chapter 4 on primary keys. One feature of a relational database is that a given table can contain more than one candidate key, but only a single primary key is allowable. A field is only a candidate key if its value is found to be unique for each row in a table. If this is a quality of a particular field, you should identify it at this point. Paradox can support a requirement for uniqueness on a nonkey field through PAL. The application of a key to keyed fields automatically enforces the uniqueness requirement. Again, the point is to shift as much of the burden as possible to Paradox for retaining the information content of a data value; if the value is incorrect, clearly it has little or no worth to an application, and thus to your need for information of value.

Required & One of the most difficult dilemmas in relational theory focuses on the issue of
missing values how to handle values that don't currently exist. In relational terminology (and practically speaking, as well), a field that is left empty in a particular record is said to contain missing information. This can occur in either of two circumstances:

- The value is not currently known.
- The feature does not apply to the current row.

These are two distinct situations, but Paradox (along with most RDBMSs) deals with them using the same technique: allowing a null in place of a value.

A null is a special kind of marker, theoretically different from a blank (which is a value) or a zero (also a value). A null is used to represent the fact that information is missing. The current version of relational theory discusses this problem extensively but provides few workable solutions, and none that can be implemented given today's RDBMS. In Paradox, a null and a blank value are indistinguishable.[3] The problem stems from the nature of a table itself. The logical structure of rows and columns assumes that the same set of columns exist for every row in the table. This means that Paradox must keep track of every column in every row, regardless of whether that column has a value, or whether that value is an applicable one. This has an impact in three areas:

- Resource requirements
- Accuracy of any query
- Calculations

Resource requirements   The need to keep track of empty columns has an impact on the use of both disk storage space and processing resources, including memory. As a result of the tendency of relational theory to break tables into their smallest components (the least number of fields), Paradox is optimized to work best on tables that have few columns. Each additional column adds a layer of complexity to the processing, and thus involves more resources, which has impact on both speed and cost (see chapters 12 and 13).

Accuracy of any query   One important reason for applying domain and other restrictions to a field is to help ensure that each value in a field is both valid and true. A null immediately raises both questions. First, is it valid? In other words, is it legal for the value to not exist, or are you waiting to discover the value? Second, is it true: does the feature just not apply? Without a method for distinguishing between the two situations, a question asked about a particular table could yield an inaccurate result.

For example, if you wanted to know how many family members had blue cars, you might query the Car Color field of the MemberCar table to extract all those records that indicated a Car Color equal to "Blue." Presumably, Paradox would locate all the records with "Blue" in that field and ignore the records without "Blue," including those with nulls. Assume the result indicated that there are five family members with blue cars. You could not be sure that five was an accurate answer to your question, because a null value in that column could represent an unknown color for a member's car that in reality was blue (the correct answer to your question thus would have been six, not five). Based on the model, Paradox should have been able to specify the answer in the context of the information that was currently known, such

· · · · · · · · ·

[3] Blank is a keyword supported through QBE and in PAL to locate fields into which no value has been entered.

as "Five blue cars, one car of unknown color." This kind of result is, however, impossible in any current RDBMS products if the question does not explicitly ask for unknowns to be included.

Calculations   In addition to the variance you must accept in extracting data when null values are allowed, you must be prepared to encounter similar variances when attempting to perform calculations on the data. If the question you were asking was what was the total cost of all the blue cars, rather than how many blue cars, any null could have a serious impact on the result.

Beyond simple summaries, there is the well-known problem with multiplication and division operations that affect zero values. This problem is extended when these operations are attempted on a value that doesn't exist, or a null. You can control how a null (or a blank) is treated in the context of a calculation (as a zero or not).[4] You can eliminate the problems encountered when nulls are allowed by forcing the users to enter a value in each field of a table. Paradox allows a field definition to include a rule that forces the entry of a value (precluding nulls). This might solve the problem of missing-but-applicable information (you just can't enter a record until you uncover any missing piece). However, this doesn't address the problem of missing-and-inapplicable information. You potentially could use a special character to indicate that value (n/a for "not applicable" has been used in this type of situation to good effect, but of course this doesn't work in a nonalphanumeric field).

Defaults   The alternative to forcing a value to be entered in a field is to rely on Paradox to enter the value for you. Here, *default* is simply a value that is entered automatically into a field if you have taken no action to add a value on your own. Paradox supports the definition of a field value default as part of the field design process along with the establishment of other valchecks.

Formats   Many values achieve meaning through their internal organization, or the way they are formatted. The example of the Street Address field explored this briefly in an earlier discussion. A street address has meaning because it associates the street number with the street name in a particular order and with a particular spacing. In this sense, the format of the value contributes to its meaning. Thus, the field design should incorporate that meaning into the field by defining (and enforcing, if possible) the expectation for that format.

The power to enforce the format of values, and specifically to enforce formatted text values, varies widely from RDBMS to RDBMS. Paradox supports formatting through the Picture valcheck. Pictures allow you to control down to the character level what is allowable in a given field. In any case, it follows that the more specific a format requirement can be, the more

•••••••••

4 Blank=Zero is an option which can be modified under the Paradox Custom Configuration program.

likely it is that the value (information) will retain meaning even when found in that field (data).

Table 5-9 summarizes the various kinds of restrictions, while Table 5-10 describes the domain and appropriate restrictions that should be applied to the fields in the case studies.

Table 5-9
Types of field restrictions.

Specified range
Unique values only
Required value (no nulls allowed)
Default value
Format requirements

Table 5-10
Case-study fields, domains, and restrictions.

Field name	Data type	Domain	Restrictions
SCHEDULE:			
Schedule date*	D	No Sundays	
Schedule start date	D		<End date
Schedule end date	D		>Start date
Schedule date printed	D	No Sundays	
APPT:			
Appointment number*	S		
Appointment date	D	No Mondays	
Appointment start time	A5		>8AM
Appointment end time	A5		<9PM
Client ID	S	Client table	
APPTSERV:			
Appointment number*	S	Appt table	
Service code performed*	S	Service table	
Hours worked	$		
SERVICE:			
Service code*	S		
Service description	A25		
Service rate	$		>$45,<$145
CLIENT:			
Client ID*	S		
Client name	A25		

Table 5-9   Continued.

Field name	Data type	Domain	Restrictions
Client street address	A25		
Client zip code	A10	City table	
Client telephone number	A12		
Primary contact name	A40		All caps
Secondary contact name	A40		All caps
CITY:			
Zip code*	A10		
City name	A25		US only
State abbreviation	A2		US only
INVOICE:			
Invoice number	S		
Invoice date	D		1st or 15th
Total amount due	$		Sum of hrs* rates
INVDET:			
Invoice number	S	Invoice table	
Service code performed*	S	Service table	
Hours worked	N		Appt times
PO:			
Purchase order number	S		
Purchase order date	D		
Vendor ID	S	Vendor table	
Vendor name	A25	Vendor table	
User name	A40		All caps
Total purchase order amount	$		Sum of PO items
Purchase order date closed	D		>Po date +60
Buyer name	A40		All caps
ITEM:			
Item number	S		
Quantity ordered	N		>=100
Price	$		>1,<500
Item description	A15		All caps
VENDOR:			
Vendor ID	S		
Vendor name	A25		Upper & lower case
Street address	A25		
City	A25	US only	
State	A2	US only	
Zip code	A10		Zip plus four
Area code	A3	Valid AC	

Phone number	A8	Three plus four

PURCHREQ:

Request number	S	
Date requested	D	
Date updated	D	>Date requested
User name	A40	

ANIMAL:

Animal ID★	S	Sequential
Animal name	A20	
Date of birth	D	
Cage number	S	Cage table
Father/animal name	A20	Animal table
Mother/animal name	A20	Animal table
Maternal grandfather/name	A20	Animal table
Paternal grandfather/name	A20	Animal table
Maternal grandmother/name	A20	Animal table
Paternal grandmother/name	A20	Animal table

CAGE:

Cage number★	S	
Cage name	A20	
Cage building	S	<43
Cage row	S	<10
Cage level	S	<4
Number of spaces total	S	
Number of spaces available	S	

ASSET:

Name of asset	A30	Upper- & lowercase
Depreciated value	$	Price-pric*DP
Description of asset	M25	
Date purchased	D	>1/1/89
Purchase price	$	
Depreciation period	N	12-mo increment
Date sold	D	>date purchased

Reevaluating the field

Once a field has been defined and thoroughly described, it is important to take a second look at the field and how it relates to the table at hand. One of the problems with the rough technique for isolating info elements into tables explored in chapter 4 is that these info elements aren't very specific until they are designed into fields. It is only after the fact that you can take the opportunity to tell—in the most specific context—whether a field truly describes a feature or attribute of the given table. Or more specifically, the question to be asked is: does the value in this field depend on the primary key value for this row in my table? If the relationship between the field value and the primary key value is not one of dependency, the field probably is incorrectly placed in the table. By definition in relational theory, all columns in a relational table must contain values that contribute to the description of the primary key (practically speaking, of the entity described by the table name).

As suggested previously by FIG. 5-1, the rearrangement required to detach an incorrectly placed field from its intuitive table assignment can involve the building of an entirely new table.

Returning to multifield keys

Now that you've taken a look at the difference between an element of information (info element) and a field definition, it should be clear that the selection of a primary key value in the previous chapter was somewhat premature. A primary key must be applied to the field (or set of fields) that uniquely identify a row. The info element identified previously as a primary key might subsequently have been isolated into more than one field. If this has occurred, you need to revisit the issue of the primary key for that table.

Specifically, you need to analyze each field that resulted from the info element identified as the primary key. A primary key that is applied to multiple fields (also termed *multifield, concatenated,* or *composite key*) requires that all the fields act equally in defining the unique quality of that row. By definition, if any field can be removed from the key and not have an impact on the uniqueness of the key, then that field should not be included as part of the key. In other words, a primary key should be defined on the column or minimum set of columns that ensure uniqueness for each row in a table.

multifield key   A primary key that is applied to multiple fields.

Including nonkey fields in only one table

This overall process of isolating atomic components into fields and fields into tables might seem like overkill. However, remember that the relational model has its basis in relational algebra, which follows precise rules in order to achieve results that are unambiguous. Given the defined properties of numbers, you can confidently predict that adding three numbers together—in whatever order you choose—always will yield the same result (e.g., $1 + 2 + 3 = 6$, $3 + 1 + 2 = 6$, or $2 + 3 + 1 = 6$). The goal in database processing is the same: you want to be confident that no matter on what form or in what order you phrase a question, the results you receive will always be the same. So you create fields that have defined properties (i.e., data type, domain, uniqueness, etc.) to ensure that when you work with the values in the fields, you will always get the correct results. Even if each of your fields are described accurately and thoroughly a particular uncertainty is added when information that you know to be the same is found in more than one place in your database. Excluding the use of primary key values, the name tags that are used deliberately to represent actual things throughout the application, all other information is represented most precisely when there is only one place (one table-and-field combination) for it to exist. For example, if one family lived at a single address, and if all the individual members of that family lived at that address as well, it would benefit the database to include the address information only in one table (Family) but not the other (Member). These benefits accrue for three reasons:

- Ambiguity is reduced.
- Maintenance tasks are simplified.
- Disk storage is conserved.

Reducing ambiguity   When information can be located in one and only one place, the question of which is most accurate or up-to-date will not exist. If you need that information, you go to the sole source. There is no need for a debate of any kind.

Simplifying maintenance   When a field contains the only description of a feature in the entire database, then if that feature changes, you are able to predict precisely which description you will need to change. Your database will remain more accurate, and will contain more information of value, if maintenance of each field value can be controlled rigorously.

Conserving disk storage   Locating a value in only one field will reduce the application's use of disk storage. It is intuitively obvious that storing a value five times will utilize five times the disk storage space than just storing it once. Although intuition isn't completely accurate in this case, the underlying concept does hold true. In general, resources are conserved if each value is found in one field only.

In this chapter you have reviewed the process of field design, which focuses on the translation of the information that you know about a value into a field structure that the application will be able to manage. Specifically, you have learned that:

Summary

- The field-design process covers the development of an accurate description of what is expected in a field: the field name, data type, domain, appropriate validity checks and other restrictions on any value in the field.
- Field design begins by isolating the fields from within previously defined info elements.
- A field should be named descriptively in the singular.
- A field's data type should represent the most specific option from the range of possibilities.
- A value exists independently from how you describe it; formatting is simply cosmetic and doesn't change the nature of the feature being described.
- Today, Paradox 4.0 does support BLOb data, but for storage purposes only.
- A field's domain is nothing more than a pool of values from which any actual value in the field will be drawn.

- A field definition can describe the allowable values in specifics outside those of a domain, including the range of values, the uniqueness of a value, whether a value is required or how it is to be handled if missing, defaults, and formatting options.
- Once a field is designed, it should be reevaluated to make sure that the defined assumptions still hold true.
- Nonprimary key fields should be stored only in one table in order to reduce ambiguity, simplify maintenance, and conserve disk storage.

Key Terms

atomicity   A quality of a value that indicates that it cannot be broken down into components without the loss of its meaning.

BLOb   Binary Large Object, any type of data which is storable in binary format.

data type   A description of a value that the DBMS uses as a way to understand some fundamental qualities of that value.

domain   The pool of values from which actual values in a field might be drawn.

multifield key   A primary key that is applied to multiple fields.

multimedia   Video and audio capabilities.

repeating group   The relational model's term for a feature of an entity that can include more than one value.

6 Relating the tables

Your tables are looking like tables now: each has a name, a primary key, and columns that describe in detail each feature of the entity in which you are interested. Thus far you have taken care to be as specific as possible, closely evaluating the information you work with to ferret out the nuances and subtleties that provide information of value and differentiate this information from valueless data.

Early on you looked at the big picture. Although you still might be working with the sketch of your application you then drew in front of you, you're probably lost in the detail by now. There is no doubt that focusing on the specifics is a sure way to lose sight of your goal.

This last step in designing a table pulls you from that detail perspective back out to the big picture. Take a look at the several different tables you have designed (see FIG. 6-1). By definition, each exists independently of any other, but that isn't the way you work with them. You deal with, that is, think about, maintain, question, and react to the information in those tables as if the whole was one (or maybe several) integrated unit(s). In this context, *integrated* refers to the existence of a mechanism, or path, by which a database can deal with different groups of information at the same time. A database design must allow and plan for this kind of integration. The database-design process carefully has isolated the data, one value from the next, and one table from the next. In a sense, thus far you have accomplished one half of the necessary translation: you have translated what you work with into data, values that the

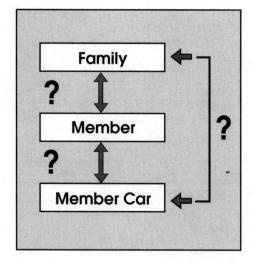

6-1
*The Family database
diagram without
any relationships*

computer can manage in a structure it understands. However, now you
must create the means for translation from the other side; you need to define
how the computer will translate what it knows into what you want. You
need to create the mechanism for integration, the paths between tables
(see FIG. 6-2).

6-2
*Evaluating all possible
paths between tables*

What a table relationship is

By definition, relational databases capture all the information in an
application solely within a table or tables. Thus, it is not a difficult task to
deduce that this additional type of information, the paths necessary for
integrating the tables, will be found in the tables themselves.

In relational terminology, a path for integrating tables is called a *relationship*. Each relationship is defined between two and only two tables and reflects the existence of a real-life connection between two entities. A relationship is created—and only works—when there is a real connection.

table relationship   A path created by data that is used to integrate two tables together.

For example, take the two tables, Member and MemberCar. The MemberCar is intended to represent the existence of a car (or cars) that belong to a given Member of the family. There is a true relationship between a given car and a person; that is, the person owns the car. Thus, there should be a relationship defined between the two tables to reflect this fact (see FIG. 6-3). In order for the values in the tables to be useful to you, there must be a relationship defined.

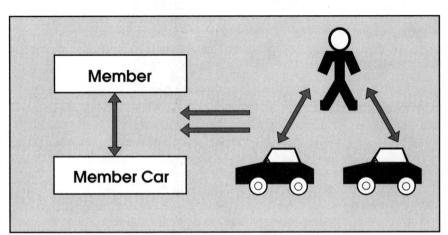

6-3
A relationship between two tables should always reflect a relationship in real life

There are different ways of defining a path between two tables, and the technique chosen depends on what kind of relationship is being drawn. There are three relational models for real-life connections to describe the three types of relationships that can exist between tables:

- One-to-one
- One-to-many
- Many-to-many

Identifying types of relationships

Each type of relationship has two components: X and Y, or more exactly, X to Y (see FIG. 6-4). Each component reflects one side of the relationship, or one perspective on what kind of relationship it is. The X side is the perspective from one table, the Y side from the other table. X and Y are interchangeable in the sense that a one-to-many and a many-to-one relationship are (in theory) exactly the same. This idea is examined more fully later in this chapter.

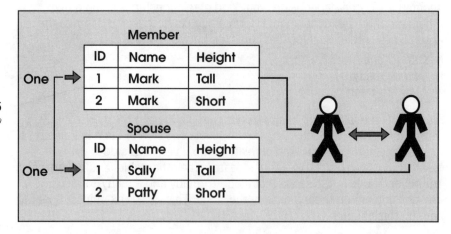

Although the descriptions of these different types of relationships can seem arbitrary, the selection of a type is not. The type of relationship must describe the actual kind of connection that exists between the real-life entities.

One-to-one
A one-to-one relationship exists between two entities when there is (and can only be) a single connection. For example, in your family database you created a table called Member to describe each member of your extended family. If you wanted to provide additional information about the husband or wife of each member, you could create a table named Spouse to describe that person who is related to the member. Each Member at most can have one Spouse; each Spouse can be related (in marriage) to only one Member. Thus, the relationship between the two entities is termed one-to-one. Because one row in the Member table represents a single member (or in the Spouse table, a single spouse), there is a direct connection between a single row in one table and a single row in the other (see FIG. 6-5).

6-5
A one-to-one relationship

A one-to-many relationship is defined between two entities when there exists the possibility for connections between one entity in one table and several entities in the other. For example, in your family database your MemberCar table describes the car or cars owned by each Member. The relationship between these two tables is termed one-to-many because one Member can own one or more (many) cars, but one MemberCar can be owned by only one Member (see FIG. 6-6).

One-to-many

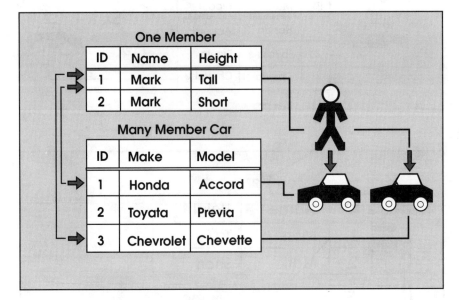

6-6
A one-to-many relationship

A many-to-many relationship exists between two entities when there exists the possibility for multiple connections from both tables' perspectives. For example, a given family might allow multiple family members to share ownership of one car. Thus, one family member could own more than one car (one-to-many from the Member side), but one car could be owned by more than one family member (one-to-many from the MemberCar side). This dual relationship is termed many-to-many and is the most complex kind of relationship to model (see FIG. 6-7). Paradox, along with most RDBMS products, has some difficulty in managing this kind of relationship.

Many-to-many

Each of these types of relationship describes a connection between two real things, not two tables. In one sense, the relationship that will be defined by the database design is not a relationship at all, but is only the potential for a relationship. The database design must allow for a potential connection between two entities, without requiring that the connection exist. This concept uncovers one of the most powerful features of relational databases. The potential for the connection exists in a table structure, while the connection itself exists in the actual records in the table. Thus the data—not

Modeling the connection

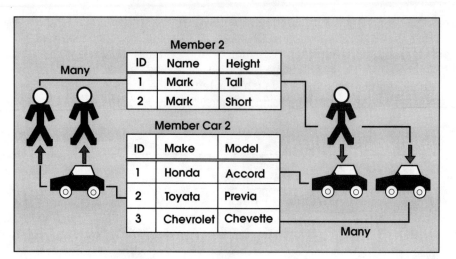

6-7
A many-to-many relationship

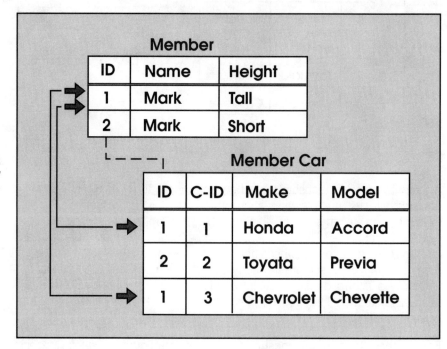

6-8
Relationships are based on matches of data

the structure—defines the relationship (see FIG. 6-8). This makes the power in the relational model threefold:

- Relationships between entities can be dynamic, reflecting reality and changing when your business does.
- Relationships that don't exist don't invalidate those that do.

- The potential for a relationship can be created or removed with simple column functions.

data-based-relationships   A quality of a relational database that sets it apart from other types of databases. The data is used to make connections.

Dynamic relationships

What this means is that the information associated with the data can be dynamic; it can change to reflect the real world. If a Member owns one car, there is a single car in the MemberCar table and a single connection between the tables. If the Member buys another car, a second record is added to the MemberCar table, and now there are two connections between the tables. If a Member sells all her cars, all records are deleted from the MemberCar table, and now there is no relationship at all.

None-to-none relationships

The potential for a relationship also allows for the possibility that there is no relationship. One-to-one more accurately should be called none-or-one to none-or-one, and one-to-many could be called none-or-one to none, one, or many. The relational design allows you to express information (this Member doesn't own a car) with the absence of data (see FIG. 6-9).

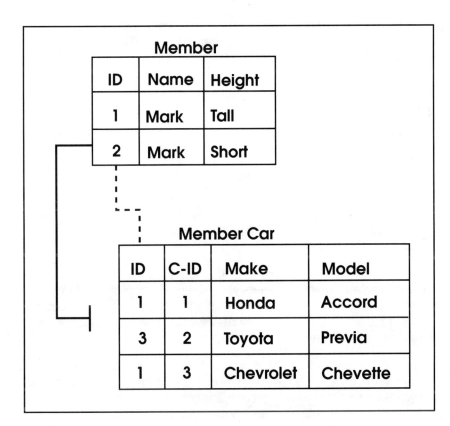

6-9
A link without a relationship

Column-based links

The data that actually forges the connection between tables must be located in the tables (where else?). The connection is actually made when the same data exists in both tables. The mechanism the relational model employs to make the connection is the match of data.

How does Paradox know, however, where to look for a match? A relational database design plans for this—in effect models the relationships—by including the same column in both related tables. Thus, the relationship between the Member and MemberCar tables is modeled by including the common element—what in reality is the same—in both tables. Because the Member and MemberCar tables both describe attributes of the Member, the Member's ID field is placed in both tables to allow for a match (look back at FIG. 6-8). This process of defining common columns is described in greater detail later.

Two tables that include a common column intended to allow for a relationship between entities are said to be *linked tables*. The potential for a relationship is called a *link*.

link   The potential that exists for a relationship between two tables by virtue of their sharing a common column.

A link is always built the same way: one of the common columns is a primary key, and that same primary key relocated into the linked table is the common column on the other side. In other words, you use the name tag for one entity to tag the related entity. A primary key, when it is located in a linked table, is known as a *foreign key* (see FIG. 6-10). Foreign keys are thus the basis for all links in a relational database design.

foreign key   A primary key value when used in another table.

The process of building a link

A link between tables is created in several steps:

1. Identify the connection and sketch the boxes.
2. Analyze from one side.
3. Analyze from the other side.
4. Refine the sketch.
5. Define the common column.

Identifying the connection

The connections that you need to identify should already be described in your documentation about the tasks you need to accomplish. Review the initial list of tasks that you created at the beginning of the database design process. Take a look at the info elements associated with each task: what tables are these elements now a part of?

Remember, what you are attempting to do is to create the opposite side of the translation process. You isolated the elements from the application, and now you need to reconnect the pieces. The connections aren't arbitrary; they are built on the needs that you already expressed quite clearly up front.

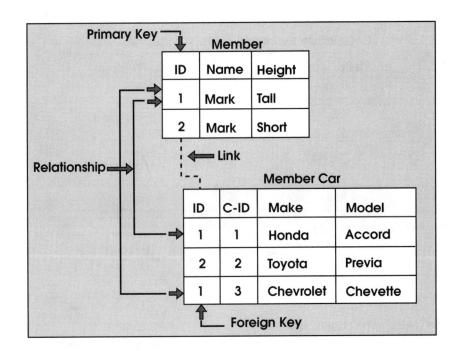

6-10
Common columns create a link, while matching data creates a relationship

Once you've looked at the list, identify the relationships needed for each task, one pair of tables at a time. You'll note that most of the tasks will be utilizing the same relational pairings. Table 6-1 identifies each task for the case studies and describes any tables that task requires. Take special note of one requirement for case study 3 (Zoo): the identification of the relationships between a specified animal and its parents and grandparents. This is a special kind of repeating group within the Animal table, one that has a consistent number of entries: every animal must have two parents and four grandparents. In effect, you have two choices. Either you can relate the table to itself, which would use the Animal ID for each relative in the principal animal's record, or you could create a separate table for ancestors that would pull out all those columns (mother, father, paternal grandmother, etc.) into a separate table. This might not be the obvious place in the design process to have identified this problem, but it is more common than not to have unusual issues and creative ideas pop up in the oddest places. Table 6-2 provides a revised take on the tables for case study 3.

Look at the tables that are indicated as being required for a single task. It is likely that these tables share a natural relationship—one that the real world dictates—because if they didn't, they probably wouldn't be covered within a single task. If more than two tables are required, look at each potential pair to determine whether there is a direct relationship or not. Then draw a pair of boxes connected by a solid line for each pair of tables. Even if you haven't determined that a relationship exists, going through the following steps will help.

Table 6-1
Case-study tasks and table(s) required.

Task	Table(s)
Print a daily/weekly/monthly schedule	Schedule Appointment
Print invoices for clients	Client City Appointment Appointment service Invoice Invoice detail
Display a daily schedule	Appointment
Display client information	Client City
Enter new appointments	Appointment Appointment service Client
Modify the appointment schedule	Appointment Appointment service Client
Enter client contacts	Client
Update client information	Client City
Print a list of purchase orders by user or item category	Purchase order Item
Print a list of vendors	Vendor
Print an analysis of processing time by buyer	Purchase order
Enter new purchase requests	Purchase request Item
Modify current purchase requests	Purchase request Item
Create purchase orders	Purchase order Item
Close a purchase order	Purchase order
Display purchase orders by user, vendor, or order date	Purchase order Vendor Item
Maintain vendor, item, and buyer	Vendor Item
Print a list of animals	Animal Cage
Print a genealogy for each animal	Animal

Print a list of available cage space	Cage
Enter new births	Animal
Modify animal records	Animal
	Cage
Display all available data about an animal	Animal
	Cage
Maintain cage data	Cage
Print a list of assets and depreciated values	Asset
Enter newly purchased assets	Asset
Delete assets that have been sold	Asset

Table 6-2
Revised tables and fields for case study 3.

Table	Field
Animal	Animal ID★
	Animal name
	Date of birth
	Cage number
Ancestor	Animal ID★
	Ancestor animal ID★
	Type of ancestor
Ancestor type	Type of ancestor
	Description of ancestor
Cage	Cage number
	Cage name
	Cage building
	Cage row
	Cage level
	Number of spaces total
	Number of spaces available

Enter the name of one of the two tables in each box. Figure 6-11 describes a sketch for one pair from case study 1. Remember that you will be going through this process once for each pair (yes, that could be a lot of times through—it just means you'll get really good at analyzing relationships!).

Pick one table of the pair. Imagine that you are "in" that table. From that perspective, how many entities in the other table could relate to you? Think of a specific example, and jot down on the side under your table box the instance you are imagining. Make a note under the other table box for each potential connection you can imagine. Is there only one possibility? Then

Analyzing the connection from one side

draw a *1* in a circle above the other table. Are there many possibilities? Then draw an *M* in a circle above the other table (see FIG. 6-12).

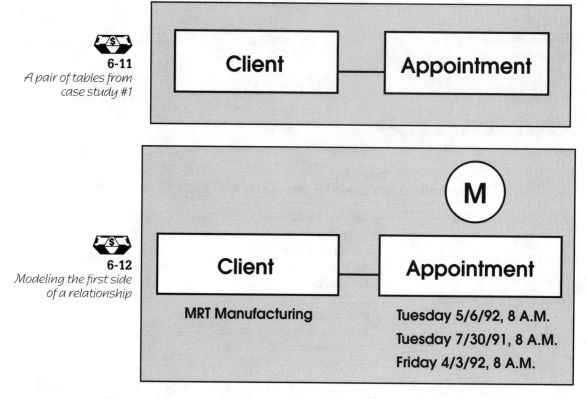

6-11
A pair of tables from case study #1

6-12
Modeling the first side of a relationship

MRT Manufacturing

Tuesday 5/6/92, 8 A.M.

Tuesday 7/30/91, 8 A.M.

Friday 4/3/92, 8 A.M.

Analyzing the connection from the other side

Choose the other table of the pair. Imagine that now you are "in" that table. From this new perspective, how many entities in the first table could relate to you in this table? Repeat the steps above, identifying the opposite side of the relationship with a *1* or an *M* in a circle over the first table (see FIG. 6-13).

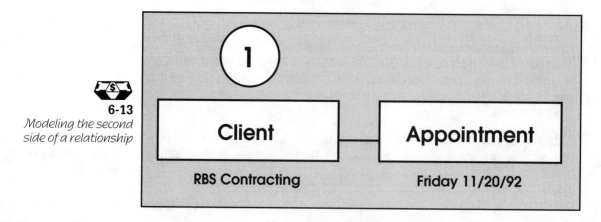

6-13
Modeling the second side of a relationship

RBS Contracting

Friday 11/20/92

A standard technique for describing table links is by connecting the linked tables in a database design diagram with a solid line (as you just did). Each line drawn represents one link. The line then can be enhanced to describe the type of relationship being represented: the *1* side of a relationship will have a single arrowhead pointing toward that table, while any *M* side of a relationship will have two arrowheads pointing toward that table. In your sketch, replace the circled *1* and *M* with the appropriate arrowhead(s) (see FIG. 6-14).

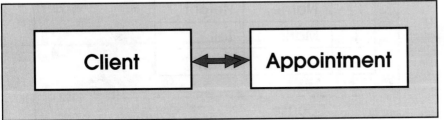

6-14
*A diagrammed
relationship*

Now that you've identified the link, all you need to do is make sure that the columns are in place to contain any matching data. You might discover that in many cases, the necessary columns already exist in the appropriate tables. The fact that you've formalized their usage in this way won't affect your data; it will just make you aware of all the potential relationships that you might want to exploit at some later date. Even if you don't need to use a relationship immediately, having identified it protects your option to change your mind and use the relationship later. Remember, relationships aren't arbitrary; they reflect true connections in the real world. So including a link you might not need right away does nothing more than more fully describe your information (which was one of the goals identified up front).

Even when the type of relationship has been determined, deciding which column should be in common between tables is not always straightforward. Each type of relationship is created using different guidelines.

Figuring out which column should be in common is not a problem when the relationship being modeled is one-to-one. The primary key for either table effectively can be used as the common column. Select one of the primary key columns and add it to the other table. Theoretically, either choice will produce the same result.

Practically speaking, it is better to evaluate the two tables to determine which is more important in the overall scheme of the database. Most database systems depend on a relatively limited number of important tables that describe the mission-critical aspects of the business. A relational design ordinarily will have many other tables that are created as a result of relational theorizing, information important in concept but of less inherent information value. If a one-to-one link involves an important table and a not-so-important table, placing the common column into the less important table is likely a better choice, because it keeps the number of columns in the important table to a minimum (see FIG. 6-15). Remember, Paradox is optimized to work with tables that have few columns.

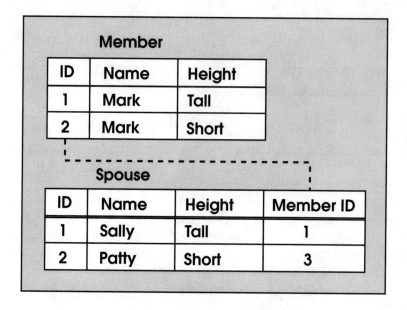

6-15
A modeled one-to-one relationship

One-to-many links

One-to-many links should be modeled by placing the primary key from the one side of the relationship into the table that is on the many side. In effect, this ties each potential many (in the MemberCar example, each car) to the associated one (the Member who owns it—see FIG. 6-16).

Many-to-many links

Many-to-many links are modeled by building what is commonly referred to as a cross or an intersection table. This table is composed of the primary key from each table on both sides of the relationship. For the family with multiple owners of cars, the tables might be reidentified as described in FIG. 6-17. Member 2 remains its own table, while MemberCar 2 now really reflects only car-specific information and thus is renamed Car 2. A new intersection table, Member by Car, is created that describes what relationships are valid between the Member and Car tables, that is, which Members own which cars, as well as which cars are owned by which Members. Figure 6-18 demonstrates how an intersection table actually is used to support these relationships.

Summary

In this chapter you have reviewed the process of modeling table relationships. You have evaluated the differences between an actual relationship (existing in real life) and a modeled relationship (a link) that only provides the potential for a relationship to exist. In addition, you have discovered that:

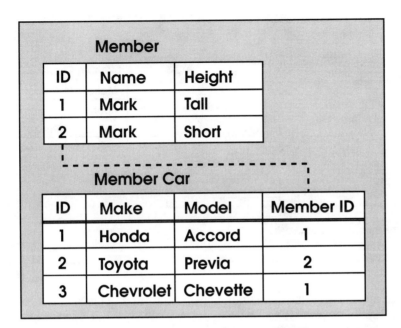

6-16
A modeled one-to-many relationship

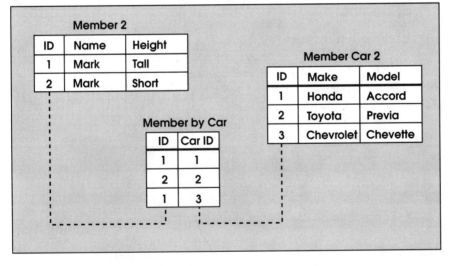

6-17
A modeled many-to-many relationship

- There are three types of relationships: one-to-one, one-to-many, and many-to-many.
- A relationship is created through matching data found in both tables, making each relationship dynamic and allowing for a relationship not to exist at all without affecting the application.
- A link is built through a column common to both tables, and is constructed of a primary key and its duplicate in the linked table as a foreign key.
- The process of building a link follows several steps. First, the connection is identified and sketched, then the connection is analyzed from both sides,

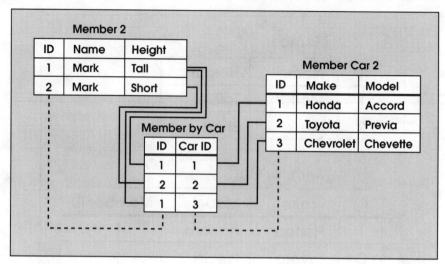

6-18
A many-to-many relationship at work

and finally the common column then is identified and placed in the appropriate linked table.

- The common column chosen differs depending on the type of relationship being modeled.

Key Terms **databased relationships** A quality of a relational database that sets it apart from other types of databases. The data is used to make connections.
foreign key A primary key value when used in another table.
link The potential that exists for a relationship between two tables by virtue of their sharing a common column.
table relationship A path created by data that is used to integrate two tables together.

7 Establishing data integrity in tables

You now have in front of you a database that covers the entire spectrum of your information. You have defined the tables, described each column in great detail, and created the necessary links between tables. You should be prepared for the next phase of database design where you consider the impact of reality on this theoretical product.

Before you move on to practical considerations and away from a focus on relational theory, it is important to take one more look at this process of translating the information you work with into data that Paradox will manipulate. The process of database design so far has focused on the issue of describing your expectations for the data. You've identified where you think relationships exist, what ranges and qualities are associated with any given value, and which values describe which entities. You should have some good documentation in hand regarding all of these issues.

However, your expectations about the data and the data itself might vary widely. What happens when they do? From the point of view of the database design, how should you be handling these expectations, beyond just writing them into your documentation?

This chapter addresses the issue of ensuring that your design expectations are met. In it you will revisit the different areas where you should have defined rules for your data, and you will reformulate those possibly loose rules into a set of constraints that Paradox can implement.

Identifying integrity requirements

What is at issue here is data integrity. This term is discussed with great seriousness in data processing circles, and is one of those magic words that separates you (the user) from them (the professional PC experts). The concept is really quite simple: the integrity of your data is a subjective measurement of its value. Value in this sense refers to how useful the data is to your application (and to you).

Integrity usually is measured on a scale (see FIG. 7-1). One side of the scale reads *Low* or *Poor*, this means that your data is so inaccurate, invalid, and out-of-date that it is useless in helping you make any decision. In effect, it doesn't reflect reality. The other side of the scale reads *High* or *Excellent* and means that your data is so useful that you not only depend on it to answer any questions you might have, but you rely on it to help you make decisions; you are confident that it reflects the truth of your business environment. As FIG. 7-1 suggests, the integrity of the data in an application reflects a balance between good and bad data—that which is correct and that which isn't. Your goal as the database designer is to do whatever you can to tilt the scales in the "good" direction.

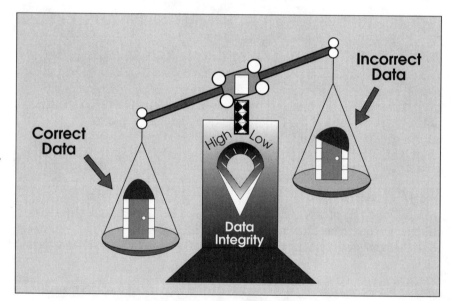

7-1
The data integrity scale

Another way of describing this continuum is to take a look at those over-used terms, data and information again. Data whose integrity is excellent retains a large portion of its information content—its meaning—even as the application is managing it. Data whose integrity is poor has lost its information content and has thus become useless.

You as the database designer must take all the appropriate steps to ensure the integrity of the data; if you don't, the users certainly will not. This is not particularly the result of industrial sabotage. Data integrity becomes *degraded*, or *compromised* (as it is usually described), from natural forces much more frequently than by any deliberate act. Data entry errors, forgetfulness in following through with all data changes related to a single real-world occurrence, uncontrolled or unvalidated movement of data between different systems: all can have a disastrous effect on data integrity.

There are three basic types of integrity that must be preserved. These three different areas of database design are all impacted by the need to capture meaning, specifically where the value of an application's data is at risk.

Understanding integrity types

- Entity integrity
- Referential integrity
- Field integrity

Entity integrity refers to how accurately a table reflects actual entities in the real world. For a table to meet relational standards (which are intended to preserve integrity), each row must reflect a different occurrence of the object or process in the real world. One real thing must equal one record in that entity's's table (see FIG. 7-2).

Ensuring entity integrity

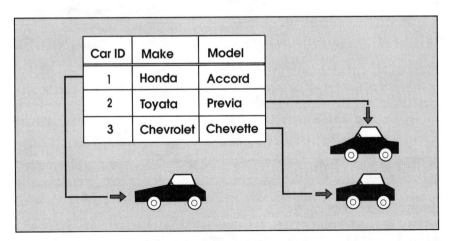

7-2
Entity integrity: one real thing for each row in a table

entity integrity   How accurately a table reflects actual entities in the real world.

This requirement is enforced in the design through the designation of a primary key. If you haven't identified a primary key for each table, you've fallen down on your job as a designer. You are opening the door for very serious questions: is this really the John Doe I want, or is it another John Doe's phone number that I am calling? Does my summary report accurately average all the purchase prices of cars that are blue, or does it count some of them twice, giving them more weight in the average?

Each table in your database must have a primary key. That key can be contained within a single field, or it can extend across multiple fields in your table. A primary key which encompasses values from multiple fields is known as multifield, concatenated, or composite key. A key should always be drawn from the single value or minimum set of values necessary to guarantee uniqueness for each record. Even so, multifield keys are extremely common in relational tables, particularly on the "many" side of a one-to-many relationship. For example, the relationship between the Member and MemberCar tables is a one-to-many relationship. The link between these two tables has been determined to be the Member #, which is the column in common between the two tables. Member # is the primary key for the Member table, and is a foreign key in the context of the MemberCar table. However, Member # is not adequate as a key for the MemberCar table; if it were, it would require that each Member own only one car (since there could only be one record for each Member # in the MemberCar table). This does not conform to reality.

Instead, a second field must be incorporated into the key in the MemberCar table. Car # when used in conjunction with Member # jointly defines a unique value (remember, the name tag) for each car in the MemberCar table. This combination of fields provides accurate attribution to each unique car in the table and at the same time quick reference to the single related record in the Member table.

It is possible to define Car # to be a unique, perhaps sequential number for each car in the MemberCar table. In Paradox, however, this would prevent you from taking advantage of some of the fundamental techniques for getting access to data found in multiple tables (see chapters 10 and 11 for discussion of multitable forms and reports).

multifield key   Primary key whose combined value is derived from more than one field in a table (also called concatenated key or composite key)

Ensuring referential integrity   The second integrity issue addresses how accurately the database reflects real-world relationships that exist between different entities. *Referential integrity* is sometimes called *relational integrity,* because it is what allows you to perform relational activities, such as a join, on your tables and have confidence in the results. Relational activities are basically those that allow you to recombine or access data from multiple tables to achieve a single goal or perform a single task.

referential integrity   How accurately the database reflects real-world relationships that exist between different entities. Sometimes called relational integrity.

Because all relationships in a relational database are created through data in the tables, data errors can destroy relationships crucial to the functioning of the application. Data that doesn't match within common columns, but which should match because there is a real connection, will cause unexpected and incorrect results in many operations. Theoretically, referential integrity is ensured through the maintenance of the primary key-to-foreign key relationship of any link. By definition, a foreign key value cannot exist (and thus there can be no link) if that value doesn't already exist as a primary key value in the linked table (see FIG. 7-3).

Name	Address	Family#
Smith	Jackson,MS	1
Jones	Kent, WA	2
Reynolds	Wash.,DC	3

Name	Height	Build	Family#
Mark	Tall	Muscular	2
Mark	Short	Thin	1
Margaret	Tall	Thin	2
Karen	Tall	Athletic	3

7-3
Referential integrity: one relationship per real life connection

Paradox only enforces referential integrity like this through a multitable form. Any access to the tables accomplished outside of a multitable form can circumvent the expected links and degrade the relational integrity of the database.

Ensuring field integrity

Field integrity is a measure of the value of a description relative to the actual fact that it is describing. Each field is intended to contain an atomic value that reflects a "truth" in the real world—a quality or attribute of the entity that it describes a quality or attribute of that particular record in the given table (see FIG. 7-4).

Field integrity is impossible to ensure, even in theory. At some point you have to rely on the value to determine whether it is true or false; the application (or Paradox) can't do that for you. However, Paradox can ensure that the field value is something like what you know it should be.

field integrity   A measure of the value of a description relative to the actual fact it is describing.

Depending on domains   The fact that each field should be declared (and based) on a specified domain helps. This is the roughest kind of

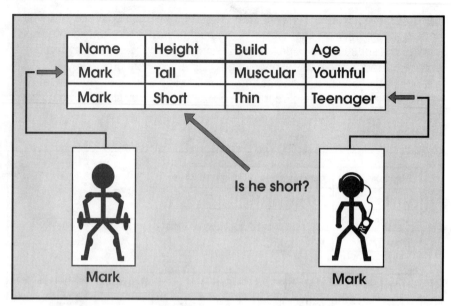

Name	Height	Build	Age
Mark	Tall	Muscular	Youthful
Mark	Short	Thin	Teenager

Is he short?

Mark

Mark

insurance, because a domain basically is unqualified; all potential values in the domain's pool of values are created equal, and whether one is more likely better than another for a given row is not known to the domain (see FIG. 7-5). Since domains are not explicitly supported in Paradox, this provides no insurance at all.

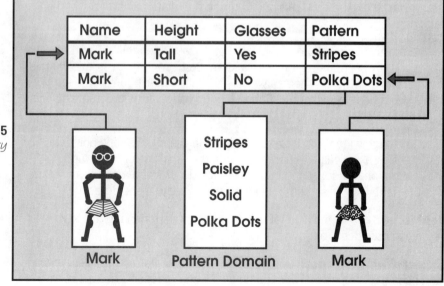

Name	Height	Glasses	Pattern
Mark	Tall	Yes	Stripes
Mark	Short	No	Polka Dots

Stripes

Paisley

Solid

Polka Dots

Mark

Pattern Domain

Mark

Defining other business rules   The definition of business rules is particularly important to the integrity of the data, because these rules tend to be more specific than the features of the data described by a data type or even through a domain.

Most commonly, a business rule describes a real fact that the business depends on in order to function properly. For example, a rule might exist that prevents the price for a particular service from increasing faster than 10% per year. Or a rule might exist that requires new employees to take two community college courses during their first two years on the job. A business might require a potential client to do at least $300,000 in gross annual sales before they will take them on. Or a business could require all employees to undergo a physical exam between the ages of 48 and 51. These kinds of rules don't fit neatly into the concept of a domain, nor do they have an impact on the type of data that a field is intended to store. Instead, they apply the same restrictions to the database as are applied to the real entities in the real world.

Describing this kind of rule in a database design is relatively simple; all you need to do is include it on the design document specifying the field definitions. However, enforcing it through Paradox can be quite difficult.

Part of the reason that maintaining data integrity is not a simple task is because all the rules—data type, domain, restrictions, business rules—must be enforced at the point that they could be compromised. In other words, the integrity of the data must be protected at those times in an application when data can be added or changed. Because part of the power of a relational database lies in its flexibility—and particularly in its support for views, each of which potentially uses a different selection of fields from the relational tables—an application that intends to enforce data integrity must do so in a wide variety of situations.

When data integrity is important

Many basic problems with data integrity are addressed directly by a system that is *object-oriented*. Roughly speaking, object orientation refers to a method of dealing with data that defines both the data and its behavior at the same time. Given this rough definition, object orientation allows the business rules (and data type and domain and restrictions) to be embedded in the definition of the object itself (the table). Therefore the object—not the application—would be the enforcer of the rules, which obviously would simplify the application immediately.

Borland International is philosophically committed to increasing support for data integrity through the movement of that functionality deeper in the product layer. The company has stated its intention of including integrity maintenance within the Borland Interbase Engine, which will make it available to all products which get at data through the Engine. Recent developments in object-oriented technology have made this possibility a reality.

Integrity maintenance is crucial in three contexts:

- Adding data
- Making changes to current data
- Deleting data

Adding data

Any data which is being entered for the first time obviously must be checked to make sure it meets all requirements. In an application that depends on data entry from a user at the keyboard, the checking can be done right on the spot (when the value is entered, it is checked). Paradox valchecks support this kind of evaluation.

However, an application might depend on data that is entered through a "back door"—not from a user but from another database or software. Databases that integrate PCs and mainframes can be linked through an import-export procedure. Data that is added to the relational tables in this way is sometimes more difficult to examine, because processing might occur in a batch mode, corresponding to the way the entries were made in the first place. Batch checking can be quite complex.

Making changes to current data

Any time that you allow a user (or the application itself) to make changes to the data, you must also allow for the possibility that the changes can violate a rule or rules you have established. Thus, any activity in the application that involves data modification also must allow for a checking process to occur. Again, if the changes are being made by a user one record at a time, the checking is not likely to be very difficult to implement; but if the changes are being made in batch mode through updates from another database, implementation could be much more difficult.

Deleting data

You might wonder how the deletion of data can affect the integrity of the database; it seems as if the validity of the value is really a moot point once it has been deleted. However, recall that integrity falls into three categories: entity, field, and referential. Referential integrity describes the validity of relationships, which are based on data found in two tables. Therefore, making changes to data in one table—including deleting data from that table—can (and should) directly affect the data in another table. This means that previously valid data can become invalid entirely as a result of the modification of another value. It is a particular problem when a record is deleted from the "one" side of a one-to-many relationship. Suddenly, any "many" records that were connected to the deleted "one" record are left stranded. These unconnected "many" records are called *orphans* in relational terminology. Orphans can cause ongoing problems for an up-and-running application, partly because they can be very difficult to find and eliminate once that relationship has been broken.

orphan record A record once on the "many" side of a one-to-many relationship whose "one" related record has been deleted.

Relational integrity should thus be of great interest at every point in an application that supports any change to the data in a table, such as through the addition of new data, the editing of current data, or the deletion of data. The description of what needs enforcing at all points should be provided by the database design.

Documenting integrity requirements

The requirements for each field in a table should be identified and described in the design document that specifies field criteria. This document is more than supporting detail for the one-page design document that describes each table and its relationship(s) to the other tables. The field specification is a necessary extension to the one-page document; without it, a design cannot be implemented. Review Table 5-10 for the complete field specifications for the case studies.

Summary

This chapter reviewed the concept of data integrity that was introduced in several previous chapters. This review should have reinforced several important aspects of maintaining data integrity, including the following:

- Integrity requirements must be identified during the design process and addressed for each table and field in the design.
- Integrity falls into three categories: entity (each record in a table is unique); referential (each record which should be related to a record in another table is related); and field integrity (each value in a field accurately represents the true description of the entity).
- Domains are an important tool in maintaining field integrity; if properly used, a domain substantially increases the probability that a value in a field will be correct.
- Other restrictions to the data should be defined to reflect specific requirements of the business. These rules tend to be unrelated to a pool of values (like a domain) or simple restrictions (like a range). Instead, business rules can combine data from several fields or even several tables in order to ensure the validity of a single value.
- Data integrity is important at any point in an application in which data can be changed, i.e., where data has been added, modified, or deleted.
- Integrity requirements should be documented as part of the database design.

Key Terms

entity integrity   How accurately a table reflects actual entities in the real world.

field integrity   A measure of the value of a description relative to the actual fact it is describing.

multifield key   Primary key whose combined value is derived from more than one field in a table (also called concatenated key or composite key).

orphan record   A record once on the "many" side of a one-to-many relationship whose "one" related record has been deleted.

referential integrity   (sometimes relational integrity) How accurately the database reflects real-world relationships that exist between different entities.

Part Three

Implementing a
Paradox design

When reality strikes: The database environment

Okay, so you're finally done with the theoretical stuff. You have thought and drawn and considered and evaluated and reevaluated until you've conceived a design that will guarantee the integrity of your data. You are prepared to base the most mission-critical decisions of your business on the data in this database.

Well, wake up and smell the roses. Not even Paradox can take your wonderfully relational and perfectly specific design and implement it without modification. And even if Paradox was fully relational (i.e., it conformed to each and every rule of the model) you probably still wouldn't implement your design as it currently stands. There are too many factors outside the database itself—in the database environment—that you must consider.

Choosing practice over theory

The relational model is intended to provide the parameters for constructing an ideal database in an ideal environment. The theory assumes that everything that is important for you as a database designer to know is covered in the rules—and everything else is handled by the RDBMS. In fact, the current version of the relational model provides rules for "everything else," too (i.e., guidelines for the developers of relational-database-management systems). These rules are thorough, although only to the extent that their effects are visible to the user or to the person managing the database (known as the *database administrator* or DBA). The idea is that as a database user or designer, you will be relying on the RDBMS to manipulate the environment; if your design choices are consistent with the model and your DBMS is relational, the result will be an ideal system.

database administrator (DBA)   The person who manages the database and applications.

The theory places great reliance on the capabilities of the RDBMS. Not only does it assume the RDBMS will provide the functionality required to be consistent with the model, but the theory also assumes that the RDBMS will be usable; that is, that it will handle the actual input and output of an application adequately. However, the huge assumptions in "adequately" hit home in two areas: performance and cost. Both of these issues depend on considerations not directly related to the theory at all, and both can have as dramatic an impact on the end result as the theory itself. These two issues are addressed in detail in chapters 12 and 13.

An attempt to make a nonrelational DBMS do what a relational design requires would be a disaster. Yet it is well documented that a gulf still exists between theory and practice, between the relational model and any DBMS products on the market (Date 1990). You are a user of a product that is advertised as relational—and a designer of an application based on the relational model. It is crucial that you be able to evaluate where Paradox differs from the model, and thus where you will need to modify your design to accommodate the difference(s). In order to make this kind of assessment, first you need to take a closer look at the definition of a relational DBMS.

Assessing the relational state of Paradox

To restate the simple definition given in chapter 1, a relational database is one that is perceived by its users as tables (and nothing but tables). A relational database (tables only) need meet nothing more than this definition. However, an RDBMS must go beyond the simple definition and modification of relational tables; it must also be able to manage—to do meaningful things with—these tables. As suggested by FIG. 8-1, the relational model actually addresses the guidelines for a relational DBMS in three areas:

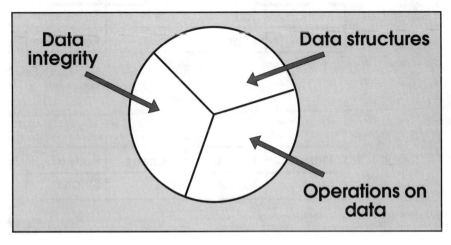

8-1
The three parts of the relational model

- Data structures
- Operations on data
- Data integrity

In fact, although the model defines an RDBMS very precisely (what do you think all those 300 plus rules are there for, anyway?), almost all of the rules fall neatly into one of these three categories. Because of the well-documented gulf between the theory and the state of the market, in 1982 Codd suggested a revised definition for relationality, which granted that a system could be relational even if it didn't match the theory in every detail (Codd 1982). A DBMS thus can be considered relational to the degree that it meets the standards in the three basic areas.

Evaluating a minimally relational DBMS

A DBMS that is relational to the smallest degree is said to be *minimally relational*. Codd suggests that this type of system must provide support for the following two features:

- Relational tables (data structures)
- The most basic relational operations (restrict, project, and join)

Relational tables, of course, follow the standard that there is nothing known in the database that is not known as data in the tables. Relational operators, on the other hand, follow the restrictions of relational algebra. These three operators are graphically described both conceptually and in their Paradox usage in FIGS. 8-2 through 8-7. Very roughly speaking, a *restrict* allows a user to extract rows from a table based on some specified condition (see FIG. 8-2). In Paradox, restricts are based upon conditionals used on a query form (see FIG. 8-3). A *project* allows a user to extract specified columns from a table

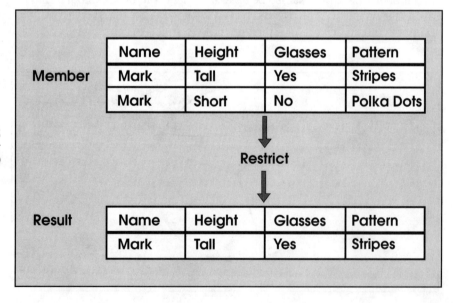

8-2
Basic relational operations: Restrict (select rows)

Member	Name	Height	Glasses	Pattern
	Mark	Tall	Yes	Stripes
	Mark	Short	No	Polka Dots

Restrict

Result	Name	Height	Glasses	Pattern
	Mark	Tall	Yes	Stripes

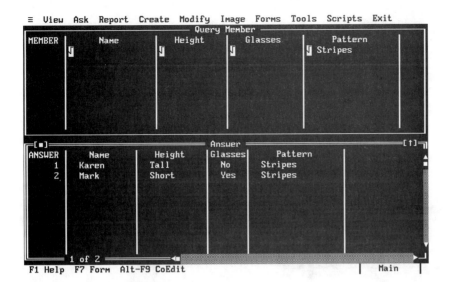

8-3
A Paradox restrict query

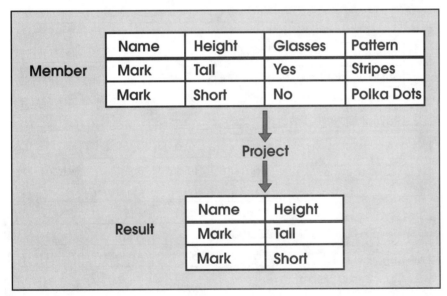

8-4
Basic relational operations: Project (select columns)

(see FIG. 8-4). Project is supported in Paradox through the Checkmark in its permutations (Check, CheckDescending, CheckPlus—see FIG. 8-5).

A *join* allows a user to combine rows and columns from two tables based on data common to both (see FIG. 8-6). Paradox-based joins are supported through the use of the Example element (F5 while on a query form) in conjunction with the appropriate Checkmarks and conditionals (see FIG. 8-7).

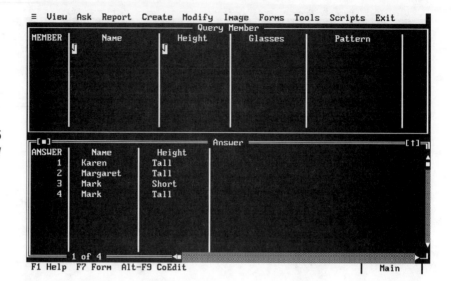

8-5
A Paradox project query

```
≡  View  Ask  Report  Create  Modify  Image  Forms  Tools  Scripts  Exit
┌─────────────────────── Query Member ──────────────────────────┐
│MEMBER │    Name    │    Height    │   Glasses   │   Pattern    │
│     √ │            │√             │             │              │
│       │            │              │             │              │
│       │            │              │             │              │
│       │            │              │             │              │
└───────────────────────────────────────────────────────────────┘
┌[■]════════════════════════ Answer ═══════════════════════[↑]┐
│ANSWER │    Name    │   Height    │                           │▲
│   1   │  Karen     │  Tall       │                           │
│   2   │  Margaret  │  Tall       │                           │
│   3   │  Mark      │  Short      │                           │
│   4   │  Mark      │  Tall       │                           │
│       │            │             │                           │
│       │            │             │                           │
│       │            │             │                           │
│═══════ 1 of 4 ══════◄─────────────────────────────────────►►│▼
F1 Help  F7 Form  Alt-F9 CoEdit                          Main
```

8-6
Basic relational operations:
Project (select columns)

Family

Name	Address	Family #
Smith	Jackson, MS	1
Jones	Kent, WA	2
Reynolds	Wash, DC	3

Family Member

Name	Height	Build	Family #
Mark	Tall	Muscular	2
Mark	Short	Thin	1
Margaret	Tall	Thin	2
Karen	Tall	Athletic	3

Result of Join

Name	Height	Build	Family #	Name	Address
Mark	Tall	Muscular	2	Jones	Kent, WA
Mark	Short	Thin	1	Smith	Jackson
Margaret	Tall	Thin	2	Jones	Kent, WA
Karen	Tall	Athletic	3	Reynolds	Wash, DC

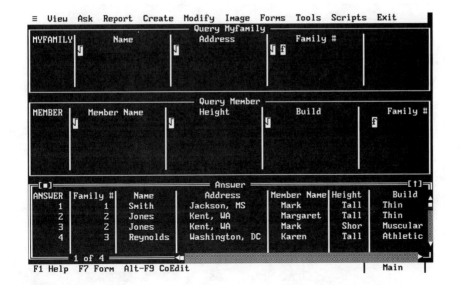

8-7
A Paradox join query

Given these criteria, Paradox is clearly at least a minimally relational DBMS.

restrict   A relational operation that extracts specific records from a relational table.
project   A relational operation by which specified columns are extracted from a table.
join   A relational operation that combines tables and brings rows together based on common values.

There are three other defined degrees of relationality that Codd also specified in 1982: a tabular system (e.g., specifically nonrelational) is one that supports relational data structures (tables) but doesn't support any relational operations. A relationally complete system is one that supports relational data structures and all the relational algebra operations (beyond the basic three), and a fully relational system is one that supports all three areas—data structures, operations, and data integrity—in their entirety (see FIG. 8-8). It is easy to see that relationality is really a spectrum into which any DBMS can fall, and on which you must judge Paradox.

The bottom line is that the more relational a DBMS is, the easier your relational design will be to implement. The less relational the DBMS, the more difficult the implementation. In a nonrelational system, the implementation of a relational design will be impossible or certainly close to it. This is because a relational design depends on the RDBMS to be able to do table manipulations in order to bring the fields and records (data values) back into the appropriate real-life combinations.

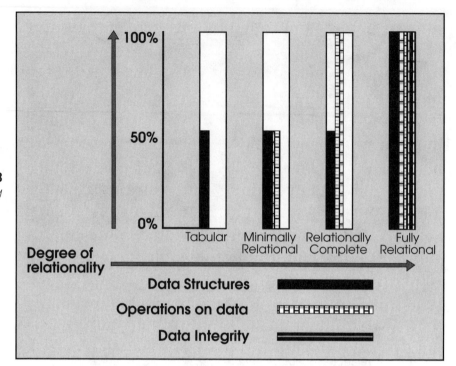

8-8
Degrees of relationality

The next sections of this chapter will lay out the basics of the relational model in each of the three areas. These summaries do not address or provide any justification for the rules (refer to the Bibliography for numerous writings on that subject); instead, the focus here is on allowing you productively to assess how Paradox measures up to the model.

Measuring DBMS support for a feature

First, understand that this is not necessarily an objective process. Simply asking whether a feature is supported by Paradox or any other DBMS (and expecting a yes or no answer) is misleading. There are definite complexities involved in any implementation. You would do better to ask several questions:

- Does Paradox allow me to do this (but I'll get hurt)?
- Does Paradox allow me to do this (and I'll benefit)?
- Does Paradox help me to do this?
- Does Paradox force me to do this?

implementation   The phase of application development during which the design is acted upon (building is begun).

These four questions really span the spectrum of the way any feature could be implemented by Paradox. As FIG. 8-9 suggests, the most powerful implementation (the most relational) is one in which Paradox takes complete control (in other words, forces the user to apply the feature). This ensures that any application (or data) always conforms to the model.

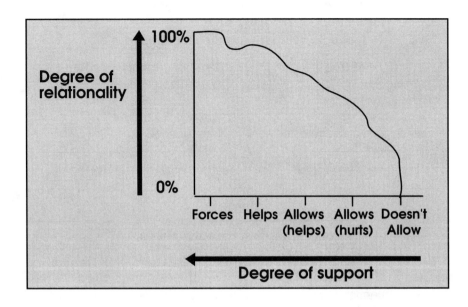

8-9
RDBMS support for relational features

An implementation that helps the user take advantage of a feature is normally fairly powerful; "helping a feature be used" implies that the feature has been made simpler or easier to use. Any feature that is easy to use is more likely to be taken advantage of than one that is difficult to master. Somewhat less powerful is an implementation in which the DBMS simply allows the use of the feature; normally this level of support is provided through a programming language rather than through any interactive system. Finally, the least powerful implementation is one that the DBMS allows to happen (again, probably through a programming language) but doesn't optimize in any way. In this case, use of the feature slows down any application to an unacceptable speed and makes an application so difficult to use that it ensures failure.

In this evaluation of Paradox, these questions are used to develop a rank. The rank of 4 supports a given feature more powerfully than one receiving a rank of 1 (see Table 8-1). Of course, no support for the feature receives a 0.

Note carefully the designations in Tables 8-2 through 8-4 that indicate the importance of each feature or class of features to relationality. A value of 5 is given to those features that are required to support a minimally relational system; these are the most important features. The lowest value, 1, is given to those rules that must be met in order to support the definition of fully relational. A value of 3 is given to those rules that must be met in order to support the definition of relationally complete. In effect, the lower the value, the less important the feature; conversely, the higher the value, the less relational a system need be to support it. For purposes of this evaluation, a combined ranking is developed which integrates the power of Paradox's support for a feature with the importance of that feature to the model.

Assessing the importance of a feature

Table 8-1
Example evaluation issues for support.

Feature	Type of support	Rank
Simple project	Query by example	4
Union of two tables	Command driven	2
Union of two tables	Query by example	4
Subtract one table from another	Menu driven	3
Join	Query by example	4

Table 8-2
Features of the relational
model regarding data structures.

Rule number	Description	Relative importance	Paradox effectiveness
RS — 1	Information all found in tables, and nothing but tables	5	5
RS — 2	No ordering of rows or columns	5	1
RS — 3	No duplicate rows	5	3
RS — 4	Information independent of site or equipment	5	3
RS — 5	Three-level architecture of views, tables, and storage	5	3
RS — 8	Each table has a primary key	5	3
RD — 2	Logical and physical structures are separate	5	5
RD — 3	There is a sharp distinction between performance issues and logical issues	5	3
RN — 1 to RN — 3	Names of domains, data types, relations, functions and columns must be distinct	3	4
RN — 4	Table and column name always used in combination	5	4
RN — 5 and RN-6	Relational operations not dependent on column names but on data	5	5
RN — 7	Names of columns must not impair commutativity of operations	3	3

Table 8-2   Continued.

Rule number	Description	Relative importance	Paradox effectiveness
RN — 8 to RN — 11	Names of columns resulting from operations are inherited where possible	3	5
RN — 12	Archived relations can have new names	3	1
RC — 1	An on-line catalog providing all pertinent database information as a table	5	3
RC — 2	DBMS must support concurrent users	3	5
RC — 3 to RC — 6	Domains, tables, and views are described in the catalog	5	1
RC — 7 to RC — 11	Integrity constraints, user-defined functions, security (authorization) information, and database statistics contained in the catalog	5	1
RV — 1	Views are supported and defined in the catalog	5	1
RV — 2 to RV — 8	How views are to be managed by DBMS	5	3
RV — 6	Different views are more or less updatable	3	1
RP — 1	Physical-data-storage techniques can be changed without affecting application	5	5
RP — 2	Logical data independence; tables can be manipulated with operators without loss of information based on algorithm VU — 1	5	5
RP — 4 and RP — 5	Location of data is independent of logical organization	3	5
RD — 4 and RD — 5	Applications independent from concurrency issues; long-term locks are not permitted	3	4
RD — 6	No features are coupled together without clearly stated, logically defensible reasons	3	3
RD — 7 to RD — 16	Implications for designers of DBMS products	3	2

Table 8-3
Features of the relational model regarding data integrity.

Rule number	Description	Relative importance	Paradox effectiveness
RS — 6	Domain is extended data type	1	1
RS — 7	Column description includes domain and additional rules	1	1
RS — 9	Appropriate views have primary keys	1	1
RS — 10	Foreign-key identification as part of column description	1	1
RS — 11 and 12	Domains and columns can be declared as composite	1	1
RS — 13	Missing data indicated with a special mark	1	1
RS — 14	All tables not stored by DBMS as one big combined table	1	1
RT — 1	Values not compared unless they are based on the same domain	1	1
RT — 2	Dates, times, and currency supported as data types; dates and times calculated, and current date and time available	1	3
RT — 3	Users can define extended data types	1	1
RT — 4 to RT — 7	Date and time components can be manipulated individually by the DBMS, and can be coupled together when necessary	1	5
RT — 8 and RT — 9	Currency data types supported as extension of integer data type integer data type	1	3
RF — 9 and FR — 10	Function and arguments names supported as part of domain and column definitions	1	1
RN — 13	Each integrity constraint must have a name	1	1
RM — 14 to RM — 20	Miscellaneous integrity constraints	1	1
RI — 1 to RI — 5	Integrity constraints are of five types: domain, field, entity, referential, and user-defined (business rules)	1	1

Rule number	Description	Relative importance	Paradox effectiveness
RI — 6 to RI — 22	How integrity issues are to be handled	1	1
RI — 23 to RI — 34	How user-defined integrity constraints are to be handled	1	1
RA — 1	Authorization is granted rather than denied	1	
RA — 2 to RA — 16	How the DBMS should grant or modify authorization; what operations can be authorized	1	3
RP — 3	Integrity independence; application is unchanged when integrity rules change	1	1

Table 8-4
Features of the relational
model regarding operations on data.

Rule number	Description	Relative importance	Paradox effectiveness
RD — 1	No fundamental laws of mathematics are violated	3	5
RE — 1 and RE — 2	Commands to find values in a domain	3	1
RB — 1	Cartesian product not an operator	3	1
RB — 2	Project	5	5
RB — 3 to RB — 12	Restrict (select)	5	5
RB — 13	Boolean extension of select	3	1
RB — 14 to RB — 23	Join	5	5
RB — 24	Boolean extension of join	3	1
RB — 25	Natural join	3	3
RB — 26 to RB — 28	Union, intersection, and difference	3	5
RB — 29	Relational division	3	3
RB — 30 to RB — 37	Manipulative operators (assignment, insert, delete, cascading update, and delete)	3	3
RZ — 1 to RZ — 40	Advanced operators (includes extend, outer joins, and recursive join)	3	3
RN — 14	Query can include an option for a name	3	3
RE — 3	Commands for the DBA to create,	3	

Table 8-4   Continued.

Rule number	Description	Relative importance	Paradox effectiveness
to RE — 19	rename, or alter domains, tables, and columns		
RE — 20	Delete duplicate rows	3	3
RE — 21 and RE — 22	Archive and restore commands	3	
RQ — 1 to RQ — 13	Qualifiers for dealing with missing data	3	1
RJ — 1 to RJ — 14	Indicators for marking errors or problems in results of operations	3	3
RM — 1	Each value is accessible through a combination table name, primary key value, and column name	3	
RM — 2 to RM — 5	Operations supported by four-valued, first-order predicate logic (at set level)	3	3
RM — 6 and RM — 7	Changes to database made in combination, and committed only when all changes are possible	3	1
RM — 8 and RM — 9	Some operations can occur dynamically without halting system; all can be executed interactively in programs, or in case of error	3	3
RM — 10 to RM — 13	What happens when operating on missing values	3	1
RZ — 41 to RZ — 44	Operations on partially normalized views and tables	3	1
RF — 1	Supports at least Count, Sum, Average, Maximum, and Minimum functions	3	5
RF — 2 to RF — 10	How DBMS should handle functions	3	3
RL — 1 to RL — 17	Relational-command design principles for DBMS developers	3	3
RX — 1 to RX — 29	Support for distributed (multiple location) databases	3	3

Refer to Tables 8-2 through 8-4 for a rundown on each of the three areas of the model, their relative importance, and their implementation effectiveness within Paradox. The summary presented in these tables is not intended to convey the depth nor the detail of the different rules of the relational model. It is simply a rough overview of the model's features and is intended to be useful only as an introduction to some of the model's most pertinent features, and not as a technical analysis of its logic. This chapter intends to provide a rough measurement of the relational nature of Paradox; adjustment of the case studies to respond to specific Paradox requirements and deficiencies is reserved until chapter 9.

Your design might need to be modified for reasons having little to do with Paradox and a lot to do with what is inherently reasonable. There are two areas that you should consider specifically:

- Ensuring security
- Choosing simplicity

Modifying a design for nonrelational reasons

Ensuring security

As chapter 7 described at length, the value of information exists as a continuum. Some information is useful and provides decision-making help; some is less useful and its benefit might not be immediately obvious. The integrity of the data is assessed with a simple question: to what degree can I depend on the accuracy of a value? The answer depends in large part on how you manage the translation process (from information to data). However, information has its own inherent value having nothing to do with its accuracy. Some information is simply more important than other information. For example, you can probably do business if you don't know the name of a client's wife, but you'll undoubtedly lose your client if you don't know his (the client's) name.

In addition to the relative value of information, but somewhat related to it, is the issue of the information's sensitivity. The sensitivity of information is a qualitative assessment that describes how secret it is. Secrecy is more an issue in some businesses than in others, and thus security is more important in some applications than in others. Security is simply the way an application enforces the need for secrecy. If an application manages sensitive information, security must be built into the system.

data sensitivity   A qualitative assessment of data that describes how secret it is.

Security can be applied at several levels within an application. Incidentally, it is an issue with the users, too; the behavior of the users will have a direct impact on the way any security is enforced. In any case, the actual mechanism for creating a secure application (in the appropriate places) in Paradox can vary. Paradox does support security at a table level or for individual scripts through the Protection Generator. See chapter 9 for a step-by-step example of enhancing an application with password security.

Relative to the database design, if your application utilizes sensitive information, you might want to consider isolating it in a table separate from those you've already defined. Capturing all the information that requires security in a single table can ease the process of building a security mechanism as part of your application. The secure table can be built in a one-to-one relationship with the already defined less-sensitive table from which the data came (see FIG. 8-10). This ensures that the separation will have no impact on your ability to access the information in exactly the same way as you could before the separation.

8-10
Sensitive data can be isolated into separate database tables

Member Table

ID	Name	Height	Build	Age
2	Mark	Tall	Muscular	Youthful
1	Mark	Short	Thin	Teenager
3	Margaret	Tall	Thin	Youthful

Weight Table

ID	Weight
1	160
2	210
3	140

Choosing simplicity

Above and beyond any other issue, considering the basic reasonableness of your relational design is an important step. Regardless of how easy Paradox is to use, working with multiple tables is simply not as easy as managing just one. Anathema to the relational model though it might be, the simplest design could in fact be the best, and a single table can be more appropriate than multiple tables. All the relational arguments aside, a single table is often easier to think about, and thus easier to use, than even the most carefully designed multitable system. Besides, some users just like the sense that they can wrap their arms around the entire set of data at one time, without having to go through any relational hoops first.

This issue is something to consider at the end, not at the beginning, of a database design process, because only at this point can you make a good assessment of what the needs of the application might be. A small number of records and relatively simple information suggest that use of a single table will not adversely affect the integrity of the data, nor the ultimate functionality of any application that uses it.

Summary

In this chapter, you took a first look at applying reality to a decidedly theoretical design. In particular, you learned that:

- It is nearly impossible to avoid choosing practice over theory, because there are elements you must consider in implementing a design that any current RDBMS, including Paradox, does not manage for you.
- Relationality is a spectrum spanning nonrelational (tabular) DBMS through fully relational DBMS (which don't exist today).
- You can assess Paradox by reviewing the summarized rules and evaluating a combination of factors.
- You need to consider adjusting a relational database design for nonrelational reasons, including the need for security for your information, and a desire for simplicity.

Key Terms

database administrator (DBA) The person who manages the database and applications.

data sensitivity A qualitative assessment of data that describes how secret it is.

implementation The phase of application development during which the design is acted upon (building is begun).

join A relational operation that combines tables and brings rows together based on common values.

project A relational operation by which specified columns are extracted from a table.

restrict A relational operation that extracts specific records from a relational table.

9 Building what you have planned

The design is formalized: the tables, fields, and relationships have all been defined. Issues of data integrity have been identified, and Paradox has been chosen as the implementation product. It is crucial to understand how that choice will impact the application as it finally appears; that understanding requires detailed knowledge of the way implementation occurs with Paradox. Rather than providing a list of concerns for you as a database developer in Paradox, this chapter will walk you through the process of implementing the design, while at the same time highlighting problems which frequently occur. You will quickly discover issues which will impact your database design choices, but from a practical point of view, not as a abbreviated list of do's and don'ts.

Maintaining perspective

The intention in this chapter is to detail the process of implementing a database design. From one perspective, that process is complete when the necessary tables are in existence. But from a longer-term perspective, implementation of the database design extends beyond the simple table creation through the establishment of mechanisms to ensure the integrity of data within those tables. And from yet a broader perspective, implementation of the database design includes the development of each table's entire family. At some point, the line between application development and database design implementation gets very fuzzy. From that point of view, implementing a database design can require comprehensive knowledge of Paradox and all of its features.

There are many excellent and exhaustive books on the market today which are intended to support a Paradox user in developing comprehensive knowledge of the product (see the Bibliography contained herein). There are books which focus on using the interactive features of Paradox, those that are specifically geared toward programmers using PAL, and those which attempt to cover both ends of the spectrum. This book is none of those.

The perspective provided here is one of concept. Database design is a conceptual art, and understanding the techniques of implementation is less crucial than understanding the concepts behind the choice of those techniques. This chapter does provide some detail as to the step-by-step, keystroke-level skills associated with building tables; but it is less important as a skills reference than as a set of suggestions intended to provoke thought about the process. Similarly, chapters 10 and 11 extend the table creation topics to include conceptual issues of form and report design. Thus, you should look to this section as more of a designer's guide than a fully-referenced text on Create and other features of Paradox.[1]

Getting organized

Overall, the steps involved with implementing a database design under Paradox are as follow:

1. Create the table(s).
2. Apply validity checks.
3. Apply password protection where required.
4. Develop PAL routines to support keys and additional integrity requirements.
5. Document table structures with a data dictionary.
6. Create query templates.
7. Design and build multitable forms.
8. Design and build multitable reports.

Once you've been through the entire process at least one time, you'll probably discover that the design components of steps 7 and 8 should occur before the creation of the first table. As chapters 10 and 11 will demonstrate, Paradox requirements for multitable forms and reports often will change your database design, in particular by reordering your field definitions but also by possibly adding requirements for new tables. For the purposes of this book, however, form and report design issues will be addressed after initial table creation, and changes in the database design as a result of form or report issues will be accomplished through the table modification process supported in Paradox.

Creating a table

The first step in implementing a design is by far the simplest. Prepare to create all your tables at once by using the list of tables in your database design document. Table creation is supported through Paradox's main menu

· · · · · · · · ·
[1] Note to experienced Paradox users: Much of the balance of this chapter deals with techniques that will be very familiar to you. You might be better served by moving directly to chapter 10.

choice `Create` (see FIGS. 9-1 and 9-2 for 3.5 and 4.0 versions). Once selected, a prompt or dialog box will appear which asks for a new table name. Enter the name of the table you want to define. Press Enter to tell Paradox you are done filling in the name.

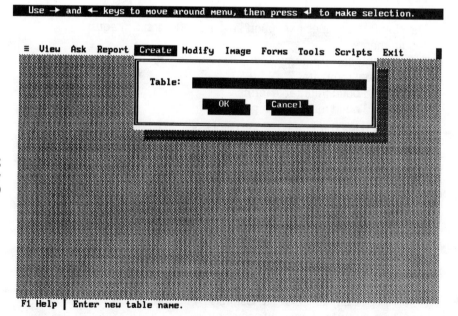

View Ask Report Create Modify Image Forms Tools Scripts Help Exit
Create a new table structure.

9-1
Main menu choice Create (3.5)

Use → and ← keys to move around menu, then press ◄┘ to make selection.

≡ View Ask Report Create Modify Image Forms Tools Scripts Exit

Table:

OK   Cancel

F1 Help | Enter new table name.

9-2
Main menu choice Create (4.0)

Paradox will respond by presenting you with an empty `Struct` table. This table is one of Paradox's temporary tables and is used as a mechanism for communication between you and Paradox relative to the structure of a particular table (in this case the table you are now creating). `Struct` is a unique table, because each of its rows represents one column in the table it is defining or describing. If the table you want to define has five fields, when you have completed Struct it will have five records (see FIG. 9-3).

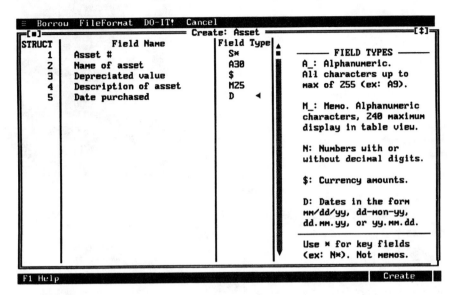

```
≡  Borrow  FileFormat  DO-IT!  Cancel
┌─[■]──────────────────────── Create: Asset ════════════════════[‡]─┐
│STRUCT │          Field Name  │Field Type│▲│────── FIELD TYPES ──────│
│   1   │  Asset #             │S×        │■│A_: Alphanumeric.        │
│   2   │  Name of asset       │A30       │ │All characters up to     │
│   3   │  Depreciated value   │$         │ │max of 255 (ex: A9).     │
│   4   │  Description of asset │M25       │ │                         │
│   5   │  Date purchased      │D      ◄  │ │M_: Memo. Alphanumeric   │
│       │                      │          │ │characters, 240 maximum  │
│       │                      │          │ │display in table view.   │
│       │                      │          │ │                         │
│       │                      │          │ │N: Numbers with or       │
│       │                      │          │ │without decimal digits.  │
│       │                      │          │ │                         │
│       │                      │          │ │$: Currency amounts.     │
│       │                      │          │ │                         │
│       │                      │          │ │D: Dates in the form     │
│       │                      │          │ │mm/dd/yy, dd-mon-yy,     │
│       │                      │          │ │dd.mm.yy, or yy.mm.dd.   │
│       │                      │          │ │                         │
│       │                      │          │ │Use × for key fields     │
│       │                      │          │ │(ex: N×). Not memos.     │
├───────┴──────────────────────┴──────────┴─┴─────────────────────────┤
│ F1 Help                              │       Create       │         │
└──────────────────────────────────────────────────────────────────┘
```

9-3
Struct table with five records

Fill in the Struct table with the field name and data type (Field Type) for each field in your design. Begin with the key fields you have specified. Paradox requires that the key fields appear first in the order of fields in your table. Add an asterisk (*) to the end of the field type for the fields you have specified in your design as key fields). In Paradox 3.5, any field of any type can be keyed (assuming it is in the appropriate—first—position in the table). None of the three field types specific to Paradox 4.0 can be keyed (Memo, Binary, and Unknown).

You can move around the Struct table with the same keypresses available in any Paradox DataEntry session. When you have finished filling in the rows (one for each field in the table you are creating), you can leave your cursor on the last row or move it to the next row (now empty). Paradox will not create an extra unnamed field when there is a blank record at the end of Struct.

Create options

Paradox provides some help in during the table creation process. As elsewhere in the product, context-sensitive help is available both through the keypress F1 or the selection of Help from the Create menu (see FIGS. 9-4 and 9-5 for menu choices in 3.5 and 4.0).

You can use the Borrow option to borrow all or part of the structure from another table which already exists. When used during a Create session, Borrow can copy the entire structure, including all fields, field types, and key

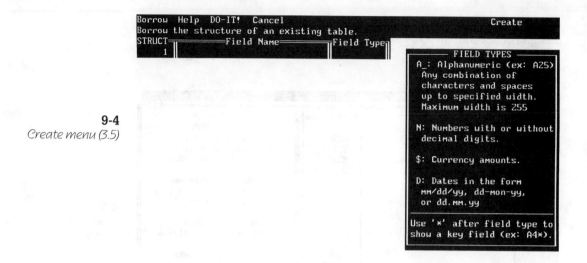

9-4
Create menu (3.5)

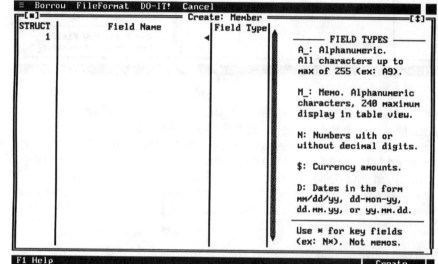

9-5
Create menu (4.0)

designations from a table you indicate. Borrow always inserts the structure from the Borrow-ed table into the current table definition immediately above your cursor position. From a relational point of view, the Borrow option won't be terribly useful, except to ensure that foreign key field names and types are captured in their exact form from the source primary key table.

Paradox 4.0 also provides an additional menu option which allows you to specify whether the new table should be created using the "old" (3.5 and before) file format or the standard 4.0 file format. The old format is known as "compatible" and can be selected from the Create menu under the FileFormat option (see FIG. 9-5). If no selection is made, 4.0 will automatically utilize the standard 4.0 file format (unless the default has been changed to `Compatible` through the 4.0 Custom Configuration Program). If you choose to create a table in compatible format, be aware that you cannot include any of the 4.0-specific field types in the table (Memo or Binary— Unknown is not available during `Create`).

Once you have completed entry of all fields, field types, and key indications, press F2 or select `Do__It!` from the `Create` menu to notify Paradox. Paradox will then proceed to create the specified table.

If you need to leave a `Create` session and do not want to save the new table definition, you can cancel without saving by selecting `Cancel` from the `Create` menu, or (in 4.0) by pressing Ctrl-F8 `WinClose`, clicking the `Close` box of the `Create` window, or selecting `!Close` from the system menu under `Create`.

Validity checks should be defined in support of the field integrity requirements outlined in your database design document. However, validity checks do not guarantee field integrity. Conceptually, validity checks are more an assistance to the data entry process than they are a protection of data in the table. Data entered or modified through `Tools|More|Add` or an import process or an insert query is not verified through a context-sensitive valcheck. Only data entered or modified through `DataEntry`, `Edit`, or `CoEdit` is subject to validity checking.

What's in validity checking

In these contexts, valchecks help protect the accuracy and validity of data that is entered into the table through keyboard entry. Validity checks are applied during a data entry or modification session at the field level. This means that if your cursor does not enter the field in question, the validity check does not apply. Even if you have created a `Required` validity check to support your intention that this particular field have a value for each and every record in the table, that `Required` valcheck won't take effect unless the user chooses (or is forced via PAL) to move into that field. This limitation and ways around it are addressed in more detail later in this chapter. Despite these limitations, validity checks are important in providing support for the requirements specified in the database design document, and they do provide a powerful aide to the process of adding or modifying data.

validity check   Also called valcheck. Paradox-specific mechanism for supporting the data entry and modification process as it occurs through keyboard entry.

Validity checks can be defined in support of the field integrity requirements outlined in your database design document. Validity checks are as close as Paradox comes to supporting the concept of domains. Aggressive use of valchecks is thus crucial in helping maintain common ground, particularly among fields drawing from the same conceptual domain.

Valchecks in Paradox

For this reason (and where appropriate), valchecks should be defined across multiple fields at once. Just as the scope of several relational fields can be bounded by a single domain, Paradox fields sharing common boundaries should be restricted through the application of identical valchecks. Refer to the following several sections to review the interactive approach to application of valchecks. PAL can be used to simplify the application and maintenance of valchecks, particularly in conjunction with a data dictionary (addressed later in this chapter).

How valchecks work

Valchecks help protect the accuracy and validity of data that is entered into the table through keyboard entry. Remember, data entered or modified through Tools|More|Add or an import process or an insert query is not verified through a valcheck. Only data entered or modified through DataEntry, Edit, or CoEdit is subject to validity checking. In addition, validity checks are applied during a data entry or modification session only at the field level. This means that if your cursor does not enter the field in question, the validity check does not apply. Even if you have created a Required validity check to support your intention that this particular field have a value for each and every record in the table, that Required valcheck won't take effect unless the user chooses (or is forced via PAL) to move into that field. This limitation and ways around it are addressed in more detail later in this chapter.

Validity checks can be important beyond the requirements specified in the database design document. In fact, one of the most beneficial uses of valchecks derives from the application of valchecks simply to aid in the process of adding or modifying data. Several types of valchecks provide exceptional support for this process and don't just verify the data, but actually encourage and facilitate its proper and speedy input. The more familiar with Paradox's valcheck facility you grow, the more you will discover uses for particular valcheck types, completely outside of the realm of data integrity requirements. As you develop these additional supportive features, include them in your database design document as well. Again, the goal is to prevent the collection of inaccurate or invalid data; easier data entry and modification of data certainly support that goal.

Applying validity checking

Once the table structure has been built, you can proceed to assign any appropriate validity checks. Consult your database design document for the specifics of valchecks that you have identified as necessary.

All valchecks must be applied while you are in either DataEntry or Edit mode, and the cursor must be current in the table you wish to create valchecks on. From either the DataEntry or Edit menu you can select ValCheck to begin the process. The ValCheck menu is prefaced by the options Define and Clear. To set up a new validity check, select Define. The available validity check types will then appear as a menu list (see FIG. 9-6).

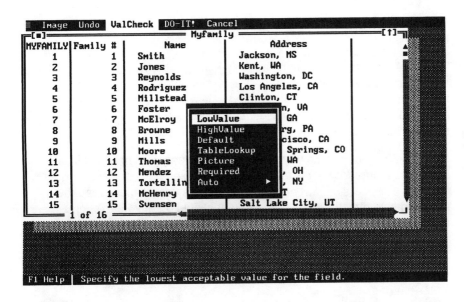

```
≡  Image  Undo  ValCheck  DO-IT!  Cancel
┌─[■]─┌──────────────── Myfamily ─────────────────┐─[↑]─┐
│MYFAMILY│Family #│      Name      │     Address      │    ▲
│    1   │   1    │ Smith          │ Jackson, MS      │
│    2   │   2    │ Jones          │ Kent, WA         │
│    3   │   3    │ Reynolds       │ Washington, DC   │
│    4   │   4    │ Rodriguez      │ Los Angeles, CA  │
│    5   │   5    │ Millstead      │ Clinton, CT      │
│    6   │   6    │ Foster     ┌──────────────┐ n, VA │
│    7   │   7    │ McElroy    │ LowValue     │   GA  │
│    8   │   8    │ Browne     │ HighValue    │ rg, PA│
│    9   │   9    │ Mills      │ Default      │ cisco, CA │
│   10   │  10    │ Moore      │ TableLookup  │ Springs, CO │
│   11   │  11    │ Thomas     │ Picture      │ WA    │
│   12   │  12    │ Mendez     │ Required     │ , OH  │
│   13   │  13    │ Tortellin  │ Auto       ▶ │ , NY  │
│   14   │  14    │ McHenry    └──────────────┘ T     │
│   15   │  15    │ Svensen        │ Salt Lake City, UT │
└────── 1 of 16 ══════◀───────────────────────────────┘
```

9-6
Validity check menu choices

F1 Help │ Specify the lowest acceptable value for the field.

Note that multiple validity checks can be placed on a single field. There is no restriction to the number of valchecks per field; however, you should be careful to ensure the valchecks you are defining are consistent with each other. Paradox does no interpretation of the valchecks you establish to make sure each makes sense, or to ensure that they work together in some logical fashion. It is possible, for example, to place a LowValue valcheck which is higher than a HighValue valcheck on the same field (e.g., LowValue = 10, HighValue = 5). This would effectively prevent entry of any value in the field, since both valchecks could never be satisfied.

LowValue & HighValue valchecks

A range of acceptable values can be specified by selecting LowValue or HighValue. LowValue sets the minimum acceptable value (an entered value must be greater than or equal to the LowValue established). HighValue sets the maximum acceptable value (an entered value must be less than or equal to the HighValue established). LowValue and HighValue are most commonly placed on numeric or date fields, although you can set either on an alphanumeric field.

To define a LowValue or HighValue valcheck, select the field to be verified and then select either LowValue or HighValue from the menu list (see FIG. 9-6). Simply enter the value for the valcheck, pressing Enter when you have finished. Paradox will give you a message confirming the placement of the new validity check.

Default & Required valchecks

The Default valcheck allows you to specify a value to be automatically filled in, assuming the user has first entered a field, and then left the field while the field's contents are blank. To apply a default valcheck, select the field for the default value and then select Default from the menu list (see

FIG. 9-6). Simply enter the value for the default, pressing Enter when you have finished.

The Required valcheck can be applied in an effort to force a user to enter a value into a particular field. However, it is only enforced when the user has first entered a field, and then attempted to leave the field while the contents are still blank. To apply a Required valcheck, selecting the field to be required, then select Required from the menu list (see FIG. 9-6).

Autoconfirm valchecks
Paradox 4.0 supports a new type of valcheck which does not specifically support data integrity but is instead intended to enhance the overall quality of a data entry session. Autoconfirm enables a user to move from the specified field directly to the next sequential field on the table or form without having to explicitly move the cursor. Autoconfirm, when properly applied, can dramatically enhance a data entry session by eliminating those extra keystrokes. Paradox 4.0 supports three types of autoconfirm valchecks:

- Filled
- Picture
- Lookup (see FIG. 9-7)

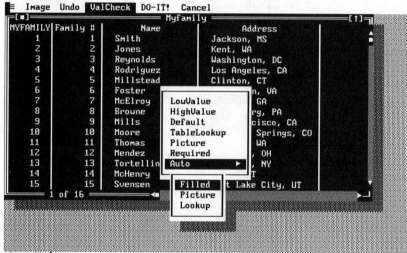

9-7
Autoconfirm validity check options

Filled Autoconfirm forces the user to the next sequential field when the user has filled a field with its maximum number of characters. This works well with Date fields (which can even be advanced by using the space bar to fill in the current date), and with shorter alphanumeric fields. Using the Filled option on a Numeric data type will not force the advance until you have entered the maximum number of digits (22 digits or 11 digits plus ten decimal places for a negative number, ten digits and 12 decimal places for a positive number). This is obviously of little help.

`Picture Autoconfirm` forces the cursor to the next sequential field when the `Picture` valcheck has been minimally satisfied (see the next section for details on `Picture` valchecks). For this reason, it works best when the `Picture` valcheck is a list of choices. `Picture` valchecks with optional endings do not work properly in this context. If, for example, your picture is a zip-plus-4 format (`#####[-####]`), `Autoconfirm` would always force cursor movement before you had the opportunity to fill in the optional plus 4. Paradox does check to make sure that a `Picture Autoconfirm` valcheck is being applied to a field that already has a `Picture` valcheck; you must be careful to apply the `Picture` valcheck first when intending to use `Picture Autoconfirm`.

`Lookup Autoconfirm` brings limited support to the data entry session. The cursor is automatically advanced only when the user takes advantage of the F1 (Help) key and subsequently makes a selection from the Lookup table by pressing F2. Direct data entry of lookup values does not invoke `Autoconfirm`. This is a particular problem if the `Lookup` valcheck established is a `PrivateLookup` only. The `Lookup` valcheck must be applied first before Paradox allows you to apply a `Lookup Autoconfirm` valcheck.

Apply an `Autoconfirm` valcheck by selecting the field for confirmation and then selecting `Auto` from the dialog box. Choose the type of `Autoconfirm` necessary from the submenu, and then Paradox will respond with a `Yes|No` menu for you to verify the placement of the new valcheck. Responding `No` at this point allows you to remove a specific valcheck without having to clear them all.

`Picture` valchecks are intended to support consistent formatting of data that could otherwise be entered in a variety of ways. `Picture` valchecks are specified through the use of picture elements (see Table 9-1). The `Picture` specifies a format which can fall into several categories:

Picture *valchecks*

**Table 9-1
Picture Elements.**

Pattern Element	Stands for
#	Numeric digit
?	Letter (upper- or lowercase)
&	Letter (convert to uppercase)
@	Any character
!	Any character (convert to uppercase)
;	Take the next value literally
*	Repeat the next element
[]	Optional item
{}	Grouped item
,	Alternative values

- List of options
- Group subsets
- Strict formatting

The picture elements can be used in a wide variety of combinations, and in conjunction with any constant (like a hyphen or parentheses), to control allowable values in a field. Table 9-2 provides a listing of some examples of each type of formats.[2] Picture valchecks are created by selecting the field the valcheck is to be applied to, then picking Picture from the valcheck list. Enter the picture elements to describe the field's values, then press Enter or choose OK to continue.

Table 9-2
Picture Examples.

Format	Requirement
[###]###-####	Telephone number with optional area code
&*?	Alphanumeric string of any length, with initial letter capitalized
#####[-####]	Zip plus four
Jam,Jelly	Either choice (Value equals "Jam" or "Jelly")

Because Picture valchecks do provide some support for the domain concept, it is important to apply identical Pictures where the data is intended to be drawn from the same source. For this reason (and others), you might want to store Picture valchecks in a table that will keep track of any available Pictures and what field types they are assigned to (or what domain they describe). Figure 9-8 provides an example of such a table. Once such a table has been defined, it is a relatively simple matter in PAL to build a small utility for applying many valchecks within a single "valcheck-assignment session." Figure 9-9 provides a listing of a simple PAL utility that might meet that requirement.

TableLookup valchecks

TableLookup valchecks are intended to help protect referential integrity as well as to assist you in the data entry process. A TableLookup valcheck is normally applied to a field which is a foreign key, and it helps link the foreign key value back to the primary key value in the Lookup table. TableLookup valchecks are an essential component involved in protecting referential integrity. In this context, the Lookup table is normally the "one" side in a one-to-many relationship (see FIG. 9-10). TableLookup valchecks help in three ways:

- They help you to maintain the proper foreign key-primary key relationship established by your database design.
- They allow you to get access to the Lookup table in order to pick the appropriate value for the current table.

• • • • • • • • •

2 Picture valchecks are consistent with the Picture option under the PAL Accept command.

```
≡  View  Ask  Report  Create  Modify  Image  Forms  Tools  Scripts  Exit
┌─[■]══════════════════ Multi-record form ═══════════════════════[↕]─┐
Description: Simulate a TIME data type with format of HH:MM and :SS optional
Picture: {0#,1#,2{0,1,2,3}}:{0,1,2,3,4,5}#[:{0,1,2,3,4,5}#]
+++++++++++++++++++++++++++++++++++++++++++++++++++++++++++++++++++++++++
Description: Simulate a TIME data type with format of HH:MMAM or HH:MMPM
Picture: {1{:,{0,1,2}:},{2,3,4,5,6,7,8,9}:}{0,1,2,3,4,5}#{AM,PM}
+++++++++++++++++++++++++++++++++++++++++++++++++++++++++++++++++++++++++
Description: Phone Number — seven digits with automatic fillin of dashes
Picture: ###-####
+++++++++++++++++++++++++++++++++++++++++++++++++++++++++++++++++++++++++
Description: Phone Number — seven digits with automatic fillin of dashes and a
Picture: [(###)]###-####
+++++++++++++++++++++++++++++++++++++++++++++++++++++++++++++++++++++++++
Description: Phone Number — seven digits with automatic fillin of dashes and a
Picture: [{1-800-,(###)}]###-####
+++++++++++++++++++++++++++++++++++++++++++++++++++++++++++++++++++++++++
Description: Date — allow only 01 for the day and have it filled in automatica
Picture: {##/01/##,#/01/##}
+++++++++++++++++++++++++++++++++++++++++++++++++++++++++++++++++++++++++
Description: Date — allow only 01 for the day and have it filled in automatica
Picture: {##/01/[##],#/01[##]}
+++++++++++++++++++++++++++++++++++++++++++++++++++++++++++++++++++++++++
══ 13 of 28 ═════◄───────────────────────────────────────────►──
 F1 Help  F7 Table  Ctrl-PgUp Prev  Ctrl-PgDn Next  Alt-F9 CoEdit │  Main
```

9-8
Picture table example

```
;Appl_pic.sc
;Procedure to apply a picture

SETKEY -25 appl_pic( )   ;Set Alt-P to pick up and put down
                                     ; picture
PROC apply_pic( )

IF TABLE ( ) = "Pictab" THEN
    pict.a = [Picture Pattern]
    MESSAGE "You have successfully grabbed a picture pattern!"
    SLEEP 2000
  ELSE
IF SYSMODE ( ) = "Edit" THEN
    Menu {Valcheck}{Define} Enter {Picture}
    SELECT pict.a
    MESSAGE "You have successfully applied picture" = pict.a
    SLEEP 2000
  ELSE
    MESSAGE "You must be in Edit mode to apply a picture valcheck!"
     SLEEP 2000
  ENDIF
ENDIF
ENDPROC
WRITELIB "main" apply_pic
RELEASE PROCS apply_pic
```

9-9
*Picture valcheck
application script*

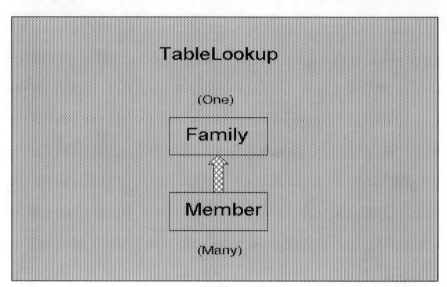

9-10
TableLookup: One in one-to-many

- They allow you to automatically copy default values from the Lookup table into the current table (AllCorrespondingFields).

Applying rules through PAL

The validity checking supported through interactive Paradox is by no means the limit of what you can do to help ensure the integrity of your data. As was suggested by the brief picture valcheck application routine shown earlier in FIG. 9-9, PAL can be an important tool for enhancing what's available interactively. The following material is not intended as a tool to help you understand or learn how to use PAL; it is simply to make you aware of some of the areas in which the integrity of your data can be supported with the help of programming.

PAL can provide important support for different integrity requirements. The next few sections address concepts for using PAL in this way. The assumption here is that PAL is already being used to run a data entry or modification session—these techniques will not work in an interactive session. A basic PAL CoEdit routine is described in FIG. 9-11. This is a very stripped down version of what you would likely use in an up-and-running application. However, it does contain the major components; it allows a user to make changes to a single table one record at a time.

Supporting key requirements through autonumbering

One of the most important supports for relational integrity occurs through Paradox's implementation of primary keys. Once a primary key has been defined on a field or set of fields, Paradox will not allow data which duplicates a previously existing key into the table. There are several different situations in which Paradox might encounter an attempt to duplicate a key (see Table 9-3). As you can see, Paradox responds in one of two ways:

```
>Go_edit.sc
;Simple procedure similar to Paradox 3.5 CoEdit model

COEDIT "Myfamily"
SHOWPULLDOWN ENDMENU
WHILE true
  IMAGERIGHTS READONLY
  WAIT TABLE
  PROMPT "[F9]-Edit        [F2]-Save&Leave"
  UNTIL "F2", "F9"
  SWITCH
    CASE retval = "F2":
      QUITLOOP
    CASE retval = "F9":
      IMAGERIGHTS UPDATE    ;allow changes to non-key fields
      FORMKEY               ;support changes in form view
      CTRLHOME              ;start on first record
      WAIT RECORD
        PROMPT "Modify record and press [F2] when
          finished"
      UNTIL "F2"
      FORMKEY               ;return to table view
      CTRLHOME RIGHT        ;return to first field in table
  ENDSWITCH
ENDWHILE
Do_It!                     ;save changes, return to view mode
ClearImage                 ;clear table from workspace
```

9-11
Basic PAL CoEdit routine

- Any previous value is updated with the newly entered value; or
- Any new value which duplicates an old value is tossed into a temporary table called KEYVIOL.

Table 9-3
When key violations might occur.

Situation	What Paradox does interactively
Edit	Updates current records
CoEdit	Provides error message and waits for user to resolve
DataEntry	Creates KEYVIOL table with new records
Tools/More/Add/Update	Updates current records
Tools/More/Add/NewEntries	Creates KEYVIOL with new records
Tools/More/FormAdd	Updates current records
ASK/insert	Updates current records
Modify/Restructure	Creates KEYVIOL with duplicate records

The KEYVIOL table holds records whose keys duplicate an already existing key. These records are called *key violations,* and they normally signal a problem which requires you to do something.

Handling key violations

Interactively, the user can respond to what is happening based upon the messages which Paradox delivers. However, once you have begun handling data entry and modification through PAL, the situation grows quite a bit more complex. A relatively simple way to handle the potential for key violations is to divide data entry and modification tasks into two parts:

- Key field maintenance, including adding new records and deleting records
- Modifying any nonkey fields

The basis of this separation is through the use of the PAL IMAGERIGHTS command. Use of IMAGERIGHTS MODIFY controls access to the key field(s) and prevents any changes to key values (allowing modification to nonkey fields only). This works great for the bulk of data maintenance tasks. For the balance, a user must specifically choose to add a new record (through the Insert key or perhaps a function key which you select), delete or modify key field values. Once the insertion key is pressed, the application will handle the addition of new records by running a script which will automatically change the imagerights (where necessary) and create new key values for you. This type of script normally helps you keep track of sequentially numbered records, and will calculate and assign new key values automatically (see FIG. 9-12). An autonumbering procedure is not difficult to create and can solve many problems (since key violations are eliminated). The only tasks which must be dealt with separately would then be deletion or a change of key value, and that is controllable through the use of a multitable form (see chapter 10).

```
;Go_Ins.sc
;Simple procedure less similar to Paradox 3.5 CoEdit model

COEDIT "Myfamily"
SHOWPULLDOWN ENDMENU
WHILE true
  IMAGERIGHTS READONLY
  WAIT WORKSPACE
  PROMPT "[F9]-Edit     [F2]-Save&Leave"
  UNTIL "F2", "F9"
  SWITCH
    CASE retval = "F2":
      QUITLOOP
    CASE retval = "F9":
      IMAGERIGHTS UPDATE    ;allow changes to non-key fields
```

9-12
Basic PAL CoEdit routine, with autonumbering

```
        FORMKEY                 ;support changes in form view
        CTRLHOME                ;start on first record
      WHILE true
        WAIT RECORD
          PROMPT "[Ins] Add record  [F2] Finished"
        UNTIL "Ins","F2"
        IF retval = "Ins" THEN
            IMAGERIGHTS
            INS
            MOVETO [Family #]
            [] = IMAGECMAX() + 1
            RIGHT
            POSTRECORD NOPOST LEAVELOCKED
            IMAGERIGHTS UPDATE
            LOOP
        ENDIF
        FORMKEY                 ;return to table view
          CTRLHOME RIGHT        ;return to first field in table
            QUITLOOP
      ENDWHILE
    ENDSWITCH
ENDWHILE
Do_It!                          ;save changes, return to view mode
ClearImage                      ;clear table from workspace
```

---

autonumbering Automatic creation of sequential numbers for key values
in new records.

Specialized business rules

Specifically, you might have established requirements for a field which
fall outside the scope of any single valcheck; for example, your business
might require that any customer with a credit line of greater than $5,000
maintain an up-to-date file with Dun and Bradstreet. Obviously, no
valcheck will support that requirement. You might require each
employee who is age 62 or older to file separate paperwork relative to
Social Security. Perhaps all your female patients have paperwork to fill
out in addition to the standard forms. As suggested by FIG. 9-13, this
simple PAL routine can be easily enhanced to call an integrity checking
procedure which would specify and check that any data just entered or
modified is consistent with these rules.[3] Business rules, like those
defined above, can be easily defined within this special procedure (see
FIG. 9-14).

• • • • • • • • •

[3] Each table on a given form would normally have its own specialized integrity checking
procedure, since you would probably be applying different rules to different fields in different
tables.

Building what you have planned

```
;Go_val.sc
;Simple procedure enhanced to call integrity checker

;******Event Handling Procedure******

PROC ehandler(etype,erec,ecycle)
  IF etype = "DEPARTROW" THEN
    check_validity()
    IF NOT retval THEN
      MESSAGE vmess + " ... press any key to continue"
      x = GETCHAR()
      RETURN 1
    ELSE
      RETURN 0
    ENDIF
  ENDIF
  IF etype = "EVENT" THEN
    SWITCH
      CASE erec["KEYCODE"] = ASC("F2"): RETURN 2      ;done
      CASE erec["KEYCODE"] = ASC("Ins")::;want to add record
        IMAGERIGHTS
        INS
        IF TABLE() = "Myfamily" THEN
          [Family #] = CMAX("Myfamily","Family #") + 1
          POSTRECORD NOPOST LEAVELOCKED
        ELSE
          MOVETO [Member #]
          IF ISBLANK([]) THEN
            [] = 1
          ELSE
            INS
            [] = IMAGECMAX() + 1
          ENDIF
          POSTRECORD NOPOST LEAVELOCKED
          RIGHT
        ENDIF
        IMAGERIGHTS UPDATE
        RETURN 1
      CASE erec["KEYCODE"] = ASC("Del"):         ;want to delete record
        SHOWPOPUP "Confirm Deletion" CENTERED
          "Delete"  : "Delete this record" : "D",
          "Cancel"  : "Don't delete this record" : "C"
        ENDMENU
        TO pc
        IF pc = "D" THEN
          IMAGERIGHTS
          DEL
          IMAGERIGHTS UPDATE
        ENDIF
        RETURN 1
    ENDSWITCH
```

9-13

Basic PAL CoEdit routine, enhanced to call integrity checker

```
    ENDIF
  ENDPROC

;******Actual Wait Loop******
autolib = "Main"
COEDIT "Myfamily"
PICKFORM 1
SHOWPULLDOWN ENDMENU
IMAGERIGHTS UPDATE
PROMPT "[Ins]-Add New Record     [F3]-Next Table     [F2]-
Save&Leave"
ECHO NORMAL
WAIT WORKSPACE
  PROC "ehandler"
  TRIGGER "DEPARTROW"
  KEY "F2","Ins","Del"
ENDWAIT
Do_It!                   ;save changes, return to view mode
ClearImage               ;clear table from workspace
```

```
;Val_rule.sc

PROC check_validity()
  PRIVATE v

IF TABLE() = "Member" THEN          ;Rules for member table
  IF ([Height] = "Tall" AND [Build]  "Thin") THEN
    vmess = "You must force your relative to lose weight"
    RETURN false
  ENDIF
ENDIF
RETURN true

ENDPROC

WRITELIB "Main" check_validity
RELEASE PROCS check_validity
```

9-14
*Integrity checking
procedure with Rules*

In addition to the business rules not supported through valchecks, two
valcheck types are in and of themselves limited in their effect. The intention
of a default value in a field is to ensure that a selected value be filled in if the
user has not selected a different value. However, if the user neglects to move
into a field on which a Default valcheck has been defined, no fill-in will
occur. In PAL, you can update your integrity checking procedure to include
confirmation of BLANK fields in order to fill in any blanks with the indicated
Default value (see FIG. 9-15).

***Enforcing* Default
& Required *rules***

```
;Val_def.sc
;Required values only

PROC check_validity()
 PRIVATE v

vmess = "OK"
IF TABLE() = "Myfamily" THEN ;Default fields in family table
  IF ISBLANK([Address]) THEN
   [Address] = "Seattle, WA"
  ENDIF
ELSE                          ;Required fields in member table
 IF ISBLANK([Pattern]) THEN
  [Pattern] = "Polka dots"
 ENDIF
ENDIF
vmess = "A default value has been entered for you"
RETURN true

ENDPROC
WRITELIB "Main" check_validity
RELEASE PROCS check_validity
```

9-15

Integrity checking procedure with Defaults

```
;Val.sc
;Required values only

PROC check_validity()
 PRIVATE v

vmess = "OK"
IF TABLE() = "Myfamily" THEN ;Required fields in family table
  IF ISBLANK([Name]) THEN
    vmess = FIELD()
  ENDIF
  IF ISBLANK([Address]) THEN
   vmess = FIELD()
  ENDIF
ELSE              ;Required fields in member table
 IF ISBLANK([Member #]) THEN
  vmess = FIELD()
 ENDIF
 IF ISBLANK([Pattern]) THEN
  vmess = FIELD()
 ENDIF
ENDIF
IF NOT vmess = "OK" THEN
 vmess = "You must enter a value in " + vmess
 RETURN false
ELSE
 RETURN true
ENDIF

ENDPROC
WRITELIB "Main" check_validity
RELEASE PROCS check_validity
```

9-16

Integrity checking procedure with Required

`Required` valchecks have the same limitation. If the user doesn't actually move his or her cursor into the field, no requirement for a value will be applied. Through PAL, however, a user can be forced to enter a value in any field or combination of fields (see FIG. 9-16).

A database design should correspond closely to an implemented design in Paradox. However, once the first phase is over, and the tables have been built and validity checks applied, it is often difficult to keep that database design in sight. Although the design document can be reviewed and updated to reflect changes in requirements, it is sometimes difficult to maintain that same responsiveness to changing requirements in the system structures. A data dictionary is intended to help manage a defined database through its ongoing maintenance. The concept of a data dictionary is by no means unique to Paradox; in fact, Paradox does not do a very good job of supporting the concept. A data dictionary is simply a document (in Paradox, a table) which contains information about all the data structures in a given application. It is called a dictionary because it is a listing of structures in a particular order, much like an English dictionary is a listing of words in alphabetical order. The data dictionary defines and expands upon the definitions of tables and fields, and provides a central clearinghouse of information about all of the application's structures. Figure 9-17 provides a simple view on a data dictionary table. There is no defined or programmed connection between the dictionary and the current condition of any table; the dictionary acts simply as a management tool and provides information on an application-wide basis.

Documenting structures with a data dictionary

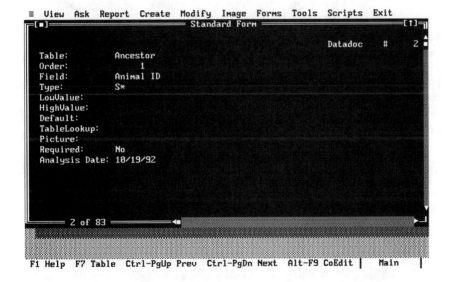

9-17
Data dictionary table

data dictionary   A file which provides a listing of data structures and their associated integrity restrictions. In Paradox, normally a table which stores table and field names along with descriptions of contents and applicable validity checks.

Even small applications with a limited number of tables and fields can benefit from inclusion in some similar table. Storing this information in a Paradox table is extremely useful, since in that form it is easy to enter and maintain.

Using a utility to generate documentation

If you are creating your data dictionary at the same time you build your tables, getting it up-to-date is an incremental process. However, if you are taking over an application from someone else for the first time, or have no database design documentation for an application which you yourself have created, PAL can be used to automate the process of building a current data dictionary. Figure 9-18 provides the code for a very straightforward creation of a data dictionary. This routine uses `Tools|Info|Inventory|Tables` in order to set up a table called `List`, containing information on all defined tables in the current subdirectory. `List` drives the rest of the work involved in figuring out what fields and field-level validity checks are defined for each table. Notice that early in the listing all nonuser tables are removed from `List` (it is not terribly useful to document Paradox's temporary tables). Also notice the places where the user can add in nonactive tables (like reporting tables); you might or might not want to exclude this kind of table from your `List`.

Applying password protection

Passwords can be an effective part of your commitment to protecting the integrity of your data. As the designer of an application, you can make determinations as to which of the application's users will be active in which ways, and can include password protection at several levels in order to support those intended uses.

`Tools|More|Protect` can be used interactively to implement a password-protection scheme. Both tables and scripts can be protected, although in this context you will be concerned only with table protection. When you create a table, you can control access to it. You can allow or deny a user's ability to get at anything within the table: the entire table itself, specific fields within the table, or objects in the table's family. You have many choices as to the type of access you grant to particular users or groups of users, both through the owner password and through auxiliary passwords which you as owner can define. Once you have protected a table with an owner password, knowledge of that password is required in order to maintain the auxiliary passwords. When you first select `Password|Table`, Paradox will prompt you for the table you wish to protect, then prompts you to enter the password. Passwords can be up to 15 characters long, including spaces. Passwords are case sensitive: upper- and lowercase characters are considered different. You must then enter the same password a second time to confirm it to Paradox. Make sure you write down the owner password, since once you have entered it, there is no way to get it from Paradox again. Even Borland's technical support cannot retrieve a password which has been lost or forgotten.

```
;Datadoc.sc

PROC data_dictionary()
        PRIVATE attr.r,                ;table attribute array
               x                       ;continue specifier

   CURSOR OFF
   CLEAR
   SHOWDIALOG "Create a Data Dictionary"
   @ 4,9 HEIGHT 17 WIDTH 60

   @ 1,2 ?? "This script scans all tables in the current directory"
   @ 2,2 ?? " but temporary tables, and builds a new table of "
   @ 3,2 ?? " attributes of those scanned tables: table names, "
   @ 4,2 ?? " field names, field types and assigned validity checks."
   @ 6,2 ??" The table storing the dictionary is named \"DataDoc\"."
   @ 7,2 ??" Passwords for all protected tables must be presented"
   @ 8,2 ??" prior to running this script or attributes for those"
   @ 9,2 ??" tables will not be collected."
   @ 11,2 ??" This procedure will delete all temporary tables!"
     PUSHBUTTON @ 13,8 WIDTH 13 "OK"
      OK
      DEFAULT
      VALUE "Continue"
      TAG "OKTag"
      TO ButtonValue
     PUSHBUTTON @ 13,35 WIDTH 13 "Cancel"
      CANCEL
      VALUE "Go Back"
      TAG "CancelTag"
      TO ButtonValue
   ENDDIALOG

   IF NOT retval THEN                  ;Cancel was selected
      RETURN false
   ENDIF

   MESSAGE "Now scanning current directory for tables..."

   WHILE true
     IF (SYSMODE()  "Main") THEN QUITLOOP ENDIF
     IF NOT ISTABLE("Datadoc")
     THEN
       BEEP SLEEP 200 BEEP
```

9-18
Creating a data dictionary with PAL

```
  MESSAGE "Attribute table must exist before processing .... "
  SLEEP 3000
  CLEARALL
  RETURN
ENDIF
SETDIR DIRECTORY()
VIEW "Datadoc"
{Tools}{Info}{Inventory}{Tables} Enter
EDITKEY
SCAN  ;List
SWITCH         ;Edit out any excluded tables
  CASE ([Name] = "List"):
  CASE ([Name] = "Datadoc"):
  CASE ([Name] = "Pictab"):
  OTHERWISE : LOOP
  ENDSWITCH
 [Name] = ""       ;Clear Name field to flag excluded tables
ENDSCAN            ;List table
DO_IT!
MESSAGE "Determining table attributes..."
ARRAY attr.r[12]
attr.r[1] = "Datadoc"          ;Create attribute array
SCAN  ;List
  IF ([Name] = "")
    THEN LOOP ENDIF            ;Skip excluded tables
  VIEW [Name]                  ;Display work table
  IF (MENUCHOICE()  "Error")       ;Flag tables that
                                   require passwords
   THEN
    UPIMAGE                         ;To Datadoc
    EDITKEY
    IF ([Table]  "") THEN DOWN ENDIF
    [Table] = [List->Name]
    [Field] = "***Protected Table***"
    DO_IT!
    DOWNIMAGE                       ;To List
   LOOP
  ENDIF
attr.r[2] = TABLE()            ;Store work table name
MENU {Tools}{Info}{Structure}
  TYPEIN [List->Name] ENTER
EDITKEY           ;Full edit to access validity checks
SCAN                           ;Struct table
  attr.r[3] = RECNO()   ;Store work table field order
  attr.r[4] = [Field Name]        ;Store field name
  attr.r[5] = [Field Type]        ;Store field type
  UPIMAGE                      ;To [List->Name] table
MOVETO FIELD attr.r[4]  ;Locate field for val check storage
  MENU {ValCheck}{Define} ENTER   ;Store validity checks
```

```
        IF NOT (MATCH(attr.r[5],"M..")    ;Make sure not
                                          Memo or BLOb field
          or MATCH(attr.r[5],"B..")) THEN
          SELECT "LowValue" attr.r[6] = MENUCHOICE() ESC
          SELECT "HighValue" attr.r[7] = MENUCHOICE() ESC
          SELECT "Default" attr.r[8] = MENUCHOICE() ESC
          SELECT "TableLookup" attr.r[9] = MENUCHOICE() ESC
          SELECT "Picture" attr.r[10] = MENUCHOICE() ESC
        ENDIF
        SELECT "Required" attr.r[11] = MENUCHOICE()
        attr.r[12] = TODAY()
        UPIMAGE UPIMAGE             ;Move To Datadoc
        IF ([Table]  "") THEN DOWN ENDIF
        COPYFROMARRAY attr.r       ;Write attributes to
                                   "Datadoc" table

        MOVETO "Struct"
      ENDSCAN  ;Struct
      DO_IT!
      CLEARIMAGE  ;Struct table
      CLEARIMAGE  ;[List->Name] table    ;Clear work table
    ENDSCAN                              ;List
    CLEARIMAGE                           ;List table
    SHOWPULLDOWN ENDMENU
    WAIT TABLE
      PROMPT "Press [F2] when finished viewing table."
      MESSAGE "Data dictionary now ready for viewing ..."
    UNTIL "F2"
    CLEARIMAGE
    QUITLOOP
  ENDWHILE
ENDPROC
WRITELIB "Main" data_dictionary
data_dictionary()
RELEASE PROCS data_dictionary
```

---

password   A series of characters used to control access to a resource; in Paradox, a key word or phrase which can be up to 15 characters in length (including spaces) and in which upper- and lowercase characters are distinguishable.

Once the owner password has been entered twice, Paradox will provide a form view of a special table which can be used to enter or modify one or more separate passwords which can be used to independently control levels of access for different users or sets of users. Each record in this special table represents one auxiliary password,[4] and normally a user would only need to

Specifying auxiliary rights

· · · · · · · · ·
[4] Auxiliary passwords are not required; an owner password might be all the protection you need.

Building what you have planned 181

use a single password from the selection (depending on her need for access to the table).

When entering an auxiliary password, you must identify the name of the password, the overall rights to the table and family, and specific rights to each field, if desired (see FIG. 9-19). This information can be entered in through form view (the default); table view is also available by pressing the F7 key or clicking F7 on the SpeedBar. The table rights which you can choose from are:

- ReadOnly
- Update
- Entry
- InsDel
- All

ReadOnly allows a user to see (view) the table, but prevents him from making any changes to it, regardless of the mode or context. Update allows the user to both view the table and make selected changes to it; nonkey fields are available for modification, but key fields are not. Under Update a user also cannot add or delete records in their entirety.

Entry supports the same rights as Update; in addition, the user's ability to add new records through Modify|DataEntry is supported. InsDel gives the user Entry rights, plus access to changing the contents of any and all fields, inserting and deleting entire records, and emptying the table of all records. All gives the user complete control of the table, including the right to restructure and delete it. All essentially provides the user with ownership

9-19
Defining auxiliary rights

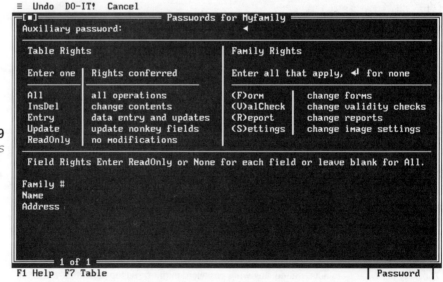

rights; however, a user with All rights still cannot get into the Password Generator in order to add or modify passwords.

You can control who can make changes to objects by indicating each or all object type in the Family rights column. (F)orms, (V)alidity checks, (R)eports, and Image (S)ettings can be protected simply by including the appropriate letter in the Family Rights field. Protecting an object prevents a user from creating, changing, or deleting any object which is of the specified type.

Specifying family & field rights

Field rights can be protected by choosing one of three levels of access for each field:

- All rights (leave the field blank)
- ReadOnly
- None

All rights preserves the user's ability to perform any operation not protected by any other means. ReadOnly allows a user to view any value in the field, but not to change it; and None prevents a user from either seeing (viewing) or changing a value in the field.

Paradox is sensitive to the relationship between table and field rights. Combinations which don't make sense (more restrictive table rights in conjunction with less restrictive field rights) are not supported through the Password Generator. You also are prevented from specifying None as the type of access granted to a field which has been defined as a key field. The minimum access granted to a key field is ReadOnly. Overall, password protection can be an effective tool in protecting database integrity.

Once you have built, protected, and documented all your tables, the next step involves looking at protecting the information content of your database at the relational level. In other words, although you can control the integrity of the data in individual tables, and to some extent you can support relational links through the TableLookup validity check feature, it is still sometimes difficult to prevent data from being corrupted simply through misuse.

Adding value through defined relationships

From the user's perspective, tables are independent entities, and there is no command or function in Paradox which will permanently tie them together. In a way, this flexibility is a positive attribute of a relational system. Remember, all the data in a relational database is stored in tables, and thus changes in data can effect changes in the relational structure. If values in linked fields no longer match, the very nature of the database has undergone a change. Although this flexibility might be intentional, from a practical perspective it is unnecessary. The types of links which are available within a database are created conceptually during the design.

values in linked fields no longer match, the very nature of the database has undergone a change. Although this flexibility might be intentional, from a practical perspective it is unnecessary. The types of links which are available within a database are created conceptually during the design. Making arbitrary changes to data, though effective in breaking down preestablished links, does not support the ongoing value of the database itself. Thus, once the independent tables have been created, it is incumbent on the database designer also to create usable links between the tables. These links fall into four categories, and can be described as the "multitable features" of Paradox (see FIG. 9-20).

- `TableLookup` validity checks
- Multitable queries
- Multitable forms
- Multitable reports

Features of a database product which contribute to the integration of relational tables are truly fundamental to its success. Paradox's four-part support for this kind of integration sets it apart from many minimally relational DBMS products.

`TableLookup` validity checks were discussed earlier in this chapter. They are an important step in the process of collecting useful relational data (which defines all the appropriate relationships accurately). The other three features fall more into the category of "applied" relational features, because they support the recombination of the data (once it has been separated into entity-based tables).

Understanding query templates

Multitable forms and reports are features which warrant special extended design and implementation discussion, and are covered in chapters 10

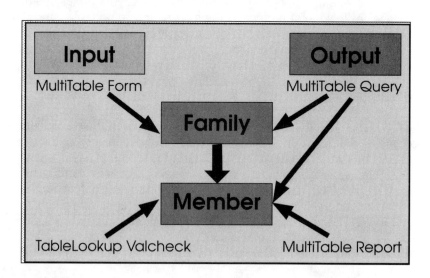

9-20
Paradox's multitable features

query-by-example (QBE) supports the combination of values from multiple fields in multiple tables in an infinite and dazzling array of possibilities. Paradox queries allow you to specify which table or tables of data to work with, which field(s) to use or display, which record(s) to use or look at, what calculation(s) to perform, and what to do with the results. Paradox queries can extract and calculate with values from tables or elsewhere, or can act right on values in the table itself. For this reason, queries can be used in a wide variety of ways to support a large number of different tasks in an application.

However, many of these tasks will involve that process of re-combining the data which was relationally isolated into separate tables. These recombinations will, in those cases, be directly driven by the relationships established by the database design. Those common columns that you established through the design process will be the columns which are used to extract and work with data from multiple related tables. Query templates are intended to reflect the nature of those database-design-driven relationships. In most databases, the number of actual relationships are fairly limited. The same set of data is used in the context of many different tasks. The query template simply eases the repetitive nature of those tasks by giving an interactive (even sometimes a programming) user of Paradox a head start on each task.

Like the template shown in FIG. 9-21, most templates are essentially empty query forms which simply define the links between tables. These forms will include any example elements which are necessary to combine data from the different query tables based upon the database design.

query template   A saved file which records the relationships between tables frequently used in combination.

A query template can be easily built by first bringing all the necessary related tables to the Desktop/Workspace. Templates can include two, three or more tables, and are entirely dependent on the tasks which an application is required to support.

Building query templates

Once the query forms are all available on the Desktop/Workspace, you can link them as you normally would, by moving into the appropriate field, pressing the F5 Example key and then typing in the connecting example element name. Examples must be defined on both sides of the link (see FIG. 9-21). You might want to make the template an inclusive join, which would simply ensure that no matter what the relationship, you would still get any available data which met the specified criteria (see FIG. 9-22). The inclusive join operator can be used on one or both sides of a link in order to force inclusion of all criteria-meeting values from the specified table without regard for any potential relationship to the other table.

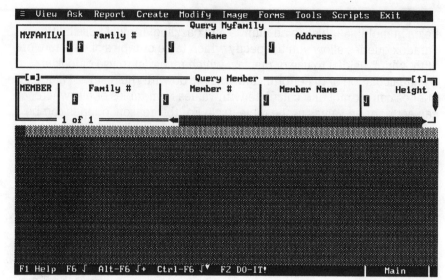

9-21
A query template

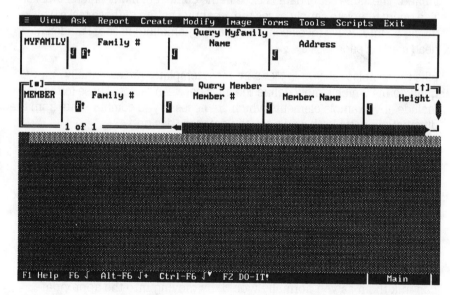

9-22
A query template with inclusive join

A template will usually not include any check marks, nor will it include any criteria. Selection of data is reserved until the template is actually used.

Normally, a query template is stored by using Scripts|Query|Save. With the query on the Desktop, you simply select Scripts|Query|Save and then type in the name of the script you want to save the query into. As a convention, you might consider naming all scripts which contain saved queries with a prefix of *q* (e.g., q__new, q__y&n, etc.).

From a database design perspective, it makes sense to build templates for the ordinary combinations of data which the tasks you perform require. This will help prevent users from forgetting links, or from attempting to create links in a query which are not supported by the database design.

Once the query has been saved, selecting `Scripts|Play` and typing in or selecting your querysave file name will bring up the template file. This quick and easy access will immediately give you a jump-start on getting the information you need and must rely upon.

Using query templates

In this chapter you have encountered techniques for implementing your database design in Paradox. These included the following pointers:

Summary

- It is important to keeping the big picture perspective throughout your implementation process so as to protect your time investment.
- You can systematically move through table creation and into building validity checks for each table.
- Validity checks in Paradox do not support and enforce data integrity as much as they assist in the data entry and modification process.
- Valchecks can be applied to support the data entry process in several areas, including Paradox 4.0's new `Autoconfirm` check for moving the cursor forward automatically.
- PAL can be used to also enhance data integrity as well as assist the data entry process by handling key violations, autonumbering, specialized business rules, and by enforcing default and required circumstances.
- A data dictionary supports the documentation of table structures and can be built with or without the assistance of PAL.
- Password protection can be an important feature of your data integrity plan and can be created and maintained through interactive Paradox.
- Query templates are important in assisting users take advantage of relationships through Paradox's QBE.

autonumbering   Automatic creation of sequential numbers for key values in new records.

Key Terms

data dictionary   A file which provides a listing of data structures and their associated integrity restrictions; in Paradox, normally a table which stores table and field names along with descriptions of contents and applicable validity checks.

password   A series of characters used to control access to a resource; in Paradox, a key word or phrase which can be up to 15 characters in length (including spaces) and in which upper- and lowercase characters are distinguishable.

query template   A saved file which records the relationships between tables frequently used in combination.

validity check   Also called valcheck. Paradox-specific mechanism for supporting the data entry and modification process as it occurs through keyboard entry.

10 Look & feel: Issues of form design

From the beginning of this database design process, it has been stressed that the way you logically store your data and the techniques you employ to use it probably will vary dramatically. The issues involved are quite different: as a user who works directly with creating input and evaluating output, you need to be able to use the information that is available to you without going through a lot of hoops before you can understand it; but, as a computer system (on the other side) the RDBMS needs to have specific and secure access to data, which is provided through the relational database design.

In essence, the rules you apply to information differ from those you apply to data. Thus, when you think about data, you think about database design; but when you think about information, you think about input design (forms) and output design (reports, graphs, etc.).

Information guidelines

In a fully relational database world, forms and reports would be easily created based upon either single tables or conceptual (multiple table) views which would be used to pull together all the data which is necessary for a particular task. Paradox is not fully relational, however, and pulling data together is not always as simple as viewing one or even multiple tables. The first requirement for building a Paradox form or report is that one table must be chosen to *drive* the form or report: any form or report object is associated with only one table, and even a linked-together multiple table object is still a member of only one table's family.

Remember, however, that in a relational database related data is found within multiple tables, and thus important forms and reports will need to be based on multiple tables. Paradox does provide mechanisms for combining data from multiple tables in both forms and reports; however, those mechanisms are dependent on the structures of the tables which you intend to combine, and (without planning) will in many cases be inadequate to support your needs.

The bottom line: in order to make a database usable, the database design must be implemented in a way that allows users to get at the data they need. Figure 10-1 describes the process by which you progressively isolate the data elements into relational tables (database design), then proceed to reconstruct related data into useful data sets (form and report development).

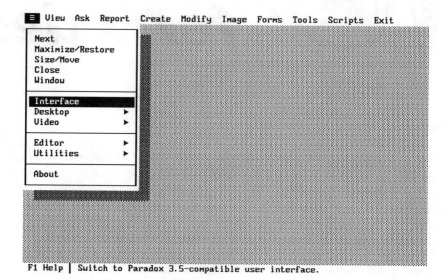

10-1
Selecting Compatible
from the System menu

Information to data to information

The tasks your application will do have driven the database design from the beginning. Refer to Table 4-1 in which the info elements for each application task are described. This early step in the database design process was supported by the list of tasks; this list is what enabled you to determine what your data requirements were. Data requirements were extracted directly from these info elements through further analysis as they were broken down into specific tables and fields.

Each task, however, was supported by some set of info elements which might or might not have ended up as fields within a single table. In order to accomplish the task, you therefore ensure that you can bring the data back together. For example, to support the modification of a daily schedule for the RTS case study, you must be able to include the appointment time(s) as well as information about each scheduled client (found in the Client, Appointment, and Appointment Service tables).

Table 10-1
Initial Form Design Requirements
for RTS: Update Schedule Task.

Table	Field
Appointment	Appointment date
	Appointment time
	Client ID
	Service Code
Appointment Service	Type of Service
Client	Client Name

This task, which includes data from three tables, could be accomplished by progressively making changes to three tables, one at a time (if necessary). However, that would be slow and complicated, and would run contrary to the primary goal of the application: it would be counterintuitive from the user's point of view. Practically speaking, the user regards the update of the schedule as one task, not three—and this is true regardless of how the database has been designed or implemented. A form is simply a way to get access to the appropriate data on screen in a usable format, regardless of how the data is actually stored. A form can enable a three-step task to occur in one step by acting as the glue to bring the three divergent data sets together.

A form is a "window[1]" on the data in a table or tables, and ordinarily can be used either just to look in at the data or to actually reach in and change the data. Paradox forms can thus be used in more than one mode (Main/View, Edit, CoEdit, or DataEntry). Paradox supports inclusion from data in multiple tables on both forms and reports. Multitable forms and multitable reports are, in fact, two of the four relational features which empower the Paradox user beyond the capabilities of many competing products. These features are what make it possible to accomplish a task like updating a schedule in one step, rather than the three outlined earlier. To accomplish that task, you must design and build a Paradox form which would allow you access to all three tables.

Designing a form involves more than simply determining what table(s) the data is to be drawn from; it involves a series of steps which will help ensure that the resulting form will meet its primary purpose: to support you in accomplishing a particular task. Those form design steps are addressed in some detail later in this chapter.

Before working through the steps of form design and implementation, it is important to take a look at the context of a form. At this point in your development process, the database is realized to some degree—you have built tables, applied valchecks, perhaps built some PAL scripts to support you in

*The look & feel
of an application*

• • • • • • • • •

[1] Not to be confused with a Paradox 4.0 screen window, which might contain a Form image of a table or might not.

data integrity. You are beginning to work with actual data—and you will quickly recognize the fact that Paradox itself has an impact on that data. You know what the Paradox interface (often called UI, or user interface) looks like. You are familiar with Paradox menus, either "ring" style (3.5) or pulldown (4.0), and you know how the color scheme acts (changes to identify what is current or selected, etc.). This is sometimes called a *look* because it is the outward appearance of Paradox, having little to do with what actually goes on inside.

You also know how to communicate with Paradox. You can make menu choices with your keyboard (cursor keys and Enter, or initial letter keypress) or with your mouse (move and click). You might know that you can bypass the menus entirely with certain Function keystrokes (i.e., F7 rather than F10|Image|PickForm), or through Alt|F10|MiniScript. When you do any of these things, Paradox responds in a consistent way, with similar colors, typefaces, messages, etc. This is sometimes called a *feel* because it has to do with what you as a user react to in the software. You could describe a stuffed animal as soft (a feel), but you can make this assessment only because you've touched it. Feel is a tactile description; you must actually work with an application to assess it.

Both the look and the feel of Paradox's UI have changed dramatically between versions 3.5 and 4.0, but each still is internally consistent (you always see either 3.5 or 4.0, but not both at the same time).

look   A subjective description of how an application appears on screen.
feel   A subjective, tactile description of how you and an application interact.

It is possible to use Paradox to build an application which looks completely unlike "native" Paradox (the software as it loads up directly out of the box). PAL provides the tools necessary to modify most aspects of what a user can see on screen. However, some customization is easy while some is quite difficult and time-consuming to implement. In any case, there are a number of decisions an application developer must make before moving forward past the basic building of the database structures.

Maintaining consistency with Paradox

One of your first decisions must address whether or not to make the application look like Paradox itself. This might seem like a strange issue, but it is crucial in determining how to go about implementing the application. An application which shares Paradox's look and feel is normally much easier to develop than one which differs in any substantive way from Paradox. Consistency with Paradox's look and feel has many advantages. Chief among them is the fact that a user who knows anything about Paradox will also (by default) know something about how your application works. This is particularly important in determining how particular keystrokes will work (seriously at issue in working with PAL), but is also important in designing the look of your application. Some components to consider in deciding on a look and feel are:

- Screen and object colors
- Display fonts
- Menu style
- Speedbar and prompting
- Messaging
- Type of windowing
- Function keys/quick keys

If you want all the applications you develop to differ from the way Paradox normally looks, you have several options. First, if you use Paradox 4.0 you might choose to run in Compatible mode rather than the Standard 4.0 mode. Compatible mode will allow you to utilize the UI from Paradox 3.5. You can change from Standard to Compatible mode by selecting Interface|Yes from the System menu (see FIG. 10-2). It is important to make this choice with an empty desktop, since Paradox will automatically clear the desktop and close all open windows when you make the change.

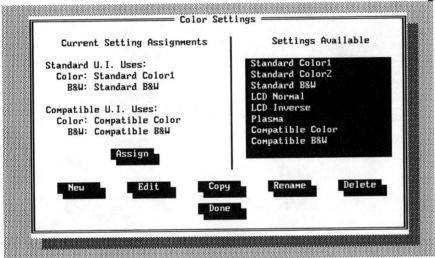

10-2
Paradox 4.0 color settings box in the CCP

You also can utilize a special script called the Custom Configuration Program (CCP) to change the look of Paradox. CCP is found in the subdirectory where the Paradox system files are located (e.g., C:\pdox40), and you Scripts|Play it like any other script. CCP can be used to change colors in every area of Paradox (including the Form Designer)[2], as well as to modify many other Paradox defaults.

•••••••••

[2] CCP can also be used to change a variety of other parameters involved with using Paradox, including machine information, report defaults (including printer setups), graph defaults, data formatting defaults, network information, PAL usage options, and ASCII file delimiter and separator choices.

CCP Paradox's Custom Configuration Program, which can be used to define Paradox defaults for use in interactive Paradox, PAL, the Form and Report Generators, and elsewhere.

To use CCP to change the colors, you first must define a color setting (which would be a New setting the first time around), and then apply this color setting to either the Standard or Compatible user interface. Figure 10-3 displays the 4.0 Color Settings dialog box (see also pp. 148-158 in the Paradox 4.0 Getting Started manual).

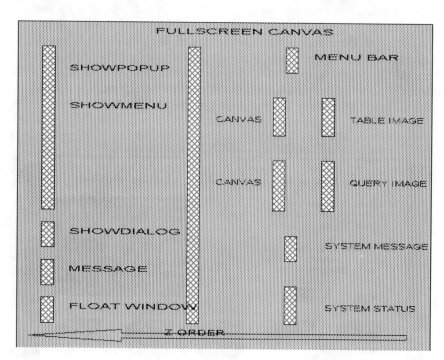

10-3
Paradox layers on the screen (p. 180 PAL Prog Guide)

What color settings are

It is important to recognize that defining color in any context involves not one but two choices: foreground (the color of text or characters displayed on screen) and background (the color of everything else). It is the combination of foreground and background which is considered a single color. Selecting a color through CCP or in the Form Designer involves two choices: picking the foreground (normally moving around the color palette in the horizontal direction) and picking the background (moving around the palette in the vertical direction).

When you control look & feel

If you intend to work with Paradox simply as an interactive user, and will never be building an application run by or using a script, your choices for look and feel will be restricted to the "look" choices and will be tied to form and desktop design. You will be able to control what you see both by building forms for use with table and query images and by designing ways to use those forms on the desktop.

If, however, you will be developing a complete application, including PAL scripts and/or procedures, you will need to consider an additional layer of complexity. The use of a script makes the canvas available. The canvas is a "shield" which drops down in front of the workspace (3.5) or current (or specified) window on the desktop (4.0) when you play a script (see FIG. 10-4). This adds a third dimension (known as the Z dimension, or *Z-order*) to the first two dimensions of the screen (horizontal and vertical, or X and Y). Designing and controlling what a user sees in a windowing environment such as Paradox 4.0 is a much more complex challenge than that posed by nonwindowing Paradox 3.5, and most of the challenges lie beyond the scope of this book.

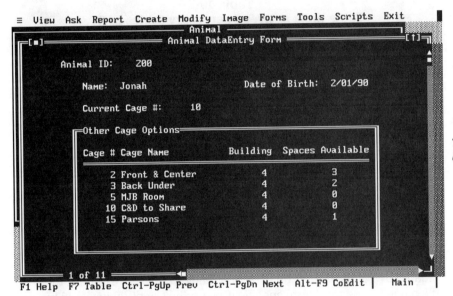

10-4
Unlinked multi-table form

There are several steps involved in designing and building a form in Paradox. They include:

- Identifying the form's purpose
- Determining the data requirements
- Planning field labels, titles, and user information to be included
- Considering the context for the form
- Planning colors and other display attributes
- Building the form

An overview of form design

The purpose of the form should always match the task it is intended to support. Updating a schedule for RTS would involve the design of a specific form whose purpose was to assist in accomplishing that goal. The purpose of the form is very useful in deciding on a title. A form title can be displayed on the form itself, as the title for a window on the desktop, or in the description of the form object used whenever the form number appears on a list of available forms. Remember, all the decisions

Identifying the form's purpose

you make during the entire form design process should be in response to the purpose of the form.

Determining the data requirements

Once you have identified the intent of the form, you should be able to determine what data is necessary to support the purpose. Again, this was answered through an earlier phase in database design (see Table 4-1). Take a look at the info elements, and determine which field(s) were created to support those elements. See Table 10-1 for an example of a preliminary form design document for the RTS application update schedule task. The first and most important question to ask is which table(s) now contain the specified fields.

Table 10-2
Table links between necessary tables in RTS.

Tables	Link
Appointment->Appointment Service	Service Code
Appointment->Client	Client ID

Single- versus multitable forms

If data from what is now a single table has been included, the form will be a single-table form and will be based on (driven by) the table which contains that data. If data from multiple tables is included, the form will need to be designed as a multitable form, with its particular rules and restrictions.

Single table forms are based on one table, and are designed as objects which are members of that table's family. There are up to 15 form "slots" available for each table. Each form is named with an extension beginning with the letter *F*, and extend from the simple form F (the standard form, created by Paradox) through F1 sequentially to F14. For example, the DOS file name for the third form specification on the Client table would be Client.F3.

Multitable forms are based on more than one table, and fall into two categories. Unlinked multitable forms include data from more than one table, but the data as displayed exploits no relationships between the multiple tables. You can create unlinked multitable forms which display data from any combination of tables (see FIG. 10-5).

Linked multitable forms are designed to exploit a defined relationship between two or more tables. When defining a form as multitable, Paradox helps you to identify the common column which defines the relationship between the tables. Once defined, the values in this common column control what is displayed on all parts of the form. For example, if a multitable form is used to support the RTS task, the one-to-many relationship between Appointment Service and Appointment might be exploited, and the one-to-many relationship between Client and Appointment might also be useful.

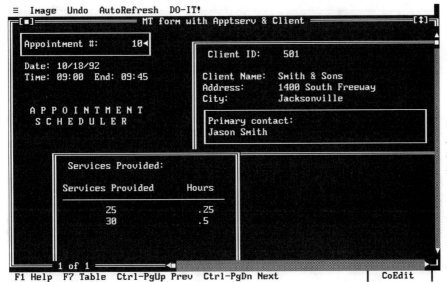

```
╒═[■]══════════════ MT form with Apptserv & Client ═══════════════[‡]╕
│ ┌─────────────────────┐                                           │
│ │ Appointment #:    10◄│                                          │
│ └─────────────────────┘   ┌──────────────────────────────────┐   │
│ Date: 10/18/92            │  Client ID:     501               │   │
│ Time: 09:00  End: 09:45   │                                   │   │
│                           │  Client Name:   Smith & Sons      │   │
│                           │  Address:       1400 South Freeway│   │
│ A P P O I N T M E N T     │  City:          Jacksonville      │   │
│ S C H E D U L E R         │  ┌───────────────────────────────┐│   │
│                           │  │ Primary contact:              ││   │
│                           │  │ Jason Smith                   ││   │
│                           │  └───────────────────────────────┘│   │
│    ┌──────────────────────┴───────┬────────────────────────────┐ │
│    │ Services Provided:           │                            │ │
│    │                              │                            │ │
│    │ Services Provided    Hours   │                            │ │
│    │                              │                            │ │
│    │        25            .25     │                            │ │
│    │        30            .5      │                            │ │
│    │                              │                            │ │
│  ═ 1 of 1 ═                       │                            │ │
╘════════════════════════════════════════════════════════════════╛
 F1 Help  F7 Table  Ctrl-PgUp Prev  Ctrl-PgDn Next   │  CoEdit  │
```

10-5
Linked RTS form for Appt->ApptServ and Appt->Client

There are limitations to Paradox's (linked) multitable form capability, however. These include the following facts:

- All tables must be linked to one master table.
- Each link must be based on the key field(s) from the linked table (so any linked table must be keyed).
- The master table is often the "one" side of any one-to-many link, but can also reflect either the "one" side of a one-to-one or the "many" side of a many-to-one relationship.
- The multitable form relationships are defined on the master table form.

In the RTS example, there are two relationships involved. The one table which is related to both other tables is the Appointment table. If your goal was to have all three tables represented, and linked, you would need to design the table on the Appointment table (this would be the master) and the other two tables would be linked in through their common columns (see FIG. 10 6). Linked tables are called *embedded* or *detail* tables in Paradox terminology.

embedded table A table which is contained within the definition of a multitable form and which can include either linked or unlinked records relative to the master table.

detail table A table which is contained within the definition of a multitable form and which includes records related to the master table records based upon the key field values in the detail table.

Beyond the need to have all tables related to a single master table, Paradox also requires that the relationships used be based on key values. That is, each relationship utilized must exist between a foreign key on the master side and a primary key on the embedded side (see Table 10-3 for the RTS example). In

Required key relationships

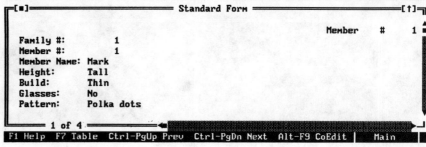

10-6
Field labels on a Paradox standard form

this example, that would work without a hitch. In some cases, however, the need for developing a multitable form might change the database design; you can choose to organize links between tables differently in order to support Paradox's multitable form feature. See chapter 11 for a discussion on modifying the database design to support either forms or reports.

Let's take a look at the relationships once again, from the perspective of the multitable form. This form will be driven by the Appointment table (FIG. 10-7). That means that the data available from the Appointment Service table and the Client table are only accessible relative to a specific appointment. If, for example, you wanted to look at all appointments for one particular client, this form would not serve your purpose. Or, if you wanted to look at all appointments for which a lab test was required, this form would also not do the job.

This form as designed is exploiting two many-to-one relationships (called *many-to-one* because the "many" side is driving the form). If you had intended to be able to update appointments from the client's perspective, you might want to show all scheduled appointments for a specified client (to look at the data from the one-to-many perspective, with the "one" side driving the form). In this case, you would be unable to include any fields from the

Table 10-3
Necessary key relationships between tables in RTS.

Tables	Link	Key Required
Appt->ApptServ	Service Code	Service Code in ApptServ
Appt->Client	Client	Client ID in Client

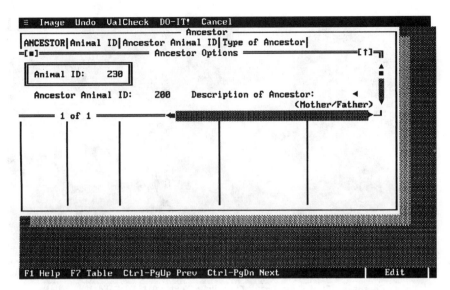

```
 ≡  Image  Undo  ValCheck  DO-IT!  Cancel
                           ─── Ancestor ───
 |ANCESTOR|Animal ID|Ancestor Animal ID|Type of Ancestor|
 ═[■]════════════════ Ancestor Options ══════════════[↑]╗
                                                        █
 ┌─────────────────────┐                                █
 │ Animal ID:     230  │                                █
 └─────────────────────┘                                ▓
                                                        ▓
    Ancestor Animal ID:    200    Description of Ancestor:  ◄  ▓
                                          (Mother/Father)      ▓
   ═════ 1 of 1 ═════           ◄─███████████████████████████▓
```

10-7
Case study #3 form with Ancestor Type options

```
 F1 Help  F7 Table  Ctrl-PgUp Prev  Ctrl-PgDn Next          | Edit |
```

Appointment Service table, since this table does not relate directly to the Client table (see FIG. 10-6).

However, when building a form from the "one" side of a one-to-many relationship, Paradox provides an extremely useful feature which enables more than one of the linked records to appear on the form at one time. A multirecord form can be utilized which would (in this case) display multiple records of data from the Appointment table (the "many"), all at the same time[3].

Planning field labels, titles, & user information

Once you have decided on the fields of data required, you can begin to organize them for their on-screen display. Normally each field's position will be preceded by a descriptive field label which identifies what is found in the field itself. Paradox's standard form uses the field name as the label for each field (see FIG. 10-8), but you are not restricted to that choice. You might want to expand on the description of the field, providing additional details as to your expectations of what value is appropriately found there; or you can choose to abbreviate the field name to conserve space on the screen. You can even choose to omit a field label altogether; although this is only advisable when what belongs in the field is indisputable based on context (e.g., a City field which is preceded by an Address field and followed by State and Zip Code fields). Regardless of the form's usage, the goal of any field label should be to support the user in understanding what any value in that labeled field actually represents.

This should also be the goal of any titles used on the form. It is often helpful to give the entire form a title which supports the user in understanding the

• • • • • • • • •

[3] Multirecord forms can be built which are not multitable. In this context, the multirecord form is much like a customized tabular view of the data.

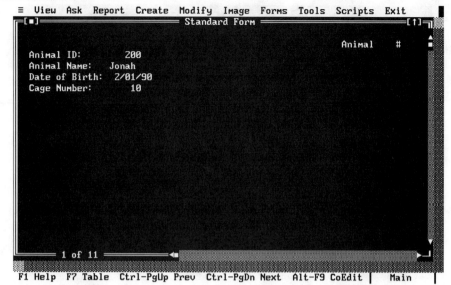

10-8
A standard form

intended usage of the form. If, for example, the form is to be used to update the appointment schedule, it might be helpful to a user to see the title "Appointment Updates" in a prominent position on the form. Depending on space requirements, you might even want the title to occupy more space than normally filled by a single-line, ordinary font display of the name. In that case you could utilize any text editor to create a special title with ASCII characters, save the lines of text into an array, and essentially "dump" the title onto the form by using the TYPEIN command. A simple version of this technique is demonstrated through the PAL code found in FIG. 10-9.

10-9
The Form Design screen

Your users might need information about the form and its intended usage which is not easily provided either through field labels or titles. You should consider using the screen to creatively display details about your business rules, validity checks, or other data attributes about which you want to inform the user. If you have, for example, included a validity check which allows only two values (Mother, Father) for your Description of Ancestor field (MH case study #3), you might want to put those choices right on your form. Type this user information directly beneath or to the side of the field.

One of the changes in the Paradox UI between versions 3.5 and 4.0 involves the new support for windowing. Allowing windows of activity dramatically changes the way a user actually sees a form. In Paradox 3.5, a form by definition occupies the entire available screen (82 columns by 25 rows); in 4.0 a form occupies a single window, which might or might not be maximized to fill the entire screen. You can layer, or cascade, multiple forms one on top of the other, or tile them to appear as discrete areas of the screen at the same time. This new flexibility should make a form designer reconsider some basic attributes of the forms he now can create.

Considering the context for the form

In particular, if support for use of multiple forms at the same time is important, the designer should make sure to reduce the area of screen utilized by each form in order to support either cascading or tiling which doesn't cut off essential data from display or access. Scroll bars which support the user in moving from currently displayed areas of a window to areas which are offscreen can be helpful, but are not nearly as easy to use as a entire form which fits neatly into its window within the limits of the space available.

In addition to space considerations, a form designer must develop an awareness of how color can impact the user. Color choices can be difficult, especially if you are new to the use of a color palette and feel somewhat overwhelmed by the number of available color combinations (128). Don't despair—there aren't that many viable color options. Few color choices create a screen display that is both readable and nondistracting. These combinations include:

Planning colors & other display attributes

- White on blue
- White on red
- White on gray
- Light blue or cyan on blue
- Light blue or cyan on red
- Light blue or cyan on gray
- Gray on white
- Gray on red
- Gray on blue
- Black on white
- Blue on white
- Red on white
- Red on blue (for small areas)

The unusual combinations (orange on black, hot pink on yellow, etc.) might be appealing or flashy in the short term, but they quickly wear out their welcome. You'll be much better off in the long term staying with the tried and true combinations.

You can, however, assign meaning to color. Color can be a very effective tool in communicating certain expectations to a user. For example, you can choose to highlight all key fields by coloring them white-on-red. You can also utilize other customized aspects of a form design to communicate with a user. Paradox supports three monochrome display attributes, which can be used in either color or monochrome systems. You can choose to display any part of your form in reverse video, intense, or blinking. Any of these can serve to draw your user's eye to important information: toward a field which must be filled in, onto instructions which detail what she should do next, or toward a list of available keystrokes.

Paradox also provides a bordering tool in the Forms Designer which can be used to surround any area of the form (or the entire form) with a border. Borders can be single-line, double-line, or composed of any ASCII character, including extended ASCII. Borders can be another effective way of communicating with your user.

Building the form

Once your design is complete, you can use Paradox to quickly implement the form. The Form Designer provides numerous tools for placing fields, creating field labels and titles, assigning color attributes, drawing borders, and linking tables together. Chapter 16 of the Paradox 4.0 User's Guide provides excellent detail as to the available tools and guidance for how to use them.

If your form design requires you to include multiple tables on the form, you will need to follow several steps, some of which occur outside of the Form Designer.

- Identify the tables to be included (you should have already done this).
- Identify the master table (you should have already done this).
- Verify that the proper key relationships exist between master and tables to be embedded.
- Build one form per table to be embedded.
- Build one form for the master table, leaving space for the embedded form(s).
- Use Multi|Table|Linked to place each embedded form on the master.
- Position the embedded form in the appropriate place on the master.

Features of a linked multitable form

Although Paradox supports the inclusion of data from multiple tables on one form, integration of the tables is not complete. A multitable form is thus a slightly awkward melding of data from different sources. Each table must exist in its own separate area of the form, and you cannot move from area to area with simple cursor key movement (normally F3 or F4 is required). You cannot intersperse fields from one table among and between fields from another. As suggested, when you build the multitable form, you must first build the forms to be embedded (one per embedded table). So in fact a multitable form is more accurately a set of related forms, each of which is attached to its separate table.

It is the master table's form which provides the integration and defines the links[4]. In a way, the master table "owns" the linked embedded tables, and when the form is in use, actions taken on records in the master table "trickle down" into linked records in embedded tables. These effects occur in several ways:

- You can't delete a master record while linked, embedded (detail) records depend on it.
- Entering or making a change to a value in a master field automatically enters or changes matching field values in any detail table.
- You cannot enter values into a detail table while the linking field value is blank.
- Once you begin an Edit or DataEntry session, you cannot switch into or out of the form without first ending the Edit or DataEntry session (Paradox applies link locking to help keep the table relationships intact).
- Once you start CoEditing tables through the form, you can switch freely to and from table view for CoEdits of the master table, assuming you have first posted any changes made to the current record.

In order to support these effects, there are certain restrictions placed on forms intended to be linked together. You can ignore these restrictions when you build each separate form, but as soon as you attempt to link the forms together, Paradox checks them out and won't allow the link if any of the rules have been broken. In particular, a master table form:

- cannot be multirecord.
- can extend over multiple pages.
- should contain all linking fields.

A linked embedded table form:

- can be multirecord.
- cannot extend over multiple pages.
- cannot itself contain any embedded form (linked or unlinked).
- cannot contain any of the fields used to link it to the master form.

In this chapter, you focused on issues involved with designing Paradox forms. Specifically, you learned that:

- Tables need to be integrated through multitable forms and reports based on the tasks defined by the application.

Summary

----

[4] Paradox also supports Unlinked embedded tables. When tables are not linked, Paradox makes no effort to relate data between them; an unlinked embedded table acts in complete independence from the master.

- Form design is first based on the attributes of the user interface.
- You can change the Paradox interface either for all your sessions (through the Custom Configuration Program) or for any specific session.
- Color settings include two components: foreground and background.
- Designing and building a form involves several steps, each of which should be undertaken carefully and with forethought.
- Paradox forms can be based on data from one or multiple tables, as long as the multiple tables (when linked) meet required key relationships.
- Linked multitable forms must be related based on the key field(s) in the detail table.
- Forms should be designed to include not only data from fields in tables, but also field labels, titles, specific color attributes, monochrome attributes, and borders where appropriate.
- Most special features of a form can be customized to enhance communication with a user and encourage accurate and valid data entry and maintenance.
- Multitable forms include several restrictions which are intended to help support referential integrity when the form is in use.

Key Terms   **CCP**   Paradox's Custom Configuration Program, which can be used to define Paradox defaults for use in interactive Paradox, PAL, the Form and Report Generators, and elsewhere.

detail table   A table which is contained within the definition of a multitable form and which includes records related to the master table records based upon the key field(s) value(s) in the detail table.

embedded table   A table which is contained within the definition of a multitable form and which can include either linked or unlinked records relative to the master table.

feel   A subjective, tactile description of how you and an application interact.

look   A subjective description of how an application appears on screen.

11 *Getting it all out: Issues of output design*

Multitable forms are a crucial element in making Paradox function as a relational database, enabling the user to deal with data stored in multiple tables somewhat as if the data were contained within a single table. However, forms only support integration of the data on-screen. When an application requires the integrated data to be presented in some other fashion, including in printed format, as a DOS file, or in a more customized display to the screen, a report can often meet that need.

Paradox reports have their requirements and limitations just as do Paradox forms. It is important to review these requirements during the database design process, as they might cause you to make changes to your design. A design might be modified if there are output requirements that cannot be met directly by a fully relational design. Thus, it is important to touch briefly on some fundamentals of report design, particularly as they relate to multitable reporting.

Output is both a noun and a verb. In different contexts, it describes either the data being extracted from a DBMS (the report in my hand is output) or the process of data extraction itself (I am outputting this report). For the purposes of this discussion, output is used as a noun, and output design refers to the design process that results in a report or graph.

What output is

By now, when you think about database design you'll probably have a sense of great order: there are rules to follow and guidelines to meet, and there are methodologies that have been developed in order to facilitate the process. However, when you think about report design, you probably have a much more limited sense of the process. Output is controlled traditionally by the needs of the user, and by nature (at least in the PC world) is pretty free-form. In fact, one of the driving forces toward PCs and away from mainframe and minicomputer systems has always been the PC's ability to put reporting (output) power in the hands of users. The number of options—how they'll look, what they'll do—has always been limited only by the number of businesses and individuals who can dream them up.

In essence, output design is a relatively free-form creation of the frame for information of value. After all, output should be a delivery system for that information. One of the most important things to recognize about output design is that how the information is delivered (the appearance of the output—the data selected, organization, and overall look) is a crucial element in the design. Formats not only make users and readers more comfortable during a learning curve, but they also actually can have an impact on, or even slant, the information given. This is particularly true in the case of a graph, which is by nature a powerful decision-making tool. Graphs almost always display highly summarized data, and thus are more an argument about the data than a presentation of the data itself.

An overview of the output design process

The output design process is much like a condensed version of the application design process. Just as application development goes through the identification of requirements, design, building, testing, installation, training, and evaluation phases (as described earlier in FIG. 2-1), so the development of output goes through similar steps. The process generally covers the following steps, which in general parallel the development of a form:

1. Identify the purpose of the report or graph.
2. Determine the data requirements.
3. Plan field labels, titles, and user information to be included.
4. Organize the output.
5. Detail the appearance.
6. Build the report or graph specification.

Just as the database design process involves the requirements identification and design phases of application development, so the input and output design processes involve similar phases. Once the design has been created, you can take it and, using Paradox, build, test, install, train users, and evaluate it. Thus, these first five steps are independent of Paradox; you can apply these techniques to output design regardless of the RDBMS you use.

Identifying the purpose for the output

First you must ask: why do I need this output? Because need normally drives your development, the answer to the question probably is close at hand. However, sometimes in the application development process, you think or hear that a report or a graph of some sort is needed, although you've never answered the question of why. This happens with particular frequency during brainstorming: what if I had all this data? what would I do with it? If you cannot document (and verify) a need, not just a desire, you probably shouldn't be spending the time to pursue a solution to it.

You also need to get beyond the simple, probably general answer. Dig deeper to figure out specifically what you intend to do with the output. Will you be making a decision based on what you see in the report? Will you be asking for a raise based on the graph you have prepared? Will you be cutting off the credit of a customer based on what you read on page 2? The purpose should be more specific than a general "need to know." In fact, the very best reports and graphs work because they answer the most specific kind of question: they meet the requirement because it has been defined so exactly.

In fact, this detailed description of your purpose shouldn't just identify the format of the output; it should define it. In other words, you should select the output format (report or graph, and even the type of report or graph) based on the requirements, not the other way around. Different purposes are better served through a report output with its textual display, excellent at integrating a number of different values, than served by a graphic display, better at focusing attention on a very few, directly related values.

However, what is a good report or graph? What differentiates it in quality from other output? In a nutshell, the best output is one that gives you the information you need and only the information you need. In fact, one of the worst things that a report or graph can do is tell you too much. Too much information will always fog the issue (and unless that is your specific goal, you'd be better off avoiding the fog). As FIG. 11-1 suggests, the best, or ideal, output normally will be focused on its purpose (often indicated in the report title or graph heading) and will include only the data necessary to achieve its purpose. Relationships that you need to highlight to convey the information are marked clearly and even set apart in some way, if through nothing else than by being juxtaposed one next to the other. This makes for an uncluttered, simple, usually short output, and in the case of a graph, allows it to be understandable.

Many applications use just a few general-purpose reports or graphs to convey all the information of value in the system. You should consider whether this is truly cost-effective. If you can more specifically identify how the report or graph will be used, you can customize each output to its intended need, creating a different report or graph for each variation. This will reduce dramatically the time it takes to use the report—to achieve its intended purpose.

Once the purpose specifically has been identified, you can proceed by focusing on what data is necessary to convey the intended information. There are two dimensions to this: what fields contain the data and what records contain the data. Remember that data in a relational database always

Determining the data requirements

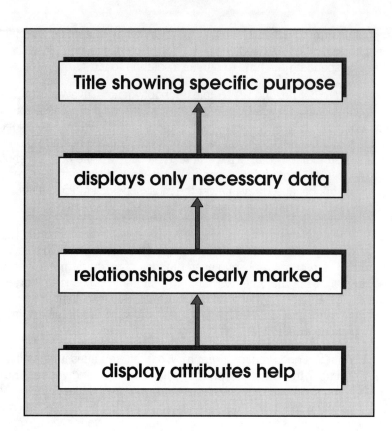

11-1
Optimal output focused on purpose with limited data (An ideal output will follow four specific guidelines)

is referenced by a combination of column and row position. Each value is found in the intersection of a column and row.

What table/fields contain the data

This is the normal focus of a report design, because the implementation of a design in any RDBMS requires the fields to be specified. If you need to figure out who in your Family database owns a blue car in order to send them a "Blue Car Owner's Newsletter," you'll need to know the name of that person and his or her address; you might also want to know what make and model of blue car it is that they own. So on your report design you'll need to specify name and address in some way. Figure 11-2 displays a report design relevant to this point.

Single- versus multitable graphs & reports

If the fields you need are found in one table, the graph or report will be a single-table report and will be based on, or driven by, the table which contains that data. If data from more than one table is included in a report, the report will need to be designed as a multitable report, with its particular rules and restrictions. Paradox does not support multitable graphs; any graph requiring data from more than one table must utilize a query to prepare the data first. Generally speaking, all graphs are preceded by a query anyway, since graphic data is normally highly summarized.

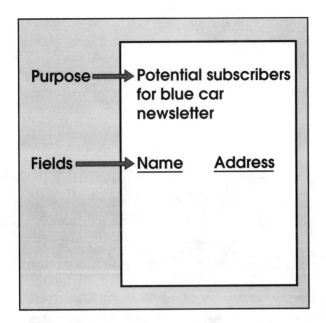

11-2
Report design specifying fields to be displayed (A report design under development)

Single table reports are based on one table, and like forms are designed as objects which are members of that table's family. There are up to 15 report "slots" available for each table. Each report is named with an extension beginning with the letter *R*, and extend from the simple R (the standard report, created by Paradox) through R1 sequentially to R14. For example, the DOS file name for the fourth report specification on the Client table would be Client.R4.

Multitable reports are based on more than one table, and include data which exploits a relationship between the tables. When defining a report as multitable, Paradox helps you to identify the common columns which define the relationship between the tables. Once defined, the values in these common columns control what is integrated as output. For example, if a multitable report is used to generate the RTS task of printing a daily schedule, the one-to-many relationship between Appointment Service and Appointment might be exploited, and the one-to-many relationship between Client and Appointment might also be useful.

Like those restrictions inherent in Paradox's multitable form capability, limitations to Paradox's multitable report capability exist as well. These include the following facts:

- All tables in the report must be linked to one master table.
- Each link must be based on the key field(s) from the linked table (so any linked table must be keyed).
- The master table is normally the "many" side of any one-to-many link but can also reflect either side of a one-to-one relationship.
- The multitable report relationships are defined on the master table form.

In the RTS example, there are two relationships involved. The one table which is related to both other tables is the Appointment table. If your goal was to have all three tables represented, and linked, you would need to design the report on the Appointment table (this would be the master) and the other two tables would be linked in through their common columns (see FIG. 11-3). Linked report tables are called *lookup tables* in Paradox terminology.

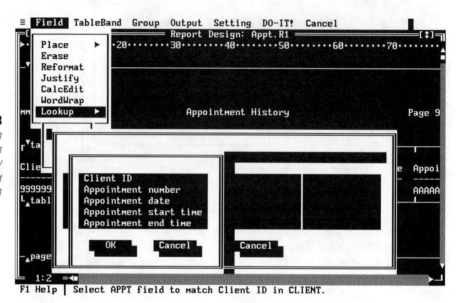

11-3
Report designed on Appointment table, with links utilized to ApptServ and to Client, including key relationships shown

lookup table   A table which is contained within the definition of a multitable report and which includes linked records relative to the master table, normally in a one-to-many relationship from the lookup table's perspective.

Required key relationships

Beyond the need to have all the lookup tables related to a single master table, Paradox also requires that all relationships used be based on key values. That is, each relationship utilized must exist between a foreign key on the master side and a primary key on the lookup side (refer to FIG. 11-3 for the RTS example). In this example, that will work without a problem. In some cases, however, the need for developing a multitable report might change the database design; you can choose to organize links between tables differently in order to support Paradox's multitable report feature (see the discussion later in this chapter on modifying the database design to support either forms or reports).

Let's take a look at the relationships once again, from the perspective of the multitable report. This report will be driven by the Appointment table; that means that the data available from the Appointment Service table and the Client table are only accessible relative to a specific appointment, which meets the requirements of this particular report. This report as designed is exploiting two many-to-one relationships (called "many-to-one" because the "many" side is driving the report).

In addition to the table/field specification, you need to consider whether or not you want to see every value in the table or tables, or if your output's purpose focuses on a specific selection of values. If there is a specific selection (or subset) required, make sure you indicate it in the report design (see FIG. 11-4). Again, this is an important technique for making a report or graph better—or more usable—by reducing the amount of information shown.

What records contain the data

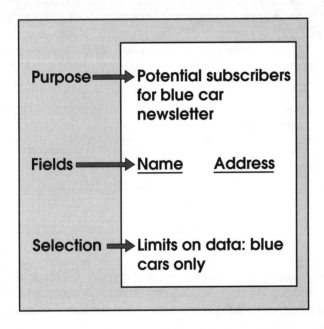

Purpose ➡ **Potential subscribers for blue car newsletter**

Fields ➡ **Name   Address**

Selection ➡ **Limits on data: blue cars only**

11-4
Documenting the report specifications

In fact, this is one area in which graphs can be more powerful than reports; graphs tend to demand reduction of information, fewer rather than more records for display. It is usually very obvious what a graph's purpose is: every report should have that same level of focus.

It is interesting to note that a well-focused graph is not usually described as organized. Because the information to be conveyed is presented in a format that reduces the pertinent facts to their most basic, you ordinarily don't look at the use of a graph as sequential, but as "one shot." In other words, you should be able to understand what the graph is saying within moments of looking at it. You ordinarily don't break a graph down into ordered, sequential facts. Even if there are several issues being covered, a graph usually allows you to review them as you need, partially because it is encompassed within a

Organizing the report with groups

single image, usually on a single page. However, this is also partly true because a graph already has selected the pertinent data for you and shows you only that. Don't be misled. Graphs must be organized, but at a different, lower level. A graph's organization usually focuses on the types of descriptive elements used, the graph values selected, and the order these appear on the axes or in the legend. In Paradox these elements include the field for values, the row and column labels, and the series (including their order).

Reports, on the other hand, tend to rely strongly on organization. When you look at a report, you expect to be led through the information in some kind of ordered fashion; if you need to find something specific within the body of the report, you expect to be able to do so quite readily. This kind of hand-holding is necessary because traditionally reports tend to tell you everything you ever wanted to know, and everything you never cared about, to begin with. Thus, the very best kind of organization comes through the identification of the purpose of the report. If the purpose is focused, the data will be restricted, and the need for organization will be minimized.

This said, the order in which data appears in a report is crucial and must be carefully planned. Order is provided in a report through some kind of sorting mechanism; a sort usually is based on a data value, and thus in your report design you must specify a *sort* by identifying which field contains that data value.

 sort The arrangement of values into a specified order, usually following the ASCII key-code order.

Many reports have so much data included that a single sort does not provide adequate organization. Thus, *multiple sorts* (also called *sort levels* or *breaks*) can be used. Multiple sorts usually are implemented using a technique called *nesting,* wherein the first sort happens first, then within the first sorted group the second sort takes place. These are sort levels because the first sort takes precedence over the second, which takes precedence over the third, etc.

Sorting by a value results in what is known as a grouping of data. For example, if you are sorting a text field you'll probably be expecting to see it in alphabetic order, and thus all the A's will be together, then the B's, then the C's, and so on. If the field you were sorting contained only a single letter (A or B or X or Z, for example), the sort would result in four groups of records: the A's would be together, the B's next, the X's next, and then the Z's. A group is a collection of records (such as each of these four) that all share a same quality, in this case, the same value in the sorted field.

If your report's purpose requires that you evaluate a variety of information, you will need to organize it adequately to meet that purpose, and your design will need to reflect that organization (see FIG. 11-5).

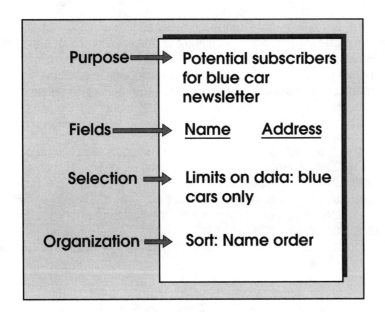

11-5
Documenting the report organization

Although the features of an output that identify its appearance might seem trivial, they often have a dramatic impact on how the output is received, and whether it is used to achieve its intended purpose. These features won't affect the essence of what is communicated, but they will help focus the user's attention on the priorities that you establish. You can look at these kind of decisions as being an extension of the organization of the output. You are attempting to control what the user looks at first (what is most important), and in so doing to affect their overall perception of the information. You can detail these choices in an output specification, or you can leave them to Paradox, which will then use its default values.[1] Appearance features to be addressed can include the following:

Detailing the appearance

- Fonts
- Spacing (single, double, extra spaces around totals, etc.)
- Break points
- Underscores
- Graph colors
- Graph fill patterns

The process of designing a graph can be quite a bit more challenging than that of creating a report design. In a way, the difference is like that between writing an abstract of an article and writing an editorial. An article abstract (like a report) is intended to reflect and summarize facts. An editorial, on the

Special concerns in conceptualizing a graph

• • • • • • • • •

[1] The Custom Configuration Program allows you to modify many default settings for reports and graphs, including report page length and width, left margin, printing configurations, and graph type, scales and divisions of axes, colors and patterns, titles and labels, and where graph output should go.

other hand, is (like a graph) intended to make an argument, to interpret the facts for a particular purpose. It is difficult to prepare a "neutral" graph, since by its nature, a highly summarized presentation of data is dependent on the assumptions made during the summarization process. In addition, a graph relies on many more presentation or appearance-detailing decisions, each of which can dramatically influence what is perceived as the message behind the graph.

For example, if a graph is intended to provide a comparison of total invoiced amounts by client, the scale at which the Y-axis is drawn can change the suggested conclusions. As demonstrated by FIGS. 11-6 and 11-7, manipulating the Y-axis can either emphasize or de-emphasize the differences between clients, arguing for either equal activity among clients or heavy activity for one client. Knowing what argument the graph is intended to support is essential in making final decisions as to all of the graph specification values.

11-6
Total invoiced amount by client graph (equal activity shown)

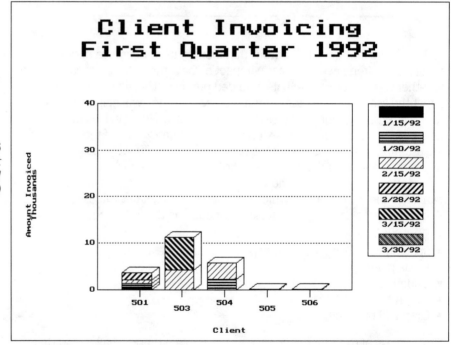

Building a graph

Once you do know what you want to argue, the creation of a graph occurs in two steps:

1. Preparation of the data
2. Development of the graph specification

Preparation of graph data

Because graphs work best with very small sets of data, normally you will need to summarize the data through a query. In the example used here, two

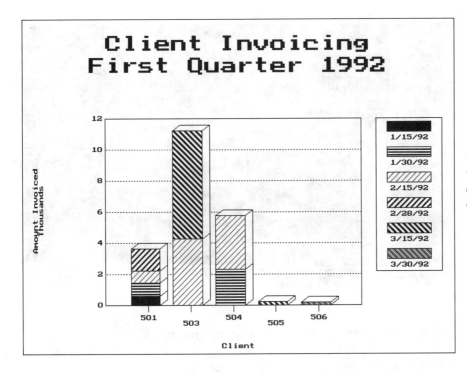

11-7
Total invoiced amount by client graph (disparate activity shown)

tables must be drawn together through a query in order to determine invoice amounts per client by month (see FIG. 11-8). Once the first summary has occurred, the result must be crosstabbed to get a table which can be easily graphed (see FIG. 11-9). The result of the crosstabulation (the crosstab table)

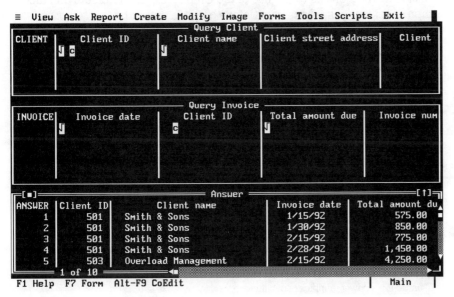

11-8
Query for invoiced amounts per client by billing cycle

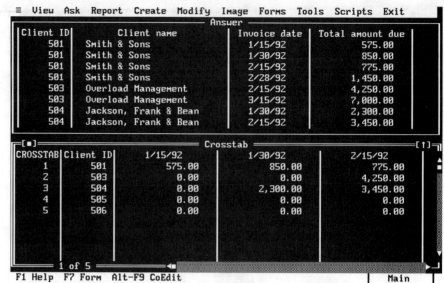

11-9
Crosstab to prepare for a graph

can then be graphed using the quick key combination (Ctrl-F6) or `Image|Graph|ViewGraph`. What displays (without further development) is the data through the default graph specification.

Development of the graph specification

Normally, the default is inadequate to support a graph for output. You must follow the development of your query/crosstabs with the building of a graph specification, which primarily involves modifying the default specifications to meet your requirements. Chapter 14 of the Paradox 4.0 User's Guide provides detailed instructions as to the use of the Graph Designer to create and modify graph specifications.[2] Once complete, a graph is output by:

1. Making the graph specification current (loading it)
2. Running the query/crosstabs to prepare the data
3. Generating the graph through Ctrl-F6 or `ViewGraph`

Building the report

Once your conceptual report design is complete, you can use Paradox to quickly implement the report. The Report Designer provides numerous tools for placing fields, creating field labels and titles, assigning output attributes, drawing borders, and linking tables together. Chapter 8 of the Paradox 4.0 User's Guide provides excellent detail as to the available tools and guidance for how to use them.

• • • • • • • • •

[2] Paradox also supports interoperability with Quattro Pro, which provides many more sophisticated graphic capabilities. If your system has enough memory to load both software packages concurrently, you can move back and forth between them with a simple Ctrl-F10 hotkey, which allows you to store and manage data in Paradox while taking advantage of Quattro Pro's power graphics capabilities.

If your report design requires you to include multiple tables on the report, you will need to follow several steps:

1. Identify the tables to be included (you should have already done this).
2. Identify the master table (you should have already done this).
3. Verify that the proper key relationships exist between master and lookup table(s).
4. `Report|Design` the report on the master table.
5. Use `Field|Lookup|Link` to define the lookup table as part of the report specification.
6. Use fields from the lookup table in any way you require, including as fields to group by, to place in the table band or any other band, to summarize, or to calculate with.

Features of a multitable report

Paradox supports the inclusion of data from multiple tables on one report, and (unlike within a multitable form) integration of the tables in a multitable report is very complete. A multitable report can thus be an elegant integration of data from different sources. You can intersperse fields from one table among and between fields from another. You can group by, summarize and calculate with lookup fields exactly as if they were in the master table itself.

The only limitation in utilizing the Report Designer to create multitable reports is in the limited type of relationships which can be exploited through the report. The Report Designer works wonderfully when the relationships involved all revolve around a single table, normally with several one-to-many relationships all looking up to the "one" side. However, more complicated relationships, such as nested one-to-many relationships between three tables (sometimes called *one-to-many-to-many*) are not supported. If your report requires this (or any other nonsupported) kind of relationship, you must first preprocess the data through a query, which is of course a powerful tool for combining data, and which has no restrictions as to key requirements for exploiting defined relationships.

This is less of a problem than you might expect, since data for reporting must commonly be preprocessed through a query for other reasons. Specifically, whenever a report is intended to output on a subset of a table (only some of the records, not all), a query is necessary in order to extract the needed records. In this case, using the query to prepare the appropriate fields is little added burden, and might even speed up the process of preparing the report.

You also have the option of programming the entire report through PAL, using various table manipulation commands and functions along with the `PRINT` command. This has the advantage in that you can create just about any conceivable output format without regard for the standards imposed through the Report Designer. The down side of programming an entire report, though, can be substantial; you have to control every aspect of the output process, from preparing the printer's setup strings, managing the length and width of the page, to calculating when pagination should occur, page numbering, subtotalling, etc.

Comparing form & report requirements

In many ways, forms and reports are conceptually the same. Both are created as ways to get at data. Not surprisingly, forms and report specifications share many common features, including field placements, field labels, and the integration of fields from more than one table.

Paradox multitable forms and multitable reports, however, approach the integration of data from multiple tables from completely opposite perspectives. To return to the RTS appointment schedule example: the form and report utilized the same relationships, but to completely different effect. The Appointment table was the master table in both contexts, but the relationships were exploited in two very different ways. As FIG. 11-10 suggests, reports (designed on the "many" side of a one-to-many relationship) and forms (designed on the "one" side of a one-to-many relationship) have opposite key requirements. What does this mean from a database design perspective? Often, it means that your key order must be determined by one or the other requirement (that of the form or that of the report), and not both. Normally, when a conflict such as this occurs, it is important to support the requirements of the multitable form, since the form can and should provide support for relational integrity. You always have choices in preparing a report output (specifically, you can always prepare a query first, and often without even slowing down your performance); you do not always have choices when it comes to data entry or data modification. Figure 11-11 provides another look at the problem of form vs. report key requirements. In this example, the requirements for preparing a multitable form and multitable report for MH case study #3 are examined.

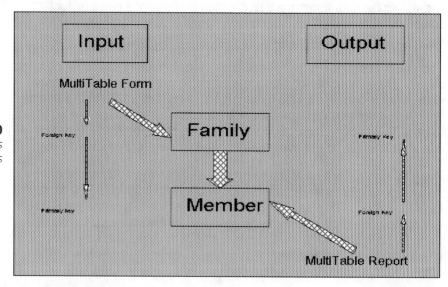

11-10
Opposite key requirements for reports and forms

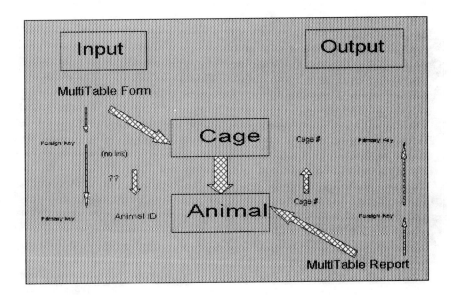

11-11
MH case study #3 requirements for reports and forms

If changes to the database structure are required once the tables have been created (and perhaps even after data has been entered), these changes can be made through the Modify|Restructure option on Paradox's main menu.

Before restructuring a table, it is essential that you make a backup copy of it. Use Tools|Copy|Table to make a copy of both the table and its family. Copy the table to a different name in the same subdirectory, or use the same name and copy the table into a different disk or subdirectory. In any case, backing it up first will protect you in case you make an inadvertent error during the restructure process. It is important to note that, once completed, restructuring cannot be undone.[3]

Selecting Modify|Restructure and entering the name of the table you intend to change will bring up the Restructure screen which is very similar to the Create screen (see FIG. 11-12).[4] You can add new fields, delete existing fields, rename or reorder current fields, change field types and lengths, and change key field designations. In this example, you will need to restructure in order to support preparation of the multitable form required by MH case

Modifying the database design

• • • • • • • • •

3 Corrupted tables from a variety of causes can sometimes be rebuilt with the use of the Tutility program. This .exe file, found in the Utility subdirectory of the Install disk, can be used to rebuild tables and table objects (including forms and reports) which have experienced problems.

4 Restructuring is used for more than making changes to the table structure. In addition, restructure can be used to recover space on your disk after deleting records, rebuilding nonmaintained secondary indexes, bringing out-of-sync family members up to date with the table they are associated with, and reformatting the table into standard 4.0 or compatible (3.5 and before) file format.

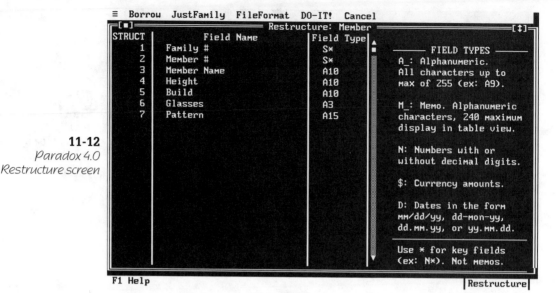

11-12
*Paradox 4.0
Restructure screen*

study #3. Be aware that changes to the Struct table through Modify|Restructure impact not only the structure of the table but any data that is stored within the table before restructuring. Deleting a field eliminates not just the column but also all the data that was in that column. This kind of deletion is unrecoverable.

Changes made during Restructure go beyond the table itself; they also flow through the entire family. Family objects are automatically restructured as follows:

- Deleting a field or changing a field type in any way will cause that field to be removed from all forms, reports, indexes, image settings, validity checks, and auxiliary password definitions.
- Deleting all fields which were on a form will cause the form to be deleted; all fields deleted from a page will cause the page to be removed from the form.
- Changing a keyed table to a nonkeyed table causes all maintained secondary indexes to automatically become nonmaintained (the default).

Added benefits of restructuring a table

Restructuring can also accomplish other tasks beyond its support for managing fields in tables. Restructuring can help:

- Recover disk space after records have been deleted
- Rebuild nonmaintained secondary indexes
- Bring out-of-date forms and reports back into sync with the table
- Change the format of the table file between Paradox 3.5 and 4.0 formats

Summary

In this chapter, you read about the basic processes involved in designing and building database outputs. Specifically, you learned that:

- Output is both the process of extracting information from the database and the result of that process.
- You need to consider how your database design will be implemented through particular output, including reports and graphs.
- Designing output is like a condensed version of database design: you must focus on the end result first: "Why do I need this output?" The description of purpose for a particular output should control its format (report or graph).
- Graphs normally present highly summarized and often argumentative information, while reports tend to display more detail.
- Reducing the amount of information in a particular output can often make the result more effective.
- Design of a graph involves both preparation of data and development of a design specification.
- Multitable reports can effectively combine data from multiple tables, as long as all tables are directly related to one single master (often the "many" side of one-to-many relationships).
- Generally speaking, it is better to optimize the database design for a multitable form than for a report, since reporting can be done through several options, whereas data entry and modification is best supported only in CoEdit through a form.

Key Terms

lookup table   A table which is contained within the definition of a multitable report and which includes linked records relative to the master table, normally in a one-to-many relationship from the lookup table's perspective.

sort   The arrangement of values into a specified order, usually following the ASCII key-code order.

Part Four

Optimizing a Paradox design

12 Evaluating application performance

You have designed your application, your forms, your reports, and most specifically your database, to perform an accurate translation of your information to and from the computer-managed data. Similarly, you've put the mechanisms in place (table links) that enable your application to recreate your information from the data being stored. You've even analyzed how the design might need to be modified based on Paradox-specific parameters. However, these considerations fail to address a critical aspect of your goal: for information to be information of value, it not only must be accurate but timely.

What makes information timely?

Timely is a term that can mean different things in different contexts. Information on a report might be timely if it reflects what happened last week; information on a graph might be timely if it shows today's sales; information that you need to modify through an application might be timely only if it reflects what is known up to the minute. Although the term *performance* often is used to describe how quickly a task is accomplished (interchangeably with the term *speed*), performance is more accurately a measure of timeliness. While speed is an objective measure of the time it takes to accomplish a task (five seconds per task, 30 minutes per task, etc.), performance is more subjective, measured relative to the timeliness requirement of the given situation. Thus, an application might run at high speed (a task happens quickly) but have inadequate performance (it doesn't happen quickly enough).

speed How fast a given task can be accomplished in an application.

In evaluating the performance of an application, you must consider what is timely: how quickly do you need a task to occur in order for the information to retain its value? Once these performance requirements have been established, you can evaluate the speed of the different system components to determine which areas need enhancement.

One of the major advantages of creating a computer-based application is that it can manage large quantities of data, but in some respects an even greater advantage is such a system's ability to manage these quantities in real time. Real time refers to the closeness of the connection between what is happening in the real world and what is going on in the database. A real-time application will maintain a close match between the two; a change in the real world will be reflected immediately in the database. Analysis done with real-time data is as accurate as possible, because it reflects what is happening now, not what happened yesterday or last week or last month.

Considering real time

real time A close connection between what is happening in the real world and what is going on in the database.

The term immediately isn't a very good way to describe the time it takes an application to reflect an activity in the real world, because there is an actual span of time involved. Ordinarily, an application is real time only when users collect the necessary information and enter it into the application at the same time. In that case, the collection and entry/modification of the information support each other, and the factor that controls the speed of the system is the users (how quickly they can collect the information) and not the application.

Thus, performance is a cumulative measurement that is affected by both the application's speed and the speed of the user.

Practically speaking, it might be tough to figure out how fast you need a task to occur, particularly if you are converting from a manual system that probably has a very different performance expectation. Because performance is hard to evaluate and even harder to specify, many application designers ignore the issue until after an application is in place. If there are complaints that the application runs too slowly, then these considerations suddenly apply. However, reacting after the fact rarely yields a satisfactory solution. Assessing performance after the fact could even force you to reconsider database design issues that more appropriately are evaluated right up front.

Assessing your performance expectations

Performance specification usually involves coming up with a maximum time for each task. For example, my daily sales report must run in under 15 minutes; my monthly sales report must run in two hours or less; data entry of one sales transaction must take no longer than three minutes. If the application performs in under that maximum time, that's great—but if it comes in above the maximum (it takes longer than specified), something must be done. The basic problem is that an application that is too slow won't get used, remembering that "too slow" can be on the user's side ("I don't know how to make this work and I don't have the time to figure it out") or on the application side ("I have to wait forever for the report to print; I can do it faster manually").

This issue follows the concept of a bottleneck: which component is slowing you down? Which component, if enhanced, will measurably affect the performance? The bottom line is that age-old equation: time equals money. It costs money to buy time; in this case, it costs money to enhance an application's performance. Your goal in assessing the value of that enhancement is to do the best job of leveraging any dollars you must invest (see chapter 13 for a more detailed discussion). This means that you should pay to speed up an application only in the areas in which you will gain the most from enhanced performance. If a user is the primary bottleneck, work at enhancing the user's speed (the basic technique: training!). However, if the application is the bottleneck, look at the pieces of the application that you can enhance.

To do your own application analysis, you need to take a look at several issues. First, where will performance be a concern (where are the bottlenecks)? Second, what are the factors that will influence that performance? Note that the goal at this point in the database design process is not to focus on the user side of the system (this is more appropriately reserved for a thorough application-design discussion). Instead, you need to focus on the database side, and to consider specifically where modifying the database design will help and where it could hinder performance.

Figuring out the bottlenecks

Each kind of input and output task varies in complexity, at least from the application's standpoint. The goal for the user, of course, is to find even the most complex tasks easy to perform. In general, just as in a manual system, the more complex a task, the more time it takes. Table 12-1 lists the

Table 12-1
Application input/output ordered by speed.

Task	Relative speed
Answer single-table question	Fast
Single-table data entry	Fast
Single-table data modification	Fairly fast
Generate single-table report	Fair
Perform single-table analysis	Fair
Multitable data entry	Fair
Multitable data modification	Fairly slow
Answer two-table question	Fairly slow
Generate graph	Fairly slow
Generate multitable report	Slow
Answer multitable question	Slow

categories of application tasks described in chapter 2, reordered based on relative speed. Note that Table 12-1 is only a very rough ordering of the relative speeds of these tasks. This table also expands the list somewhat, adding some new subcategories to those tasks; Paradox's speed is impacted differently for tasks involving one table and tasks involving multiple tables. Obviously, multitable tasks will be common in relational applications, but you will pay a price for that functionality in speed. Before you specifically address how these issues will affect your database design, you need to consider what factors influence speed in general. If each of your application tasks meet your performance goals, no redesign of your database might be necessary.

To understand why an application slows where it does, you need a sense of the basic components of a PC. Consider this an extremely rough overview of which PC components contribute to making a task occur and which usually affect how fast or slow the task occurs. There are many more highly technical books available on these topics; this is by no means a comprehensive discussion.

Understanding PC speed

You need to start with a brief review of the elements of a PC. Figure 12-1 graphically describes the basic categories: hardware and software. These components work together to accomplish any task (relative costs are discussed briefly in chapter 13).

Software provides the basic set of instructions which you, or your application, use to accomplish any task. Because your task involves data, and specifically involves data in relational tables, your software (Paradox) is a relational

Software components

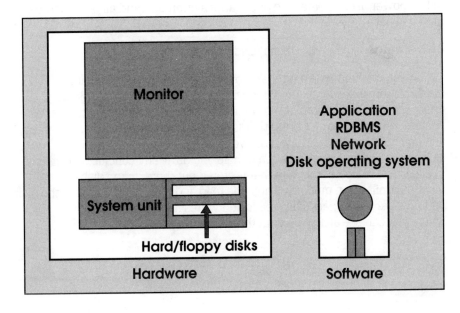

12-1
Elements of a PC

DBMS. Paradox in turn works with the operating system (DOS)[1] to manipulate the various hardware components of the PC. Paradox also must work with any network operating system, an additional "layer" of software that is required for linking multiple PCs together in a network, if your application needs to use data on a PC that is not your own, or if your data needs to be shared. Different RDBMSs can accomplish the same task at different speeds, because the mechanism each uses is likely to be different. Any software review that compares different RDBMSs is likely to compare speeds to perform the same task (see Miller, ed. 1991). You need to be aware that your choice of Paradox affects how quickly your application tasks are accomplished. Luckily, Paradox 4.0 has been benchmarked as the fastest multiuser database program in its class (Software Digest's NSTL, May 1992).

Hardware components
The hardware components that have a direct and measurable impact on speed fall into three areas. Each of these is a resource with a finite limit:

- Disk drive
- Memory
- Processor

The disk drive(s) in your computer are used to store data. Disk speed is a measure of how quickly data can be read from or written to it. When an application needs to use data, it first must find it on the disk and then make it available to use (read it). The faster the disk speed, the faster that data can be retrieved, and the faster your task that needs the data can be completed. In general, any task that must use data from disk storage will be slower than one that doesn't; because database applications by definition use data (and usually lots of it), they also tend to do a lot of disk reads and writes. This is one reason why PC database application developers are said to be "power users"; database applications often demand all the resources they can get.

disk storage   Magnetic media used to store data permanently.

Memory is the hardware area that provides a temporary holding and manipulation space for all the things the computer needs to do. Memory (more specifically, random access memory, or RAM) is similar to the top of your desk: it is where you bring things together, review, write, summarize, and generally get things done, with your information. For a computer to do anything, to perform a calculation or help you draw any conclusions, or even to allow you to look at the data that is stored out there on the disk, the data must be available in memory. Thus, the read and write functions that the disk performs are more specifically reads and writes from the disk into memory, where you can see and work with the data.

• • • • • • • • •

[1] At least until Paradox for Windows makes the Windows operating system available to Paradox users as well.

memory   Random access memory (RAM), used temporarily to store and process data.

In general, the more memory you have available on your PC, the faster things will work. This is because displaying or manipulating data already in memory is substantially faster than having to go out and retrieve it off of a disk (even the fastest disk). In fact, purchasing memory can be the cheapest way to improve performance across the board (see chapter 13).

The processor is the hardware component that provides the capability actually to do things to the data. When you buy a PC, the first question asked (even before the manufacturer's name) is what type you're buying: a 386, a 386SX, a 486, or a 486DX2. Each of these refers to the type of processor that the PC uses. The more powerful and sophisticated processors are those most recently developed; generally, a 486 is faster than a 386, which is faster than a 386SX, which is faster than a 286/AT, etc. Again, speed is almost always what you're paying for when you purchase a more expensive machine.

A discussion of which kind of machine will give you the best performance for dollars spent is again outside of the scope of the book. However, be aware that database applications in general push all available hardware resources to their limits. All of today's RDBMSs are designed to run on faster hardware; no matter what you do to maximize performance through your database design, you might never get the performance you require from a Paradox application without investing in hardware at the 386 level or above, and without buying at least 4 megabytes of RAM.

Before you even consider modifying a database design in order to make an application work faster, take special note: relational theory is intended to provide the best solution to the needs of a relational database system in most circumstances. Most of the situations under which you might decide to modify a design are specific to the current form of an application. Beware that in optimizing your design for a certain task or set of tasks you don't reduce the flexibility and power inherent in a truly relational database. You might not think you need flexibility, but recall the discussion in chapter 2 about growth; even if you don't need to do some particular task today, there might be a good chance that you'll need to do it tomorrow. If in optimizing for today you've reduced your options for tomorrow, you might not be making a good buy.

Modifying a design for performance reasons

All this considered, there are three major areas in which a relational database design might need modification in order to meet or enhance minimum performance requirements.

- Building indexes
- Minimizing the width of the primary tables
- Recombining tables for speed

Building indexes In general, the slowest tasks are those that manipulate the largest amounts of data. However, what are these tasks, and how can you make them faster? The tasks most related to these issues are:

- Reports
- Queries
- Sorting

You need to revisit the concept of a primary key just for a moment. Recall that Paradox implements a primary key through the building of an index, a machine-readable file that keeps track of each primary key value and where it actually is located in the table. The goal for a primary index is to make sure that each value in the table is unique, but a benefit of that index is that rows in the table can be obtained much more quickly than without an index.

Paradox supports the use of additional indexes that can be built simply for the purpose of speeding up the tasks in an application. This kind of index, called a *secondary index* because it is built on a nonprimary key field or set of fields, acts just like a primary index, except that it doesn't force values to be unique. A secondary index records the values in specific fields (the indexed fields), keeping them in order just as a primary index does, and keeps track of where each of these values is located in the table itself. So building a secondary index on a field or a set of fields that will be used to get at data in a table is a good way to immediately speed up tasks that use that table in this way. An index really helps only when you are looking to find a value in that field of the table (in performing a search); searches commonly are performed either in answer to a query (question) or as part of the preparation or organization of data for a report.

secondary index An index built on a nonprimary key field or set of fields.

The down side to an index has to do with keeping it current. Although a primary index is always up-to-date (it has to be in order to control the uniqueness of the values), a secondary index might or might not reflect the current values in the table. Paradox allows you to specify whether a secondary index will be kept up-to-date like a primary index; this is called a *maintained index*. The default when creating an index is to keep it in a nonmaintained state, at least until you need to use it; when an index is nonmaintained the updating occurs when Paradox detects that it is needed (normally during a query or reporting session). The real trade-off here is whether you want the best performance during your data maintenance sessions, in which case you'll choose nonmaintained indexing, because that way no time is devoted to secondary index maintenance during the DataEntry, Edit or CoEdit session (or at any other time when data is being modified); or whether you'd rather have the speed during a query or reporting session, in which case you'll have to live with it if the data maintenance process takes a little longer.

Your database design should specify which fields should be indexed, but how do you determine this? You need to build a field usage matrix that you can use in this evaluation and in considering other issues as well. The basic technique is to build a two-dimensional structure (a table!) that will contain one dimension for each task and one dimension for each table/field combination in your database (see FIG. 12-2, which describes a matrix for case study 3). Whether you select rows or columns for each dimension depends on how many tasks the application will perform relative to how many fields there are in the application. The fewer of the two should be in the column dimension. Once you've created the matrix, go through your lists of input and output tasks, and place a checkmark in the columns that are being used in that task. Place a

Analyzing your field usage

Task/field matrix	Print animal list	Print genealogy	Print cage space list	Enter new births	Modify animal records	Display animal data	Maintain cage data
Animal ID							
Animal Name							
Date of Birth							
Cage #							
Ancestor Animal ID							
Type of Ancestor							
Description of Ancestor							
Cage name							
Cage Building							
Cage Row							
Cage Level							
Total Spaces							
Available Spaces							

12-2
Input/output tasks and field matrix for case study #3

special mark (an asterisk or check) in that column or columns that describe a field that is used specifically to direct that task (see FIG. 12-3). Here "specifically direct" refers to a field value being used in a search or linking process.

Once you've created this matrix, it should be easy to see which fields should be indexed. Add that designation to your database design with a symbol (like a bullet) placed next to the field name in your list of tables and fields (see Table 12-2).

Even if the appropriate fields have secondary indexes, your application still might not meet your performance expectations. So what other design areas should you look at?

12-3
Input/output tasks and field usage (filled-in usage matrix for case study #3)

Task/field matrix

	Print animal list	Print genealogy	Print cage space list	Enter new births	Modify animal records	Display animal data	Maintain cage data
Animal ID	✓			✓		✓	
Animal Name	✓	✓		✓	✓	✓	
Date of Birth	✓			✓		✓	
Cage #						✓	
Ancestor Animal ID		✓		✓		✓	
Type of Ancestor				✓		✓	
Description of Ancestor		✓		✓		✓	
Cage name	✓		✓			✓	✓
Cage Building			✓				✓
Cage Row			✓				✓
Cage Level			✓				✓
Total Spaces							✓
Available Spaces			✓				✓

Table 12-2
Tables and fields for case study 3
including critical-link indicators.

Table	Field
Animal	Animal ID*
	Animal Name++
	Date of birth
	Cage number
Ancestor	Animal ID*
	Ancestor animal ID*
	Type of ancestor
Ancestor type	Type of ancestor*
	Description of ancestor
Cage	Cage number*
	Cage name
	Cage building++
	Cage row++
	Cage level++
	Number of spaces total
	Number of spaces available++

++Secondary index recommended

Minimizing the width of the primary tables

In general, all relational DBMS are intended to perform their best (i.e., fastest) when manipulating tables that have few columns and lots of rows. Narrow (fewer than 20 columns) is in almost every case better than wide, at least from a performance standpoint. After all, a theoretically sound relational database usually consists of many tables with relatively few columns in each.

For this reason you might want to consider reducing the size of the tables you work with most frequently. If you ask questions about or produce reports on the information in a table that is relatively wide, you might consider dividing your data into most-frequently-used and less-frequently-used categories. You can create easily a separate table with a one-to-one relationship to the first table, keeping both sets of data available at the same time through a link. You wouldn't see any functional difference in your application; things would work exactly the same way. However, you would notice a substantial improvement in performance when you need to do those tasks that use only one (narrower) table's data. To make this kind of evaluation, look at your task/field matrix. You'll be able to see graphically which fields fall into the most-frequently-used category, and which don't.

Recombining tables for speed

On the other side of the fence, you should be aware that having more tables will exact a different price. Every time you must access data from multiple tables at the same time, you will pay, simply because multitable tasks always take longer than those involving a single table. The question is whether that price is worth it. Remember, theoretically at least, the isolation of fields and tables is a good thing, even a requirement in many cases. In practice, it is almost always advantageous. However, in some situations, you might have a need to recombine fields that describe different entities into a single table—a relational no-no—because if you don't, the performance price you pay every time you need the combination is just too high. So how do you assess whether to change your design? Which price is worth paying? Ask yourself the following questions about how you will actually use your application:

- Do I ever deal with these entities separately?
- How frequently do I take advantage of a particular link?

Although two entities might be separate in theory, if in practice you always use them together, theory might just be wrong. Take another look at your task/field matrix. Are the same tables always used in combination, or more specifically, is there ever a situation in which a table is used independently? If not, you might want to consider combining it with its master, the table with which it is always used. Even if you do use a table separately on occasion, your overwhelming usage of it in combination with another table (particularly if those combination usages are in the context of queries or reports) might be incentive enough for recombining them.

Summary

This chapter has addressed performance issues associated with an application. In particular, you have looked in detail at various aspects of information, including the facts that:

- Information of value must be timely, or it loses its value.
- Real-time applications are those that place a priority on being consistent with what is happening in the real world.
- You can figure out what you expect from an application's performance by evaluating the maximum time you'll allow a task to take before the application loses its value—before your users refuse to use it.
- The bottlenecks in an application's speed fall into a few specific categories, including software and hardware components.
- It is possible and even, under some circumstances, advisable to modify a database design for performance reasons. In particular, you will want to evaluate building indexes, minimizing the width of your primary tables, and recombining your tables in order to enhance your application's speed.

Key Terms

disk storage   Magnetic media used to store data permanently.

memory   Random access memory (RAM), used temporarily to store and process data.

primary key   The field or fields used as the identifier for each record in a table.

real time   A close connection between what is happening in the real world and what is going on in the database.

secondary index   An index built on a nonprimary key field or set of fields.

speed   How fast a given task can be accomplished in an application.

13 Evaluating the cost of a database

Your theoretical design already has changed shape; the impact of reality frequently forces modifications despite the requirements of theory. You've had to make changes in your table structures and modify your data integrity requirements as practical considerations have taken a front seat.

The considerations you will address in this chapter might come late in the process as laid out in this book, but they probably will come first in your business. Every choice you make about an application involves the issue of money, because every choice you make in your business concerns that resource. Cost hits you everywhere, from the biggest picture (what's my bottom line with this application?) to the smallest detail (should I add one more field to my database design?). Even those issues that involve nothing more than your time involve cost; after all, time is money.

Throughout the design process you have deferred cost concerns to this chapter. The process of figuring out how much an application will cost and determining what the benefits of buying it will be is called cost justification. There are a number of formal methodologies that you can work through to develop extensive and detailed documentation about each aspect of the application-development process; it certainly is not the intent of this chapter to address the issue at that level. Instead, this general overview is intended to make you aware of the major cost areas and help you assess which of those might apply in your situation, and to what degree. It is not intended to balance them against the benefits you specifically will experience, although that evaluation is implicit in every cost decision you must make.

Identifying the cost components

First, you need to consider the two areas in which the costs of an application must be determined:

- Start-up costs
- Maintenance costs

It is all too common to look closely at the costs involved in developing and implementing an application, but ignore the longer term (and often more substantial) costs of operating it. This happens in large part because the start-up costs are heavily out-of-pocket; you can easily see any new equipment, new staffing, and consultant involvement as one big package. However, the costs an application will cause you to incur over time are also substantial; in fact, the biggest cause of application failure is a lack of planning about long-term issues, including maintenance and enhancement costs.

The costs involved in an application fall into two categories, which, as you might expect, are the same two categories that make up the application itself: users and application software. You must consider both aspects; don't fall into the trap of ignoring the costs associated with the users. Although this book is focused on the database design issues involved in building an application (the computerized side of the equation), the user development and ongoing support issues are just as crucial, and unfortunately more frequently ignored.

You can break the costs down into two additional categories: out-of-pocket and time. In most businesses, out-of-pocket expenses make it directly into the accounting system and demand thorough cost justification and explanation. However, unless they are associated with (and billed by) a consultant, time costs often are hidden. This fact represents a real failure in cost assessment and justification, because in many cases the efficiency of business operations (time savings off the accounting record!) is involved directly in the push for new application development.

In addition, many businesses will implement a new application with the expectation that, over time, it will reduce the cost of doing business. The expectation is that the new application will make the users more efficient, thus allowing them to get more accomplished faster, thus (potentially) reducing the need for certain kinds of personnel. This attitude represents a common fear of many workers, a fear that is particularly acute relative to PC-based systems. Fear just might be responsible (at least partially) for the substantial resistance many users experience when beginning work with a new application (Henderson, ed. 1990).

Interestingly enough, newly computer-based applications rarely, if ever, result in a reduction of staff. Much more commonly, the efficiencies engendered by a new application will provide the "breathing room" necessary to support business growth. This might not be possible immediately, because users will experience a learning curve with any new system; besides, any time freed up as the result of a new application is more than likely immediately absorbed by new tasks that only make themselves known once the system is underway. However, in the long term there is no doubt that computer applications make it possible for a business to grow and be competitive in a business world that is increasingly computer-dependent.

The costs involved in getting a new application up and running are tied directly to the application-development process. To begin the cost evaluation, you first need to revisit the application life cycle discussed in chapter 1. You probably want to define further the term start-up as that part of the process associated with the first time through the cycle. You could consider the second time around as part of the ongoing costs of system maintenance.

Assessing start-up costs

In general, application-design costs should represent 30%–35% of the overall application-development costs (see FIG. 13-1). This reflects the relative time

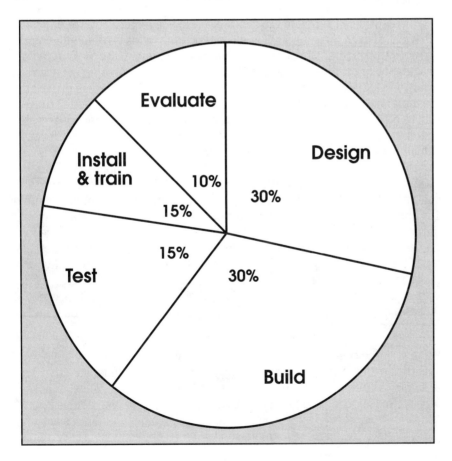

13-1
Design components of application development costs

differential between the various phases of development. If the time/cost percentage is much less than that, you'll probably experience an immediate need for redesign.

Estimating disk storage requirements

Hardware costs must include an assessment of the disk storage capabilities an application will require. Making this kind of assessment might be difficult, particularly so for a newly computerized application. It is important, however, to come up with at least a rough "guesstimate." Not allocating enough disk space to an application obviously will affect your ability to store additional data, but less obviously will likely affect the ability of your application to perform its tasks and to get things done. Like most RDBMSs, Paradox does have hidden disk storage requirements, hidden because they are not fully documented, but nonetheless required. For example, a user needs to have around three times the disk space occupied by a table available for any query on that table. This space is required for scratch and/or temporary tables used by Paradox when executing a query. These hidden requirements might create an additional requirement of 20%–25% more disk space across the entire application, depending on the size of the tables themselves and the kind of processing your application must do.

In general, you can estimate the disk storage space required by figuring out the width of each table (adding up all the column widths) and multiplying the width by the number of records you anticipate locating in the table. A table to contain clients, for example, would be fairly easy to estimate; the rate with which you add new clients might be fairly low, and thus once you guess at the table size, you'll probably be fairly close for an extended period of time. On the other hand, the tables that contain daily business transactions—sales, appointments, contacts, etc.—are likely to grow much more quickly. If you estimate that the history you intend to keep immediately available in the system will cover six months, and you do 1,000 sales per month, you can estimate that six months' worth of records will total 6,000 records. If the table contains a total width of 300 characters (15 columns with an average width of 15 characters plus some extra for table name, etc.), this would mean it would occupy approximately 1,800,000 bytes (or 1.8 megabytes) of disk storage for that six-month period. Adding the 25% reserve, that gives you a requirement for 2.25 megabytes of storage for that one table. Adding up the other five tables in the database design, the total estimate for this application is about six megabytes of storage required to handle six months of data. This is not an unreasonable guess for a relatively small application, like the one built and used by case study 3.

Relative to the cost of other components, disk storage is usually relatively cheap. The difference between a 40-megabyte and a 60-megabyte drive, for example, is often less than 15% of cost for 50% more storage. Thus, it makes sense to make good guesses about storage required, and then double it, or add at least another 50% (just in case). In addition, bigger hard disks are increasingly a requirement for more sophisticated applications. For example, any application running under OS/2 normally requires a minimum of around 100 megabytes (just for software).

Time requirements vary from case to case depending on a number of factors. The most crucial factor, of course, is the expertise of the individuals who are spending the time. The more skilled an individual is, the more likely any design or programming task will be accomplished in an efficient manner, and the more time probably will be conserved.

Estimating time requirements

This time variance is one of the most important reasons to consider utilizing a consultant when developing an application. Even if an in-house person has the skill which would lead you to feel comfortable in supporting an in-house development, the likelihood is that the process will still take longer, in most cases much longer. This is also why consultants tend to charge substantially more than the rate that could be used to bill in-house time: expertise equals time, which equals money. As a rule of thumb, system design consultants in today's market will charge a rate that ranges from $85 to $140 per hour depending on the local market, their experience, and the software products they specialize in. You can estimate that the time of an in-house person who is paid $38,000 (plus benefits) will be worth about $28 per hour.

Table 13-1 lists the basic application start-up expense points and presents some rough estimates for those costs, using the requirements developed in case study 2 (EB). The table compares projected start-up hours associated with two different implementation methods. First, the in-house option is explored, in which all development is handled by an expert user or users who are employees of the business. Second, the option to contract out the development process is presented, in which two time estimates must be considered: in-house time (still a requirement) and consultants' time.

You'll note that the hours involved for a nonprofessional to create a design are substantially more than those for a consultant. In total, the man-hours are reduced from 405 to 235, almost in half. You also should take a look at some differences in time that might not be so apparent.

First, the time involved in getting the management and users "on board" can vary substantially; having a professional involved is something like placing a stamp of approval on the process. Suddenly users (and managers) feel more inclined to accept the process rather than pick it apart. Second, note that the consultant time to create the database design depends on in-house time gathering the input and output requirements and the documents to support those requirements. Without that in-house preparation, creating the database design will take at least 50% longer, and the likelihood of redevelopment (changes to the basic requirements) being required is extremely high. Third, make careful note of the assumption that the manager involved has prior experience in management information systems (MIS). Without that experience, it would be difficult to consider an in-house development.

Table 13-1
Some start-up expense points and estimated costs.

Assumptions:
1. Installation time is ASAP
2. All hardware is installed previously and working.
3. Application development is being managed or performed in-house by a manager with substantial MIS experience.
4. Manager and user time can be charged at $28 per hour.
5. Consultant time is billable at $85 per hour

Expense point	Hours	Cost
Time expenses with in-house development:		
Discover requirements/study feasibility	30	$ 840
Get management on board	20	560
Get users on board	25	700
Evaluate hardware & site requirements	30	840
Develop database design specifications	75	2,100
Build and test application	125	3,500
Install system and train users	30	840
Follow up/review	20	560
Training (10 users @ 5 hrs each)	50	1,400
	405	$11,340
	(Man hours)	(Total $)
	(10.1 weeks)	
Time expenses with consultant development:		
In-house time:		
Discover requirements/study feasibility	20	$ 560
Get management on board	10	280
Get users on board	15	420
Gather input/output documents	15	420
Evaluate consultants	15	420
Manage design and development	10	280
Follow up/review	15	420
Training (10 users @ 5 hrs each)	50	$ 1,400
Consultant time:		
Evaluate hardware & site requirements	10	850
Create database design	30	2,550
Build and test application	50	4,250
Install system and train users	10	850
Follow up/review	15	1,275
	235	$13,975
	(Man hours)	(Total $)
	(5.8 weeks)	

Regardless of the developer's expertise, not having a person experienced in managing the process is asking for the most unlikely and thorniest problems to emerge. Chapter 14 of this book does address some issues relative to the design project, but without experience even the techniques described there will be unlikely to bring in the project in a timely fashion simply due to the complexity of the process.

These are a few of the issues to consider before entering into an agreement with a consultant. In addition, you might keep some other issues in mind. First, your consultant will never know your business as well as you do, and thus a consultant-developed application will never be as reflective of your business as an application developed in-house. Second, an in-house development will likely yield an application that is slower, less flexible, and of lower quality overall; it is unlikely that your in-house expertise will match a consultant's, and the quality, speed, and flexibility of an application are directly related to the developer's expertise. Third, you must consider the effect of this project on in-house resources: an in-house developer will be unavailable to support other projects or requirements (including those already up-and-running) and the stress that probably will result can be quite substantial. And fourth, doing the work in-house doesn't mean just-after-5:00 p.m. The less frequently any developer works on an application, the longer it takes to get anything done.

If you do decide to hire a consultant, at a minimum make sure to cover the following bases.

Be in charge   Take the time to discuss your general business needs first. If the consultant isn't interested in listening, it is a good clue that he won't be receptive to your input throughout the process. Also, be prepared for ongoing interaction. Don't send the consultant off to work and ignore him until the application is complete.

Keep an open mind   You hire consultants for their expertise; take advantage of it! Even if you have gone through a design process on your own, listen closely to their questions. Questions are often the key to solutions.

Get any agreement in writing   In particular, make sure that you both buy off on the database design, whoever might be responsible for producing it. The biggest threat to a consulting project is a lack of clear specifications. Also, if the agreement includes a range of hours or costs (e.g., 75–100 hours, or $5,000–8,000 dollars), budget for the upper end of the range. If the project comes in under that, you'll feel good and look good to any manager evaluating what's happening. If not, at least you knew what to expect.

Always check references   No matter what a consultant's PR says, there is no better way to find out if he is legitimate than by asking a prior client. There are many fly-by-night consultants out there, too many of them in the computer consulting business. Make sure that you've got a good chance of getting what you pay for. Find out about reputation. If your consultant has been around long enough to develop a client base, he or she probably will have been in touch with the larger Paradox community. Inquire about your consultant's involvement with local Paradox user's groups, with any of Borland International's programs, and even with the Paradox forums on CompuServe. Higher profile doesn't necessarily equate to higher quality, but at least you'll be able to get a sense of the seriousness of their specific commitment to Paradox.

Initiating application development

Before spending any money, and certainly prior to entering into any contractual agreement regarding an application, it is crucial that you identify your end result. Having this established will make it possible to discuss your needs with the consultant and should open the needs up for further discussion with other employees in-house. Figure 13-1 describes this as "discovering the requirements," and as outlined in chapter 1 (and chapter 14 in more detail), it is often in the nature of a quest.

It is particularly important to hunt for needs, or at least to touch base, with both the users and the managers who will be involved with the application, particularly if they are two different groups of people. Soliciting agreement on the end result and providing a way to impact the process once the design is underway will go a long way toward making sure that the system is accepted once it is ready to implement. If the goals aren't at least somewhat uniform up-front, you can bet that you won't get uniform usage at the other end.

Don't step off a plank. Conserve your time and money resources until you are thoroughly convinced that the application is worth developing, that it will be cost-effective to bring to implementation, and that you fully understand what will be involved in the process. Once you have arrived at a good understanding of the issues involved, you stand to make a decision that is appropriate to the situation, not a decision driven by anxiety, peer pressure, or "system envy," a dread disease that strikes when you know your competitor has invested in state-of-the-art technology (but you haven't).

Table 13-2 reviews some of these considerations, particularly as they relate to the decision on proceeding with an in-house rather than a contracted application development.

Working through the design process

Once there is agreement as to the end result desired, and you have decided to either forge ahead in-house or contract the job out, the design process commences for real.

Considering off-the-shelf options

Once the design project is complete, and you have in your hand a design document that combines the best of theory and practice, it is time to start building a system, right? Wrong. It is only after you have made the investment in the design process that you are in a position to evaluate some of the other application options, particularly those that might be available at substantially lower cost than a custom, "just for you" development.

Table 13-2
Comparison of in-house and contracted application development.

Issue	In-house	Contracted
Total out-of-pocket dollars spent	Substantially lower	Substantially higher
Level of business knowledge reflected in system	Excellent	Fair
Quality of result	Fair	Excellent
Flexibility of result	Poor	Excellent
Total time expended	Substantially higher	Substantially lower
RDBMS product knowledge required of manager	High	Low
Knowledge of comparable systems available	Poor	Excellent
Stress level of manager	High	Low
Availability of manager/ developer to other projects	Poor	Excellent
Probability of need to hire temporary support	High	Low

You probably aren't in business alone. In fact, I know of no business that has no competitors, friendly or not. Even the government parallels private industry in many respects. From an application standpoint, this means that there is a good chance that someone else has already gone through the process that you've just emerged from. If your application need is one that spans multiple industries, like the need for an accounting system, it is very likely that you'll be able to locate a previously built system that meets your needs. A previously built application usually is called *off-the-shelf software*, because you might be able to walk into a computer store and buy it right off the shelf. Applications that aren't quite this easy to come by might still be considered off-the-shelf, because you'll still be able to purchase, install, and have the system up-and-running within hours if not days. Compare this to the months it typically takes to get a complete PC-based application up-and-running (years if the project is minicomputer- or mainframe-based) and you can quickly see the cost benefits.

If your application need is specific to your industry, you might find that a generic application probably won't fit it. However, the vertical software market is flourishing; unless you've already done some investigating, you'll probably be surprised to find how many options there are for applications that have been custom designed for someone else in your same business. Obviously, if you can piggyback on someone else's design headaches, the cost will quickly justify itself. The best place to look for vertical market software is in the trade publications for your industry.

The best part about having completed your design process is that you are truly in a position to assess the off-the-shelf product, not only from a functional standpoint, but from a performance perspective as well. You will be able to look at the application's documentation; better yet, you'll actually be able to talk intelligently with the vendor, carefully assessing whether or not the system will work for you with your specific needs. You won't have to be at the mercy of a software salesman!

You could discover that even if the basic package doesn't work for you, there are some elements of it that will. If the software meets 85% of your requirements, you might be able to live without the missing 15%, at least for some period of time. In fact, many businesses end up regarding software as disposable, in the sense that if they can justify the cost in under 24 months, buying a whole new system after 36 months is not unreasonable. You'd probably be surprised to know how many cost justifications arrive at a break-even point less than 24 months out: in the range of 60%, which is substantially more than you might think (Henderson, ed. 1990).

You also need to investigate whether or not the missing 15% could be made available to you through customization of the software. Many software developers, particularly in the vertical market, are also in the business of customizing their software to individual customer's needs. You'll be surprised to discover how willing most software developers are to help create a custom system. Of course, the moment you move into customization, you begin to run into the same issue that drove you to consider off-the-shelf in the first place: namely, the costs involved. Even so, you might end up with the best of two worlds: customization to support your specific needs, and a price that severely undercuts the potential cost of a completely custom implementation.

Off-the-shelf systems usually range in price from the most simplistic, $99 accounting system, to substantial vertical market applications that run into thousands of dollars. The variance is great because the level of functionality ranges dramatically.

Let's take an example. You have designed a fairly simple application (similar to case study 3: the zoo), and the process took you a total of 50 hours. At an in-house rate of $28/hour, the design cost you $1,400. Assuming this is 30% of the overall cost of system development and implementation, this leaves you with a suggested balance of about $3,260 that it will cost you to complete the process in-house. You have located a vertical market software that will meet about 80% of your requirements; the cost of this software is $1,799. The vendor has estimated that customization to address the missing 20% will take 40 hours; at their billable rate of $80 per hour, this adds up to $3,200 for a total off-the-shelf software cost of $4,999. Compared to an in-house cost of $4,660, you'll pay almost $350 more for the off-the-shelf option, and, of course, that option puts the expense out-of-pocket rather than absorbed by overhead.

If you do decide to build your own custom system, look closely at the layouts in chapter 14. You must make sure specifically to provide adequate time for all the steps of the process, particularly on the post-implementation end— and don't make the mistake of reserving the off-hours to get the development done. Not only will that slow you down dramatically (how coherent are you after a full day's work?), but the decisions you make will not likely be of the quality you should be demanding. Even with substantial on-hours time allocated (and by substantial I mean at least 40% on a weekly basis), you must be prepared for the first round of the life cycle to take months, not weeks. Furthermore, you must be prepared for even your best estimate of the costs involved to be at least 10% low.

Building an application

On the plus side, however, an application that you have created specifically for your needs should be more flexible, more powerful, and better supported by the users than a simple purchase.

Any application will require maintenance. You need to assess the costs and budget for them, or you'll end up playing continuous catch-up and being frustrated in the bargain.

Evaluating ongoing expenses

Just a brief mention of the costs on the user side of the application: any dollars you devote to enhancing your user skills (e.g., training) will directly affect your other long-term costs. You should see an immediate payoff in productivity, and a long-term benefit from reduced outside consulting services.

The application environment must be maintained in order for you to continue to support the application. Maintenance usually involves both the time and expense of keeping your application environment operational. The maintenance costs that your application depends on might be fairly low, involving simply the vigilance (time) of your system or database administrator, or these costs could be relatively higher and involve an actual change to the fundamental elements of the computer system your application is based on. This type of change is addressed briefly below. There are three major areas that potentially are affected by these changes, which of course parallel those fundamental elements of the application environment:

Maintaining the application environment

- Hardware
- Operating systems software
- Paradox

Upgrading your hardware   Historically, the hardware segment of the computer industry has been the fastest developing. The available hardware tends to be two to three generations ahead of the PC on the average user's desk. Each generation represents a dramatic leap forward in the power and speed of the hardware, so two or three generations of difference make for a definite loss of potential for an application.

Even though I have assumed for the purposes of this book that the hardware supporting the application already is up and running, practically speaking it is rarely optimized, and at some point you must consider upgrading. Upgrading usually becomes an issue as a business grows. Even if you have taken into consideration your business plan and any growth you might have projected (see chapter 2), those concerns always are balanced against the cost factor. If building an application to support two years of growth is prohibitively expensive (at least from a hardware point of view), most businesses will opt to build to meet today's requirements, then upgrade as they need to do so.

As the potential of the hardware has increased, its cost has dropped, and so as you consider when to buy you always have to balance not only what you can get in today's market, but what you could get for the same money if you waited until tomorrow's market. In 1993 you can get a 386 machine for well under $1,000, which is remarkable considering that you couldn't buy a PC (the 8086-based original) for less than five or six times that in 1982. So far the industry shows no signs of slowing that type of progress.

Upgrading operating system software   One of the biggest questions in the PC industry in 1993 is what platform will support PC growth in the next ten years. This term usually refers to the operating system that will support the different software and applications. This is of concern in two major areas: the operating system on your PC, and the operating system used to link your PC to others. In 1993 the PC world is still DOS-based, although Microsoft Windows is making strong inroads into that assumption. A large percentage of software and applications are still designed to live within the limits of that fairly unsophisticated system, although beefed-up hardware is more the norm than not (including lots of RAM). However, other operating systems are making inroads into the PC world, including Unix/Xenix and OS/2. These more advanced systems are designed to take advantage of the capabilities of more advanced hardware; Windows has really slowed this migration as users choose to remain in the DOS world while upgrading the functionality and usability of their operating system. Windows applications are a different breed from standard DOS applications, because they are designed to utilize Windows' friendlier, more powerful graphical user interface (GUI), and also support the use of a mouse. Products like Paradox 4.0 are taking on a GUI interface even without being Microsoft Windows products.

In 1993 the networked PC world is still substantially based on Novell Netware, although other network operating systems are increasing their market shares. There are a number of issues, many extremely complex, involved in a network operating system, all outside of the scope of this book. For your purposes, you should just be aware that as improvements to all types of operating systems are made, you will need to evaluate how these improvements might affect your PC, your network, or your application. A shift of operating system is usually quite expensive, because more advanced systems cost exponentially more; where DOS usually is bundled free with any hardware, Unix or OS/2 normally must be purchased. In addition, a change to a nonnetwork operating system involves the migration of any currently running applications and retraining of all users. These are often substantial expenses that might run close to 70% of the expenses of the original application development (with the sole exception of the database design process, again usually 30% or so of the overall). However, it might be a justified expense depending on the benefits that might accrue, particularly if those benefits allow a necessary requirement to be fulfilled that previously was not being met.

Changing your RDBMS   As you make different choices regarding your hardware and/or operating system environments, you might consider reevaluating your choice of Paradox as well. Because, like all software, database management systems are designed to run with specific operating systems, an operating system change might require a change to another DBMS. The release of Paradox for Windows changes the equation for the Paradox user and poses a challenge: which environment is most suited for my application needs? Migration of an application from one RDBMS to another (even from Paradox 4.0 to Paradox for Windows) is also painful to contemplate for reasons similar to those described above: redevelopment costs can be substantial, but again, the benefits could outweigh cost considerations.

Even if your application environment is a stable one, you still need to consider the costs associated with ongoing application maintenance. Growth, as always, is a major factor. An implementation of a design that performed suitably when originally installed could become too slow, in which case one of the alternatives is to rework the implemented application, fine-tuning it to meet performance goals.

Maintaining the application

You also must be aware that once the application has been installed for some period of time and the evaluation phase of the development has occurred, your requirements will be modified. This is a natural process that leads to a better application, one that more closely meets the end result laid out in the beginning of the design process.

This maintenance of the application will cost you. As always, you have the choice of keeping the maintenance tasks in-house, in which case your primary cost will be the time of your in-house developer. You can plan on an average of 10% of your development time being required to support the application on a monthly basis for the first six months, and about 5% thereafter. Major redevelopments are not included in this rough estimate. Taking the example of case study 2 detailed in Table 13-1, you can estimate about 40 hours per month for the first six months at an estimated cost of $1,120. You'll see a gradual reduction in support time after that, probably settling to 20 hours per month ($560).

Of course, you also have the choice of contracting out the work. All legitimate consultants provide long-term support to their clients, some at their standard hourly rate, others based on a maintenance schedule drawn up in advance. If you are developing a substantial application (over 100 man-hours) with a consultant, you should consider some kind of maintenance agreement with your consultant that will ensure that support is available when you need it and at a cost you can predict. Again, as a general rule, you might consider a prepaid agreement that provides you with roughly 10% of the initial development time on a monthly basis for the first six months, and another 5% per month thereafter. Taking case study 3's estimate detailed above, 10% of the 115 consultant hours runs 11.5 hours, or about $850 per month for the first six months. Thereafter, you'd probably be safe estimating $400 or so per month for regular ongoing support (see Table 13-3).

Table 13-3
Estimated application maintenance costs.

Assumptions:
1. Manager and user time can be charged at $28 per hour
2. Consultant time is billable at $85 per hour
3. Time and costs are on a per month basis

Type of maintenance	In-house time	In-house cost	Consultant time	Consultant cost
First six months	40	$1,120	11.5	$977.50
Post six months	20	$ 560	5	$425

Modifying a design for cost reasons

If these costs seem overwhelming or perhaps out of line with the benefits you anticipate from the development of a new system, it makes sense to take a second look at your end result. Is the application that you propose truly mission-critical? What benefits will accrue if you proceed with the development? Will you be unable to support business growth without it?

Rather than coming up with a *yes* or *no* answer, you'll more likely come up with a maybe, meaning that in some ways the application is critical, but in other ways it will provide nice additions to the way you do business. Many businesses begin to apply priorities to the design elements laid out in the database design, then decide to continue the development with a phased approach, rather than a one-shot deal. This is a very workable way to proceed, because it will allow you to spread the development costs out over a longer period of time, but will provide you the knowledge that each phase, once implemented, will fit neatly into the overall design that was developed right up front. There won't be a compatibility issue; you'll know where you stand at each step of the way so that you are in a position to reassess continually the cost/benefit of continuing to proceed.

In other words, you should never modify a design for cost reasons. The design should reflect the requirements of your business, and a good design should be able to support those requirements for a good long period of time. Even if the continuing development costs prohibit the implementation of the entire design, having the overall document available for phased implementation will always be more beneficial than actually making changes to the fields or tables to reduce the implementation cost. This said, you might in fact consider modifying your design permanently; however, if you do so at this point in the process, at least you're doing so in full knowledge of what you risk: loss of usefulness, compactness, accuracy, or speed.

Is good design worth the cost?

If you've gone through all the details contained within these first 13 chapters and find that you're more overwhelmed than when you started, you're probably in good company. The database design process is not a straightforward one, and a good design does not come cheap. Chapter 14 is intended to help support your function through a database design project, but it doesn't necessarily make the process any easier.

I've always been of the opinion that money paid to a consultant for a database design represents the best value you'll find for those database dollars; at this point you might agree. However, the costs, although high, should be paid in full knowledge of the benefits that a good relational database design will bring. This book has focused on the process, but the result is where you'll find your justification. If you design relational tables, you'll get a useful and compact database. If you design detailed integrity constraints, you'll get accurate data. If you consider speed issues where appropriate, you'll get an application that meets your performance requirements. Finally, if you're aware of the costs up front, you'll be sure to get a cost-effective application.

Summary

This chapter presented several considerations involved with evaluating the costs of developing a database. These included the following:

- The process of designing a database is not cheap. No matter who the specific players involved, you should still expect a substantial commitment.
- Cost justification should always include both start-up and maintenance costs.
- Costs can be further divided into user-based and application-based costs.
- Expect the design component of application development to encompass 30–35% of the overall time.
- Your hardware should be optimized to the degree possible, particularly to include enough disk storage space and enough RAM to cover potential growth.
- There are pluses and minuses to extending the process to include a consultant.
- There are guidelines to working with a consultant; evaluate these carefully to protect yourself.
- You should consider an off-the-shelf software solution, but only after you've completed the design process and thus have something to evaluate the software against.

14 Facilitating the database design project

The process of taking a database design from concept to design specification is not simple. The bulk of this book is devoted to helping you understand how the process works, what the appropriate steps are, and in what order they should occur.

This chapter is focused on making it all easier. In particular, most of the suggestions for data collection and analysis have been distilled into forms which you can tear out, copy and put right to work. The intention is to tie the concepts down to a practical database design project: the project which you must undertake.

Identifying the roles

Once you have sketched out a draft which identifies relative cost and time constraints on your project, you also will probably have made a determination as to who you can afford to involve in the project. If a consultant is to be used, make sure she is informed and involved right from the beginning of the process, and not brought in midway through. Make a decision about your role and stick with it.

Whether or not a consultant is brought in, every design project requires an in-house project manager. The design project manager (DPM) will be responsible for the overall progress of the design project, and will be the individual accountable for meeting goals and deadlines. The DPM alone might be staffing enough to get your particular project done (and you can very well serve as the DPM). However, a project of any larger size, particularly when a consultant has been provided a contract, requires the involvement of a DPM normally on at least a half-time basis. Whatever the case, responsibilities of the DPM can include:

- Development of a project schedule, including milestones
- Development of a project budget, including contingencies
- Management of consultant relationships and design team members
- Coordination of progress meetings with management
- Distribution, collection and analysis of preinterview questionnaires
- Coordination of interviews with management and users
- Collection and analysis of source documentation
- Preparation of design document
- Presentation of design document to management and users

design project manager (DPM)   Individual in charge of overseeing the database design project from start to finish.

The DPM might or might not require additional staffing help. Depending on the project scope, administrative support might be required. Also depending on scope, the DPM could choose to enlist the support of other potential system users to collaborate on a design team. The design team could then work through the questionnaire analysis, interviewing, and source documentation analysis as a joint effort.

Whether a design team is developed or not, the DPM acts as the primary contact within the company for any consultant(s). The DPM also acts as the interface between the design team and all other interested parties.

Development of a design project schedule and budget is an essential first step. It is incumbent on the DPM to assess the general scope of the project and lay out the plan. Some flexibility is obviously required, but the more exact a schedule, the more likely a timely result. Likewise, development of a design project budget is an important early step in the process. The DPM should be able to include any consultant time and billing and estimate the time requirements for in-house staff as well.

Formalizing the project schedule & budget

The DPM should recognize the importance of communication throughout the project. It is particularly important for management to remain fully informed as the project unfolds. One way to facilitate this is to schedule periodic progress meetings at which project status can be identified and the schedule and budget can be verified. The more knowledgeable and involved management remains with the project, the more buy-in you'll discover at the other end. Remember, this is only the design phase for an application development process which could extend over substantially more resources (the other 70%). The last thing you want to do is sink the project in the early going through a simple lack of communication.

Keeping management informed

Preparing the way for users

Getting potential users to be interested and committed to the success of any system under development is a task best started from the beginning of the project as well. In this regard, the Preinterview Questionnaire described as FIG. 14-1 can be a helpful tool. Communicating the basic intentions behind the database design project and requesting user responses can be an effective means of beginning the interactive design process.

Pre-Interview Questionnaire

Name | Job title

Computer Skill Level:
- [ ] New User
- [ ] Some Experience
- [ ] Programmer

Source Documents:
- [ ] Hand-done report
- [ ] Spreadsheet report
- [ ] Other DB report
- [ ] Entry form
- [ ] Client/customer list
- [ ] Catalog
- [ ] Index
- [ ] Business plan
- [ ] Strategic plan
- [ ] Annual/quarterly reports
- [ ] Guide
- [ ] Employee handbook
- [ ] Tax returns

What kind of things do you do?
- [ ] Entering data
- [ ] Network admin
- [ ] Data maintenance
- [ ] Links to mainframe
- [ ] Training new users
- [ ] Handling new info requests
- [ ] Maintaining equipment
- [ ] Designing reports
- [ ] Word processing
- [ ] Contact management
- [ ] Backup data
- [ ] Answering questions
- [ ] Scheduling
- [ ] Other
- [ ] Printing reports
- [ ] Mailing lists
- [ ] Programming
- [ ] Data analysis
- [ ] Researching problems
- [ ] Summarizing material

Please describe other things you do:

How much time do you spend using the computer (daily)?
- [ ] 0-1 hour
- [ ] 1-3 hours
- [ ] 4-5 hours
- [ ] 6 or more hours

How much time do you anticipate using the computer with the new system (daily)?
- [ ] 0-1 hour
- [ ] 1-3 hours
- [ ] 4-5 hours
- [ ] 6 or more hours

Will you be responsible for any aspect of the new system?
- [ ] Yes, primary responsibility
- [ ] Yes, secondary responsibility
- [ ] Yes, but only on occasion
- [ ] No, never

What problems do you anticipate with the new system?
- [ ] It will keep me from getting my job done
- [ ] I won't know what's going on
- [ ] It won't do what I need it to do
- [ ] It will slow me down
- [ ] I'll know too much about what's going on
- [ ] I don't know what it will do
- [ ] It will make my job harder
- [ ] It will cost too much
- [ ] Other_____

Do you have any questions about this process? Note them here.

What is the best time of day to schedule an interview with you?
- [ ] Breakfast/before 8:00 AM
- [ ] 8:00-10:00 AM
- [ ] 10:00 AM-12:00 Noon
- [ ] Lunch: Time _____
- [ ] 12:00 Noon-2:00 PM
- [ ] 2:00-4:00 PM
- [ ] 4:00-6:00 PM
- [ ] After hours: Time _____

Do you have any suggestions that might help this process?

14-1
Pre-Interview Questionnaire

Understanding the scope of work

Chapter 2 dealt in great detail with the concept of an end result: figuring out the purpose of the database you are developing. Sometimes getting an answer to that main question is extremely challenging, particularly if the system you are contemplating is one which will be serving multiple users. An end result you might envision can be quite different than others involved perceive. A large part of this problem has to do with perspective.

Top-down design demands that you reach as high up into your organization as your planned system might filter. Even if the total impact of the system is derived from a one-page report presented at the annual meeting of the board of directors, that one-page report might very well be your most valuable indicator as to what is and is not important in the database system. The more you step back, the more likely the entire big picture is to come into focus.

top-down design   Allowing the requirements of the upper levels in an organization to drive the integration of lower level needs.

Managers often have surprising insight into not only your needs but the requirements of other users and even other parallel departments. So your first task is to pull out your organization chart and figure out how high up to go. Again, start at the top and work your way down until you reach a point where the system will have some visibility. Schedule a meeting and use it as a brainstorming session. Plan to take full advantage of any time made available to you. Take a look at FIG. 14-2 for an idea of how you might utilize or gather information from a management interview.

Management Interview Form

Name		Job title	

| Computer Skill Level:
☐ New User
☐ Some Experience
☐ Programmer | Job Description:
☐ Project Manager
☐ Department Head
☐ Specific Title:_____ | ☐ Vice President
☐ Supervisor | # people you supervise:

Job type of people you supervise: |

Computer Hardware

| CPU:
☐ 286
☐ 386
☐ 486
☐ Macintosh
☐ NeXT
☐ Other_____ | Printers:

Modem: | Monitor:
☐ CGA ☐ EGA ☐ VGA ☐ SVGA

Connectivity:
☐ Token Ring   ☐ Client/Server
☐ Peer to Peer   ☐ Ethernet
☐ WAN   ☐ MainFrame
☐ Other_____ |

Computer Software

| Operating System:
☐ DOS
☐ OS2
☐ Windows
☐ UNIX
☐ Other_____ | Network:
☐ 3Comm
☐ Netware
☐ LanMAN
☐ Banyan Vines
☐ SQLServer
☐ Other_____ | Are you satisfied with your hardware/software? | Software Applications:
☐ M/S Word   ☐ Word Perfect
☐ Excel   ☐ Lotus 1-2-3
☐ Quattro Pro   ☐ ObjectVision
☐ EMail:_____   ☐ Other_____ |

Your goals for the system (include reasons why you are undertaking this project):

Current systems you want to integrate into this system:

Anticipated benefits of system:

User interviews will be as critical to the project as management sessions. Each interview should be seen as an opportunity both to collect information and to share it. The more any user is aware of the design process and priorities being expressed throughout, the more likely it is that he will buy into the process and be willing to make a commitment to actually use whatever software is developed as a result. Without the commitment of the users, a design project will end up as just that: a design, with no effective path to implementation.

From the users you will collect the necessary details (see FIG. 14-3). Each user will probably have their unique perspective on both the problem(s) to be solved and the best solution to each. Gathering these perspectives is an exercise which can yield dramatic payoff in the long term. In fact, what often

14-3
User Interview Form

User Interview Form		
Name		Job title
Computer Skill Level:	**Job Description:**		
☐ New User	☐ Project Manager	☐ Report Designer	☐ Service Technician
☐ Some Experience	☐ Office Manager	☐ Data Entry	☐ Programming
☐ Programmer	☐ Other_____		

Computer Hardware

CPU:	Printers:	Monitor:			
☐ 286		☐ CGA ☐ EGA ☐ VGA ☐ SVGA			
☐ 386					
☐ 486		**Connectivity:**			
☐ Macintosh		☐ Token Ring		☐ Client/Server	
☐ NeXT	Modem:	☐ Peer to Peer		☐ Ethernet	
☐ Other_____		☐ WAN		☐ MainFrame	
		☐ Other_____			

Computer Software

Operating System:	Network:	Software Applications:	
☐ DOS	☐ 3Comm	☐ M/S Word	☐ Word Perfect
☐ OS2	☐ Netware	☐ Excel	☐ Lotus 1-2-3
☐ Windows	☐ LanMAN	☐ Quattro Pro	☐ ObjectVision
☐ UNIX	☐ Banyan Vines	☐ EMail:_____	☐ Other_____
☐ Other_____	☐ SQLServer		
	☐ Other_____		

Tasks the System is to Achieve:

Anticipated Benefits of System:

ends up as a corollary result to a database design project is a reengineering of the current business processes. As the project unfolds, the opening of communication and flow of information from user to user to manager to manager to user can be facilitated to the point that discussions are no longer limited to "What do we do now?" but extend into the realm of "What should we do tomorrow?" These discussions can lead to creative solutions to previously undiscussed problems.

There are several sources of information important to a developing database design. Some of these flow naturally from the interview process, while others require some sleuthing to uncover. As in the interview process, the intent is to gather information at the source, in the form that it is actually used. A design project might be aided by sources including:

- Reports currently being generated (either manually or through another computer system or software)
- Forms which users, managers, customers, clients, patients etc., fill out
- Nonreport documents, including telephone lists, inventory catalogs, document indexes, personal calendars, department schedules, job descriptions, diskette inventories, library indexes
- Business plans (short- and long-term)
- Annual reports or other periodic publications about the business, including financial reports or statements
- Employee handbook or other published guides, including information on regulations or codes

source documents   Materials which are in use prior to the implementation of a new application and which act as guidelines for the design process; can include reports, organization charts, business plans, etc.

Each of these documents can contain information which is best integrated into the database under design. The sleuthing process can sometimes yield more useless detail than raw gold, but it is often an unexpected source that ends up changing the entire nature of the design. It is sometimes helpful to summarize the documentation with a cover sheet (see FIG. 14-4). Standardizing the format for the information as you collect does nothing but ease the burden further down in the process.

Once all the information has been collected, the challenge lies in sorting through it to figure out what your particular database system needs to know about. Normally, this is matter of identifying priorities and sticking with them. Having an end result to measure the information against makes it possible to decide with some sense of confidence on what is or is not important.

It can be helpful to keep track of information as you collect it on another standard type of form. Figure 14-5 describes a table template, which can be used both to help collect and describe information when it is revealed through an interview or document review process.

Reviewing source documents

Describing a design

Document Cover Sheet

Name of Document:		Document source (provider):

Type of Document:

☐ Computerized report (from PC) ☐ Computerized report (from mini/mainframe) ☐ Manual report
☐ Entry form filled out by _____ ☐ Telephone list ☐ Inventory catalog
☐ Document index ☐ Personal calendar ☐ Group calendar
☐ Department schedule ☐ Project schedule ☐ Job description
☐ Library index ☐ Business plan ☐ Annual report
☐ Quarterly report ☐ Financial report ☐ Financial statement
☐ Employee handbook ☐ Mission statement ☐ Other _____

Period covered by document:
☐ From _____ ☐ To _____

Frequency of publication:
☐ Annual ☐ Semi-annual ☐ Quarterly ☐ Monthly
☐ Weekly ☐ Daily ☐ Every _____ ☐ Whenever data changes
☐ Whenever _____

How document will be integrated into system:
☐ Source for new report
☐ Data source only
☐ Other _____

14-4
Source Document Cover Sheet

The one-page diagram

In the end, the most effective communication tool relative to the database design remains the one-page diagram. A completed design project might yield a stack of documentation, which (depending on tactics) can include many interview records and many source document summaries. But as long as the end result is in clear focus, all the detail can be distilled to a very clean set of tables and relationships. From Paradox's point of view, there couldn't be anything easier to implement than a carefully developed relational database design document. Thus in the end the process supports its goal: to create a database design which supports an application yielding information of value—information that is useful, accurate, cost-effective, and timely.

Key Terms

design project manager (DPM)   Individual in charge of overseeing the database design project from start to finish.

source documents   Materials which are in use prior to the implementation of a new application and which act as guidelines for the design process; can include reports, organization charts, business plans, etc.

top-down design   Allowing the requirements of the upper levels in an organization to drive the integration of lower level needs.

Table Template

_____

Table

Field Name	Field Description	Key	Data Type(Only One):	Val Checks	Domain
		☐ Primary ☐ Foreign	☐ D: Date ☐ S: Short ☐ $: Currency ☐ N: Numeric ☐ A5: Time(Alphanumeric) ☐ A_: Alphanumeric ☐ M_: Memo ☐ B: BLOb	☐ LowValue ☐ HighValue ☐ Default ☐ TableLookup ☐ Picture ☐ Required ☐ Auto	

Field Name	Field Description	Key	Data Type(Only One):	Val Checks	Domain
		☐ Primary ☐ Foreign	☐ D: Date ☐ S: Short ☐ $: Currency ☐ N: Numeric ☐ A5: Time(Alphanumeric) ☐ A_: Alphanumeric ☐ M_: Memo ☐ B: BLOb	☐ LowValue ☐ HighValue ☐ Default ☐ TableLookup ☐ Picture ☐ Required ☐ Auto	

Field Name	Field Description	Key	Data Type(Only One):	Val Checks	Domain
		☐ Primary ☐ Foreign	☐ D: Date ☐ S: Short ☐ $: Currency ☐ N: Numeric ☐ A5: Time(Alphanumeric) ☐ A_: Alphanumeric ☐ M_: Memo ☐ B: BLOb	☐ LowValue ☐ HighValue ☐ Default ☐ TableLookup ☐ Picture ☐ Required ☐ Auto	

Field Name	Field Description	Key	Data Type(Only One):	Val Checks	Domain
		☐ Primary ☐ Foreign	☐ D: Date ☐ S: Short ☐ $: Currency ☐ N: Numeric ☐ A5: Time(Alphanumeric) ☐ A_: Alphanumeric ☐ M_: Memo ☐ B: BLOb	☐ LowValue ☐ HighValue ☐ Default ☐ TableLookup ☐ Picture ☐ Required ☐ Auto	

14-5
Table template

Database designs for case studies

Case study 1: RTS

Type of business: Financial planning sole proprietorship

Employees: 1 full-time, 1 part-time

Statement of purpose: This financial planner has a need to keep track of what he does and when. He needs to be able to manage his time spent from a historical perspective for billing purposes, and he also needs a way to help him schedule his future time commitments. In addition, he needs to keep better tabs on his client contacts, including who he has talked to, when the contact took place, what recommendations he made, and what follow-up was required.

End result: Manage time

Database design solution: Fig. A-1

Field requirements: Table A-1

Table A-1
Field definitions for case study 1.

Field name	Data type	Domain	Restrictions
SCHEDULE:			
Schedule date*	D	No Sundays	
Schedule start date	D		<End date
Schedule end date	D		>Start date

Field name	Data type	Domain	Restrictions
Schedule date printed	D	No Sundays	
APPT:			
Appointment number*	S		
Appointment date	D	No Mondays	
Appointment start time	A5		>8AM
Appointment end time	A5		<9PM
Client ID	S	Client table	
APPTSERV:			
Appointment number*	S	Appt table	
Service code performed*	S	Service table	
Hours worked	$		
SERVICE:			
Service code*	S		
Service description	A25		
Service rate	$		>$45,<$145
CLIENT:			
Client ID*	S		
Client name	A25		
Client street address	A25		
Client zip code	A10	City table	
Client telephone number	A12		
Primary contact name	A40		All caps
Secondary contact name	A40		All caps
CITY:			
Zip code*	A10		
City name	A25	US only	
State abbreviation	A2	US only	
INVOICE:			
Invoice number	S		
Invoice date	D		1st or 15th
Total amount due	$		Sum of hrs*rates
INVDET:			
Invoice number	S	Invoice table	
Service code performed*	S	Service table	
Hours worked	N		Appt times

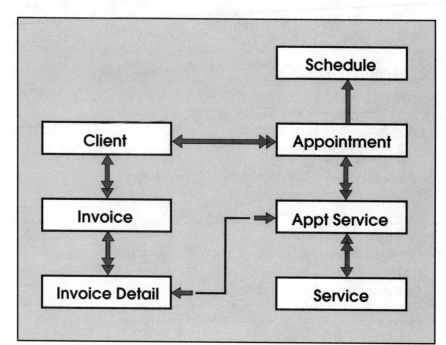

A-1
Database design for case study #1

Case study 2: EB
Type of business: Purchasing group within a large retail corporation
Employees: 11 full-time (within the group)
Statement of purpose: The purchasing group of a nationwide retail sales
company needs to manage the process of buying nonmerchandise supplies
for their stores and corporate entities. The group processes requests for
supplies that are submitted by various users, forwarding these requests to a
vendor or to a corporate warehouse location as indicated.
End result: Manage purchase orders
Database design solution: Fig. A-2
Field requirements: Table A-2

Table A-2.
Field definitions for case study 2.

Field name	Data type	Domain	Restrictions
PO:			
Purchase order number	S		
Purchase order date	D		
Vendor ID	S	Vendor table	
Vendor name	A25	Vendor table	
User name	A40		All caps

Field name	Data type	Domain	Restrictions
Total purchase order amount	$		Sum of PO items
Purchase order date closed	D		>Po date +60
Buyer name	A40		All caps
ITEM:			
Item number	S		
Quantity ordered	N	>=100	
Price	$	>1,<500	
Item description	A15	All caps	
VENDOR:			
Vendor ID	S		
Vendor name	A25		Upper- & lowercase
Street address	A25		
City	A25	US only	
State	A2	US only	
Zip code	A10		Zip plus four
Area code	A3	Valid AC	
Phone number	A8		Three plus four
PURCHREQ:			
Request number	S		
Date requested	D		
Date updated	D		>Date requested
User name	A40		

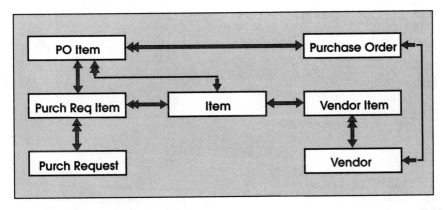

A-2
Database design for case study #2

Case study 3: MH

Type of Business: Small zoo

Employees: 15 full-time, 9 part-time

Statement of purpose: The owner of this small zoo has a need to keep track of his animals. He needs to know the genealogy for each animal and where it is currently caged in order to plan mating schedules.

End result: Find mates

Database design solution: Fig. A-3
Field requirements: Table A-3

Table A-3
Field definitions for case study 3.

Field name	Data type	Domain	Restrictions
ANIMAL:			
Animal ID*	S		Sequential
Animal name	A20		
Date of birth	D		
Cage number	S	Cage table	
Father/animal name	A20	Animal table	
Mother/animal name	A20	Animal table	
Maternal grandfather/name	A20	Animal table	
Paternal grandfather/name	A20	Animal table	
Maternal grandmother/name	A20	Animal table	
Paternal grandmother/name	A20	Animal table	
CAGE:			
Cage number*	S		
Cage name	A20		
Cage building	S		<43
Cage row	S		<10
Cage level	S		<4
Number of spaces total	S		
Number of spaces available	S		
Client name		Client name	
Client address		Client street address	
		Client zip code	
Telephone number		Client telephone number	
Primary contact		Primary contact name	
Secondary contact		Secondary contact name	
CITY (new)			
		Zip code*	
		City name	
		State abbreviation	
INVOICE:			
Invoice number		Invoice number*	
Invoice date		Invoice date	
Total due		Total amount due	
Invoice Detail INVDET (New):			
		Invoice number*	
Services performed		Service code performed*	
Hours worked		Hours worked	

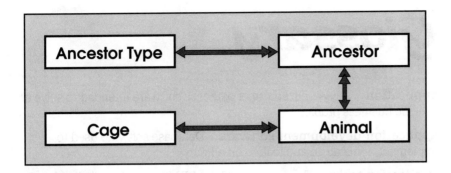

A-3
Database design for case study #3

Case study 4: Household

Type of business: N/A
Employees: N/A
Statement of purpose: All you need to do is keep track of the total value for all your depreciable assets so you can give it to your accountant once a year.
End result: Keep list of assets
Database design solution:
Field requirements: Table A-4

Table A-4
Field definitions for case study 4.

Field name	Data type	Domain	Restrictions
ASSET:			
Name of asset	A30		Upper & lower case
Depreciated value	$		Price-pric*DP
Description of asset	M25		
Date purchased	D		>1/1/89
Purchase price	$		
Depreciation period	N		12-mo increment
Date sold	D		>date purchased

Glossary

application   A customized use of database software intended to solve a specific business problem.

application-development software   Database software used to implement or install an application on a PC.

application tasks   Things you need the DBMS to do, usually involving input or output from the database.

atomicity   A quality of a value that indicates it cannot be broken down into components without the loss of its meaning.

autonumbering   A DBMS function that builds a primary key value without the need for user input.

backup   The process of making a copy of the application programs and data (often in some kind of compressed mode).

column   Used interchangeably with field to refer to one descriptive element or attribute of a table (the vertical of the table).

data   Facts (plural), or a fact (singular), meaningless because it lacks context.

data independence   A quality of data that describes the fact that it is accessible through a logical format, and whose users need never know how it is physically stored.

data integrity   The accuracy and validity of data in an application relative to the requirements of the business.

data security   The control the DBMS exerts over who can do what in an application.

data sensitivity   A qualitative assessment of data that describes how secret it is.

data type   A description of a value that the DBMS uses as a way to understand some fundamental qualities of that value.

database administrator (DBA)   The person who manages the database and applications.

data-based relationships   A quality of a relational database that sets it apart from other types of databases. The data is used to make connections.

database management system (DBMS)   Software designed to allow you to manage a wide variety of data types to meet a variety of needs.

disk storage   Magnetic media used to store data permanently.

domain   The pool of values from which actual values in a field might be drawn.

easy-to-use   A DBMS that is intuitive and provide lots of help through detailed menus and well-defined choices, and also screens that look a lot like the physical objects you are already familiar with.

end result   The output of an up-and-running application, and the goal of the application-development process.

entity   Anything that has definite, individual existence in reality or in the mind; anything real in itself.

entity integrity   How accurately a table reflects actual entities in the real world.

export   A translation of data from your DBMS to the format of another software program.

field   Used interchangeably with column to refer to one descriptive element or attribute of a table (the vertical of the table).

field integrity   A measure of the value of a description relative to the actual fact it is describing.

foreign key   A primary key value when used in another table.

form   An image on the computer screen that is used to access data; to input new data, or to look at or modify data that has already been input.

identifier (ID)   The field or fields (or during the design process, the info element) that can be used to identify uniquely each row of a table.

import   A translation of data from another software program into your DBMS.

implementation   The phase of application development during which the design is acted upon (building is begun).

index   A separate and relatively small file used to keep track of values (in the case of a primary index, it tracks primary key values), and that allows a DBMS to access to particular value without searching the table itself.

information   Organized data.

information element (info element)   An item of information that has not yet been defined or broken down into a specific field or fields.

information of value   Information that you are comfortable basing a decision on, or that helps you make a decision.

join   A relational operation that combines tables and brings rows together based on common values.

life cycle   A development process that spans the life of the system being developed and usually encompasses steps from the identification of the requirements through the installation, training, and evaluation of the system.

link   The potential that exists for a relationship between two tables by virtue of their sharing a common column.

local area network (LAN)   A group of computers physically linked together with cables, usually utilizing a special operating system to manage the interactions of the multiple users.

logical table   A table that is conceived by application users to think about and manipulate data.

maintenance   The ongoing work done to an application that is required in order to ensure that it continues to work.

memory   Random access memory (RAM), used temporarily to store and process data.

multifield key   A primary key that is applied to multiple fields.

multimedia   Video and audio capabilities.

naming conventions   Rules for naming that you follow as standard practice rather than by necessity.

orphan record   A record once on the "many" side of a one-to-many relationship whose "one" related record has been deleted.

performance   The speed of an application measured against the application's requirements.

primary key   The field or fields used as the identifier for each record in a table.

program   A set of directions you create and save that tell a DBMS what things to do and in what order.

programming language   Those features of the DBMS that allow you to automate or customize the use of the other features.

project   A relational operation by which specified columns are extracted from a table.

query   A technique for asking questions or doing analysis on data managed by a DBMS.

real time   A close connection between what is happening in the real world and what is going on in the database.

record   Used interchangeably with row to refer to one occurrence of an object or process within a table (the horizontal of the table).

recovery   The process of returning an application to a prefailure state after a problem has occurred.

referential integrity   Sometimes relational integrity; how accurately the database reflects real-world relationships that exist between different entities.

relation   A special kind of table that has been modified to follow the rules of the relational model.

relational DBMS (RDBMS)   DBMS software that (to one degree or another) follows the rules laid out by the relational model.

relational model   A set of rules based on relational algebra that describe data structures using mathematical principles. The model describes three aspects of database management: data structures, data integrity, and data manipulation. The data structures are intended to reduce redundancy in data storage, and also to provide efficiency, security, and integrity across databases that are both shared and integrated.

repeating group   The relational model's term for a feature of an entity that can include more than one value.

restrict   A relational operation that extracts specific records from a relational table.

row   Used interchangeably with record to refer to one occurrence of an object or process within a table (the horizontal of the table).

secondary index   An index built on a nonprimary key field.

sophistication   The degree of automation of an application that makes use of the system as easy as possible.

sort   The arrangement of values into a specified order, usually following the ASCII key-code order.

speed   How fast a given task can be accomplished in an application.

system documentation   The written-in-English, published version of what the system does, usually including details from the user's perspective as well as from the programmer's perspective.

table   A set of columns and rows that describes a single object or process and that is the fundamental data structure of any relational database.

table relationship   A path created by data that is used to integrate two tables together.

user   A person who works with an application, either to maintain the data or to rely on it, to aid in the decision-making process.

view   A combination of fields from tables that acts like a table itself. A view normally is used for a specific input or output process.

Bibliography

Codd, E.F. 1970. A Relational Model for Large Shared Data Banks. *Communications of the Association for Computing Machinery*, 13 (6).

Codd, E.F. 1990. *The Relational Model for Database Management: Version 2.* Reading, MA: Addison-Wesley Publishing Company.

Date, C.J. 1990. *An Introduction to Database Systems: Volume I.* Reading, MA: Addison-Wesley Publishing Company.

Guralnik, David B. ed. 1976. *Webster's New World Dictionary of the American Language.* Cleveland: The World Publishing Company.

Henderson, Lee, ed. 1990. *Management in the 1990s.* Cambridge, MA: MIT Press.

Miller, Michael, ed. 1990. *The Info World Test Center Software Buyer's Guide: 1991 Edition.* San Mateo, CA: IDG Books Worldwide.

Mullin, Mark 1989. *Object-Oriented Program Design with Examples in C++* Reading, MA: Addison-Wesley Publishing Company.

Parsaye, Kamran, Mark Chignell, Setrag Khoshafian, and Harry Wong 1989. *Intelligent Databases: Object-Oriented, Deductive Hypermedia Technologies.* New York: John Wiley & Sons, Inc.

Salcedo, Gregory B. and Martin W. Rudy 1990. *PC WORLD Paradox 3.5 Power Programming Techniques.* San Mateo, CA: IDG Books Worldwide, Inc.

Stonebraker, Michael, Jeff Anton, and Eric Hanson 1987. "Extending a Database System with Procedures." *ACM TODS,* 12 (3).

Tsichritzia, Dionysios and Anthony Klug (eds.) 1987. "The ANSI/X3/SPARC DBMS Framework: Report of the Study Group on Data Base Management Systems." *Information Systems,* 3.

Vang, Soren 1991. *SQL and Relational Databases.* San Marcos, CA: Microtrend Books.

Ward, M. 1990. *Software That Works.* New York: Academic Press.

Zenreich, Alan and James M. Kocis 1990. *Paradox Programmer's Guide: PAL by Example.* ScottForesman Professional Books.

Index

A

accuracy of database, 9

application-development software, 8, 27

applications, 7-9, 20-22, 26-27, 30-32

  application-development software, 8

  brainstorming for ideas, 41, 43

  cost of initiating development, 242

  depth of detail, 40

  developing applications, 245

  diagram of proposed application, 44

  end result identification, 35-36

  growth and expansion, 36-40

  life-cycle of application, 31-32

  networking local area networks (LAN), 37

  performance criteria, 38, 224-234

  programs (*see* scripts)

  scripts, 12

  sketch of proposed application, 40-41, 42

  sophistication of application, 27

  speed of processing, 38

  storage of data, 38-40

  tasks, 20, 45

    decision-oriented, 21

    maintenance tasks, 21-22, 27

  user-interface, 26-27

    identifying users, 45-46

    growth in number of users, 36-38

atomicity, 91, 114

attributes, 65

automated features, 19-20

autonumbering, 85, 87, 187

  key requirements, 170-172

auxiliary rights passwords, 182-183

B

backup processes, 22, 27

binary large object (BLOb) values, 91, 114

bottlenecks, 226-227

brainstorming for ideas, 41, 43

budgeting for database design/implementation, 251

C

calculated fields, 108

case studies, xviii-xx, 258-263

  EB case study, xix, 260-261

  household case study, xx, 263

  info elements, 71-73

  MH case study, xix, 261-262

  RTS case study, xix, 258-259

  tasks analysis for the applications, 46, 48, 49

  user identifications, 47, 48, 49

Codd E.F. relational-theory development, 13, 147

coding conventions used in book, xviii

color use, 194

  forms, 201-202

columns, 23, 87, 64-67

  attributes, 65

  fields, 65

  links common-column identification, 127

  relationships column-based links, 122

compactness of database, 9

consultants database-design, 241-242

conventions used in book, xviii

cost of database, 9, 235-249

  application development costs, 242, 245

  budgeting for database design/implementation, 251

  consultants to help with design/implementation, 241-242

  cost components, 236-237

  disk-storage requirements, 238-239

  environment maintenance, 245

  hardware upgrades, 245-246

  maintenance costs, 247-248

  modifying design to fit costs, 248-249

  off-the-shelf design options, 242-244

  ongoing expenses of database use, 245

  operating-system upgrades, 246-247

  RDBMS upgrades, 247

  software upgrades, 246-247

  start-up costs, 237-242

  time requirements, 239 241

Custom Configuration Program (CCP), 193-194, 204

R